Challenging Knowledge

The University in the Knowledge Society

SRHE and Open University Press Imprint
General Editor: Heather Eggins

Current titles include:

Catherine Bargh et al.: University Leadership
Ronald Barnett: The Idea of Higher Education
Ronald Barnett: The Limits of Competence
Ronald Barnett: Higher Education
Ronald Barnett: Realizing the University in an age of supercomplexity
Neville Bennett et al.: Skills Development in Higher Education and Employment
John Biggs: Teaching for Quality Learning at University
David Boud et al. (eds): Using Experience for Learning
David Boud and Nicky Solomon (eds): Work-based Learning
Etienne Bourgeois et al.: The Adult University
Tom Bourner et al. (eds): New Directions in Professional Higher Education
John Brennan et al. (eds): What Kind of University?
Anne Brockbank and Ian McGill: Facilitating Reflective Learning in Higher Education
Stephen Brookfield and Stephen Preskill: Discussion as a Way of Teaching
Ann Brooks: Academic Women
Sally Brown and Angela Glasner (eds): Assessment Matters in Higher Education
John Cowan: On Becoming an Innovative University Teacher
Gerard Delanty: Challenging Knowledge: The University in the Knowledge Society
Heather Eggins (ed.): Women as Leaders and Managers in Higher Education
Gillian Evans: Calling Academia to Account
Sinclair Goodlad: The Quest for Quality
Harry Gray (ed.): Universities and the Creation of Wealth
Andrew Hannan and Harold Silver: Innovating in Higher Education
Norman Jackson and Helen Lund (eds): Benchmarking for Higher Education
Merle Jacob and Tomas Hellström (eds): The Future of Knowledge Production in the
    Academy
Mary Lea and Barry Stierer (eds): Student Writing in Higher Education
Elaine Martin: Changing Academic Work
Ian McNay (ed.): Higher Education and its Communities
David Palfreyman and David Warner (eds): Higher Education and the Law
Craig Prichard: Making Managers in Universities and Colleges
Michael Prosser and Keith Trigwell: Understanding Learning and Teaching
John Richardson: Researching Student Learning
Stephen Rowland: The Enquiring University Teacher
Yoni Ryan and Ortrun Zuber-Skerritt (eds): Supervising Postgraduates from Non-
    English Speaking Backgrounds
Maggi Savin-Baden: Problem-based Learning in Higher Education
Peter Scott (ed.): The Globalization of Higher Education
Peter Scott: The Meanings of Mass Higher Education
Anthony Smith and Frank Webster (eds): The Postmodern University?
Colin Symes and John McIntyre (eds): Working Knowledge
Peter G. Taylor: Making Sense of Academic Life
Susan Toohey: Designing Courses for Higher Education
Paul R. Trowler: Academics Responding to Change
David Warner and David Palfreyman (eds): Higher Education Management
Diana Woodward and Karen Ross: Managing Equal Opportunities in Higher Education

Challenging Knowledge

The University in the
Knowledge Society

Gerard Delanty

The Society for Research into Higher Education
& Open University Press

Published by SRHE and
Open University Press
Celtic Court
22 Ballmoor
Buckingham
MK18 1XW

email: enquiries@openup.co.uk
world wide web: www.openup.co.uk

and

325 Chestnut Street
Philadelphia, PA 19106, USA

First Published 2001

A catalogue record of this book is available from the British Library

ISBN 0 335 20578 X (pb)   0 335 20579 8 (hb)

Library of Congress Cataloging-in-Publication Data

Delanty, Gerard.
    Challenging knowledge: the university in the knowledge society /
Gerard Delanty.
        p.   cm.
    Includes bibliographical references and index.
    ISBN 0-335-20579-8 – ISBN 0-335-20578-X (pbk.)
        1. Universities and colleges–Social aspects.   2. Education, Higher–Social
    aspects.   3. Knowledge, Sociology of.   I. Title.

LB2324. D45 2001
378–dc21

                                                                            00-060677

Typeset by Graphicraft Limited, Hong Kong
Printed in Great Britain by St Edmundsbury Press, Bury St Edmunds, Suffolk

Contents

Preface and Acknowledgements

The background to this book lies in three quite separate areas that I have been interested in for some time: the sociology of knowledge, the social theory of modernity and the debate on the idea of the university from the Enlightenment to the global age. It is the aim of the book to bring these quite diverse topics together in order to rethink the question of the identity of the university in the twenty-first century. I have attempted to look at the university as a key institution of modernity and as the site where knowledge, culture and society interconnect. In essence, I see the modern university as a producer and transformer of knowledge as science and knowledge as culture. It cannot be reduced to either science or culture for it is an institution that mediates, or interconnects, several discourses in society, in particular the encounter between knowledge as academic discourse and culturally articulated cognitive structures. Such a cautiously 'universalistic' view of the university suggests that its key role is linked to reflexive communication and citizenship. In particular, such a role will today entail the articulation of technological and cultural citizenship. In this way I have attempted to show that the identity of the university is determined neither by technocratic/managerial strategies nor by purely academic pursuits: in the 'knowledge society' knowledge cannot be reduced to its 'uses' or to itself because it is embedded in the deeper cognitive complexes of society, in conceptual structures and in the epistemic structures of power and interests. Rather than being a passive actor, drawn helplessly into the market, it can have a transformative role. Thus rather than speak of the demise of the university as a result of the postmodern scenarios of the fragmentation of knowledge, the retreat of the state and the embracing of market values, this sociologically constructivist approach facilitates a new identity for the university based on its ability to expand reflexively the discursive capacity of society and by doing so to enhance citizenship in the knowledge society.

This book is a development of my contribution to a debate in a special issue of *Social Epistemology* (vol. 12, 1998) on the university as a site of knowledge production. The theory of modernity underlying it draws from my *Social Theory in a Changing World* (published by Polity Press, 1999) and a plenary paper presented to the conference 'Reorganizing Knowledge/ Transforming Institutions: Knowing, Knowledge and the University in the Twenty-first Century', University of Massachusetts–Amherst, USA, 17–19 September 1999, published in *Organization*, 8 (21) 2001.

An earlier draft of the book was read by Ron Barnett, Steve Fuller, Heidi Granger, Tim May, Andrew Marks, Piet Strydom and Frank Webster. I am grateful to them for their detailed and helpful comments. The theoretical structure of the book has been considerably improved from advice by Piet Strydom. I am also grateful to John Skelton of Open University Press for suggesting that I write the book. I would also like to acknowledge the advice of the referees consulted by Open University Press, as well as the valuable corrections of the copy editor. The shortcomings of the book in no way reflect their advice and the arguments put forward do not necessarily re-flect their views.

Gerard Delanty,
May 2000

Introduction: Challenging Knowledge

The history of western social and political systems of thought can be said to be the expression of a deeply rooted conflict between two kinds of knowledge: knowledge as science and knowledge as culture. The origins of this go back to the classical Greek opposition of *logos* and *doxa*, knowledge versus opinion, a conflict which also established the superiority of knowledge over democracy. As is well known, Plato rejected the world of ordinary knowledge as illusion and democracy as the expression of political degeneration, and not without reason, for when Athens became a self-governing democracy one of its first acts was to sentence Socrates, the paragon of knowledge, to death by drinking poison. It would appear that knowledge and democracy are incompatible and that nothing can bridge the worlds of the cave and the academy.

Moving from Plato's Academy to Immanuel Kant's plea to the Prussian king to have a university founded on the principles of reason, we find a second instance of the precarious relation between knowledge and democracy (Kant, 1979). In what was to be one the most influential visions of the modern university, Kant gave expression to patrician republicanism which confined democracy to academic discourse. In distinguishing between public and private reason, with the former pertaining to academic discourse and the latter being outside argumentation, Kant excluded from the university anything that might be disruptive of the smooth functioning of society. Public reason, institutionalized in the university, was thus de-politicized. The subject of my book is precisely this question of the relationship of knowledge and the culture of democracy with respect to the university. Is a democracy of knowledge possible? Of what would it consist and what kind of university would it call into being?

The current situation of the university reflects the contemporary condition of knowledge. The most striking aspect of this is the penetration of communication into the heart of the epistemic structure of society precisely at a time when this is also happening to democracy, for both knowledge and democracy are being transformed by communication. In the past, in the age of modernity, from the Enlightenment to the postwar period, the institution of knowledge existed in a space outside the flow of communication. This place has been occupied mostly by the university. Knowledge has been seen as a site, a place, that can be occupied by something called a university. In this conception, knowledge was located in the university, not in society, which like the *polis* for Plato, enjoyed the epistemic status of the cave. Communicative forms of action found little resonance in the university, confined as they were to the prepolitical private domain or the public realm from which the university excluded itself. Though universities were always important sites of intellectual resistance to power, the institution was primarily designed to serve the national state with technically useful knowledge and the preservation and reproduction of national cultural traditions. As the protector of the cognitive structure of the modern national state, the university represented an epistemic paradigm in knowledge whose chief characteristic was its autonomy. Underlying this was a model of consensus about the social and political order. In the broader historical context, dissensus in society has only rarely penetrated into the university, exceptions being in the foundation of the University of Berlin, the foundation of University College London and University College Dublin in the nineteenth century and which inspired some of the most important debates on the 'idea of the university'. The university formed a pact with the state: in return for autonomy it would furnish the state with its cognitive requirements. The great social movements of modernity – the workers' movement, the anti-slavery movement, colonial liberation – had little to do with the ivory tower of the academy and its posture of splendid isolation.

This mode of knowledge was challenged in the late 1960s, and in many countries there was considerable reform in the university by the mid-1970s. But these reforms had little impact on the actual production of knowledge and many merely concerned the institutional organization of the university, with demands for student representation and the democratization of an ancient institution. Although the university became for the first time in its history an important site for the radicalization of democratic citizenship, disciplinary-based knowledge continued more-or-less unscathed in what was still an industrial society. What is occurring today in our postindustrial society is a crisis not only in the structure of authority and in the cognitive structures of society as was the case a few decades ago but in the very constitution of knowledge as a result of the extension of democracy into knowledge itself. While in the early 1970s the university did embrace the democratic ethos of citizenship in its strong advocation for civic, political and social rights in movements ranging from the civil rights movement to democratic socialism and feminism, these concerns were relatively extra-epistemic in that they were not directly connected with the production of knowledge itself but with radical democracy and such cognitive ideas as justice, happiness, equality, emancipation. Despite widespread cultural critique, the mode of knowledge was not itself transformed by democracy.

It is a feature of democracy that it is anarchic: it is a space that is inhabited by no one social actor (Lefort, 1986: 279). In the western liberal democracies this pure kind of democracy has been modified by the rule of law, and in the field of knowledge this legal form of democracy, along with democracy's other sides – pluralization, or the representation of interests, and citizenship, or public participation – are limited since knowledge is an open structure and when social forces enter into it the result very often has been ideology. Yet, something like a democracy of knowledge rooted in citizenship can be possible. What makes this prospect more likely today is that the challenge does not just emanate from democratic forces in civil society, as was the case in 1968, but stems to a large degree from changes within the structure of knowledge and its relation to cultural production. Indeed, I would suggest that the intrusion of civil society into the university may even be less revolutionary. The current situation, in my estimation, is a good deal more interesting in that there is far greater questioning of knowledge going on, not only in the academy though, but in society more broadly, and this is leading to a different kind of cognitive structure and to a different and more reflexive role for knowledge. Examples of questions that cut across the epistemic/cognitive, or knowledge/culture, divide are those pertaining to biotechnology, bioethics, nature, ecology and sustainability, the growth of populations, information technology and multiculturalism. In other words, some of the fundamental cultural questions today relate directly to knowledge. My contention in this book is that if the university does respond to the changing nature of knowledge production and of shifts in cognitive structures, it will have to address the challenge of technological and cultural citizenship, which can be seen as the basis of a new cognitive structure.

According to Gibbons *et al.* (1984) a new model of knowledge, called Mode 2, is replacing the Mode 1 of organized modernity. It is characterized by the proliferation of many knowledge producers working in the context of application, which is mostly problem specific. In this situation the university is no longer the primary site of knowledge production, having been challenged by a range of new knowledge producers. Disciplinary boundaries are becoming blurred as multidisciplinarity becomes the norm, and as the new phenomenon of 'postdisciplinarity' takes over (Turner, 1999). What this amounts to is not quite clear. For some it could mean the end of knowledge, or at least of a particular conception of knowledge as self-legislating or legitimated by reference to meta-narratives, as Lyotard argued (Lyotard, 1984). It is clear that there has been widespread de-legitimation of the university in what is also the last great crisis of modernity itself. This crisis is particularly manifest in the battle over knowledge. Just as the beginning of the twentieth century witnessed the end of the nineteenth-century mode of knowledge and dominant cultural model, so too, today, we are witnessing the end of the mode of knowledge that emerged along with organized modernity and its cultural model and institutional framework. Specialization within disciplinary and national boundaries has ceased to be the exclusive kind of knowledge that is being produced today and the university is no longer the privileged site of knowledge. Battles over knowledge in the context of the identity of the university, which first erupted in 1968, have today taken a more radical form and have penetrated into the cultural model of society. With the dissolution of the old socialist movement and the coming of new politics, the university has become a major site of battles of cultural identity, confrontations which have had major repercussions for the very meaning of a discipline-based knowledge as well as a historically formed canon (Bloom, 1987). In these debates the postmodernist attitude to identity – the rejection of a stable concept of the self in favour of multiplicity and heterogeneity – has penetrated into the cognitive structure itself, making dissensus rather than consensus the order of the day.

This all means that the notion that the university as based on a founding cognitive 'idea' – as in the famous works of Newman (1996) or Jaspers (1960) – is no longer tenable: there are many ideas of the university since there are many cognitive structures in contemporary society. With the loss of a self-legitimating idea, or a foundational cognitive model, and the emergence of a multiple order of cognitive models, the question of identity arises. The current situation, then, is one of crisis for the university, as is witnessed in the expanding debate on the identity of university in the past few years (Barnett, 1994; Berube and Nelson, 1995; Scott, 1995; Sommer, 1995; Readings, 1996; Rothblatt, 1997a; Bowen and Shapiro, 1998; Delanty, 1998a,b). Having rationalized knowledge, the university would be in danger of rationalizing itself out of existence were it not for the fact that one dimension to this rationalization of knowledge is the increase in reflexivity. In this reflexive turn in knowledge production, the university has become a focus of cultural reinterpretation about the meaning of knowledge and modernity. The loss of certainty that began with the crisis of nineteenth-century culture has now penetrated into the heart of science with epistemological uncertainty in science being reflected in the crisis of the identity of the university and in the management of risk.

The main changes in the mode of knowledge are the following. First, the historical pact between the state and knowledge that was formed in the late seventeenth century is slowly beginning to unravel. Although still the primary financier of knowledge, the state is no longer the sole guardian of knowledge production. It is true that the state is increasing its subsidization of knowledge, but knowledge is also being produced by other sources. Processes of globalization are also affecting the confinement of knowledge production to the nation state (Scott, 1998b). Of all social resources, it is knowledge, because of its depersonalized and universalistic nature, that lends itself most easily to globalization. Second, contemporary society is coming to depend more and more on knowledge, in economic production, political regulation and in everyday life. This warrants the claim that we are living in a knowledge society as the latest phase of the postindustrial/ information society (Stehr, 1994; Castells, 1996; Böhme, 1997). The third change in the mode of knowledge is that as a result of mass education, social protest and the new social movements, and the rise of new kinds of information technologies, knowledge is more spread through society than ever before; it is no longer confined to elites but is more publicly available. Thus lay knowledge can no longer be separated from professional knowledge (Wallerstein *et al.*, 1996). This insight is the basis of the reflexive thesis, namely that in late modernity, knowledge is increasingly about the application of knowledge to itself rather than to an object. Fourth, and lastly, the relative democratization of knowledge has been accompanied by the growing contestability of knowledge claims. As more and more actors are being drawn into the field of knowledge production, the self-legitimation of the older knowledge elites becomes less certain. In the context of the risk society, the culture of expertise enters into crisis, with the widespread loss of scientific legitimacy and growing public calls for the accountability of science and technology (Beck, 1992).

My thesis, then, is that the current situation amounts to a major epistemic/cognitive shift. Changes in the mode of knowledge are related to a transformation in cultural models and underlying these changes are more far-reaching changes in the institutional framework of society. The current situation is one that requires the articulation of technological and cultural forms of citizenship to complement the older civic, political and social rights of citizenship. This thesis is not quite the same as Castells' argument concerning the information age or other accounts of the knowledge society (Stehr, 1994), for these ultimately tend towards a technological determinism. Knowledge is more than information for it has a far broader range of applicability than information, which is instrumental knowledge: it is related to the cognitive structure of society. This, too, is one of the major limits of the theory of the new production of knowledge, a thesis which reduces knowledge to the application of information (Gibbons *et al.*, 1984). I do not see knowledge only as a matter of expertise. By knowledge I mean the capacity of a society for learning, a cognitive capacity that is related to the production of cultural models and institutional innovation. In the contemporary context, the penetration of knowledge into all spheres of life is clearly one of the major characteristics of the age. We are living in a knowledge society in the sense that social actors have ever greater capacities for self-interpretation and action (Giddens, 1990, 1991; Melucci, 1996). Professional knowledge and lay knowledge are less separate than they used to be. The idea of the knowledge society refers also to something more basic: the opening up of new cognitive fields which have a reflexive relation to knowledge.

In view of the previous analysis, what can we say about the identity of the university today? The postmodern interpretation (Lyotard, 1984; Crook *et al.*, 1992; Readings, 1996) would claim that the university has reached its end and with the closure of modernity has collapsed into a bureaucratic enterprise bereft of moral purpose. Its founding cognitive ideas – the universality of knowledge, the quest for truth, the unity of culture – are becoming irrelevant and the social and economic reality has instrumentalized the university to a point that has made its autonomy neither possible nor desirable. The question we now have to ask is what does the future hold? In my view, Readings offers a starting point: the model of the university that prevailed in liberal modernity and which partly sustained the mass university of organized modernity is in decline today, for its presuppositions have been undermined by social change. The disciplinary structure of knowledge and the nation state no longer totally define the cognitive field of knowledge. Consensus on what constitutes knowledge has been replaced by dissensus, and culture, once preserved and reproduced in the university, is more contested than ever before. If the university is not to degenerate into technocratic consumerism by which students become mere consumers of knowledge and the university a transnational bureaucratic corporation legitimating itself by the technocratic discourse of 'excellence', it will have to discover another role. However, it is clear that the postmodern position has little to offer in terms of an alternative scenario.

The argument in this book is the following. A new role and identity for the university is emerging around the democratization of knowledge. By democratization I mean the participation of more and more actors in the social construction of reality. Given that the university is no longer the crucial institution in society for the reproduction of instrumental/technical knowledge and is also no longer the codifier of a now fragmented national culture, it can ally itself to civil society. No longer the privileged site of particular kinds of knowledge, it can become a key institution in a society that is coming to depend more and more on knowledge. In liberal modernity, knowledge served the state, providing it with a national culture and professional elites; in organized modernity knowledge serviced the occupational order of mass society while enhancing the power and prestige of the state. Today knowledge has become more important and at the same time no longer emanates from any one particular source. This restructuring in the mode of knowledge implies not the end of the university but its reconstitution. The great significance of the institution of the university today is that it can be the most important site of interconnectivity in what is now a knowledge society. There is a proliferation of so many different kinds of knowledge that no particular one can unify all the others. The university cannot re-establish the broken unity of knowledge but it can open up avenues of communication between these different kinds of knowledge, in particular between knowledge as science and knowledge as culture. Of what would a communicative concept of the university consist?

The university must give expression to the new social bond that is emerging in postmodern society, that is communication. Contemporary society is integrated not by national culture, nor is it integrated by the functional prerequisites of the occupational system, be they those of money or power; it is integrated by communication. Under the conditions of societal complexity, neither values nor roles can integrate society, as Luhmann has argued, for complex societies are instead based on differentiated systems of communication. Historically, the site of societal communication has been the public sphere, as described by Habermas in his seminal book (Habermas, 1989). As has been well established in the huge reception of that work, the public sphere has been considerably 'refeudalized' or colonized by the media of money and power and all that remains is the 'phantom public sphere' (Robbins, 1993a). While most critics have rejected Habermas's early call for a return to the Enlightenment model of the public sphere, Habermas himself has more recently advocated a critical concept of the public sphere as lying in the oppositional currents in contemporary society (Habermas, 1996). Taking up this development, my argument is that the real challenge of the university is to occupy the space of the public sphere, a position which Habermas himself put forward in debates on university reform in Germany (Habermas, 1969, 1971a,b, 1992; see also Chapter 4). Even though knowledge is more available than ever before in society and also more central to the working of society, it is also more diffuse. The all-powerful mass media tends to trivialize debate and contribute to the weakening of the cognitive capacities of society. The new mode of knowledge production has not led to the articulation of new cultural models capable of exploiting the democratic potential of the transformation in knowledge. Perhaps this is the mission of the university. The university must recover the public space of discourse that has been lost in the decline of the public sphere. In Habermas's epistemological terms, it must relink knowledge and human interests (Habermas, [1968] 1978). But this will involve an extension of the scientific communication community to include lay knowledge as well as rethinking the relationship between the sciences in the light of the end of positivism (Delanty, 1997). In this respect the university is a key institution for the formation of cultural and technological citizenship.

I am not suggesting that the university can provide spiritual, cultural or political leadership for society, for that is not the role of the university. It is the task of the university to open up sites of communication in society rather than, as it is currently in danger of doing, becoming a self-referential bureaucratic organization. Readings formulated this quite clearly in his advocation of the university as a community of dissensus. Following Lyotard, he argued for the recognition of a distinction between the political horizon of consensus that aims at a self-legitimating, autonomous society and the heteronomous horizon of dissensus. The community of dissensus does not seek an idea of identity, a consensus on the nature of knowledge, or a meta-narrative of unity: 'the University will have to become one place, among others, where the attempt is made to think the social bond without re-course to a unifying idea, whether culture or the state' (Readings, 1996: 191). Thus rather than seeking the unity of culture, a consensus-based community of communication, the point is to institutionalize dissensus and to make the university a site of public debate, thus reversing the decline of the public sphere. I agree that the university is only one institution in society having a diminished importance with respect to culture, state and economy, but one whose significance may increase as a result of the diffusion of knowledge within society. Viewing the university as a site of interconnectivity, communication becomes more central to it. The university cannot enlighten society as the older model of the university dictated. What is needed is a more communicative concept of the university.

Three kinds of communicative interconnecting can be specified: (1) new links between the university and society; (2) new links between the sciences, and (3) changing relations between the university and the state. With regard to the first, the role of the university will change accordingly as more communication occurs between expert systems and public discourse. In this context the university is an important site of public debate between expert and lay cultures. Demands for accountability are growing and the nascent 'audit culture' has already made its impact on the university, in particular in the UK (Power, 1997). If the university is to adapt to social change it will have to evolve ways of responding to this and the more general de-legitimation of science.

Second, cross-disciplinary communication between disciplines and the sciences as a whole will become more important and will change the internal structure of universities. The principal carriers of the university's socio-critical function, which in recent years in the Anglo-Saxon world have shifted from sociology and politics to literature and history, must be spread out into other disciplines across the sciences (Bender and Schorske, 1997). One of the unexplored tasks of the university is to be a site of interconnectivity between the diverse forms of knowledge that are now being produced. If multidisciplinarity is not to degenerate into an empty and instrumentalized 'postdisciplinarity' determined by bureaucratic and financial goals it will have to find new ways of coping with the dissolution of the disciplinary structure of departments. At the moment the solution is purely managerial (Turner, 1999) or entrepreneurial (Slaughter and Leslie, 1997) exercises in 'academic capitalism'.

Third, with the state becoming increasingly a regulatory agency and less exclusively a provider state, the university will be forced to negotiate with non-state actors. This is one of the most difficult challenges facing the university and is beyond the scope of this book. It will suffice to mention here that one avenue that remains to be explored is the creation of a diversity of universities, designed to fulfil different functions. The solution may be in more and smaller universities rather than in economies of scale. With the retreat of the state from taking responsibility for society, the university can take on a greater role in the articulation of the values of technological and cultural citizenship. Given that this new culture of citizenship must be transnational, the university as a cosmopolitan communication community is ideal for this task.

Finally, I would like to clarify the question of what kind of knowledge is produced by the postmodern university in the age of technological and cultural citizenship. There are four kinds of knowledge, to which correspond four knowledge producers. The university fosters the following kinds of knowledge: (1) research, (2) education, (3) professional training, and (4) intellectual inquiry and critique. The first pertains to basic research and the accumulation of information. The second relates to human experience and the formation of personality (once known as *Bildung*). The third concerns the practical task of vocational training and accreditation for professional life, while the fourth deals with the wider public issues of society (*Ausbildung*) and relates to the intellectualization of society. Corresponding to each of these are the roles of the expert, the teacher, the professional trainer and the intellectual. With respect to citizenship, the domains of education and intellectual inquiry and critique relate to cultural citizenship, and the domains of research and professional training relate to technological citizenship. The fulfilment of these two kinds of citizenship is the social responsibility of the university. To find ways of linking these roles and cognitive frameworks into a communicative understanding of the university seems to be what the university needs to achieve today if it is to be able to take on the task of becoming one of the key institutions in the public sphere and in which citizenship is brought forward on to new levels. Although it may be losing its traditional monopoly on knowledge, the fact is that the university is still the only institution in society where these functions can be found together. It is only in this limited sense that we can speak of the 'universalism' of the university.

My overall conclusion is that the central task of the university in the twenty-first century is to become a key actor in the public sphere and thereby enhance the democratization of knowledge. The university is the key institution in society that is capable of mediating between the mode of knowledge, the articulation of cultural models and institutional innovation. The epistemic/cognitive shift that we are witnessing today is one of linking communication in culture, and more generally in society, to the production, organization and diffusion of knowledge. There are many examples of how this is occurring in the world today. In China, for instance, the university was an important site in democratization (Calhoun, 1994) and in the Islamic world the 'Islamization of science', which has been produced by Islamic intellectuals in western universities, has been as much a challenge to western values as to Islamic values. This leads Bryan Turner to the conclusion that the university is caught in a contradiction between national culture and cosmopolitanism, for it is still in essence a national institution but it is the nature of knowledge that it cannot be controlled by national boundaries (Turner, 1998). In Mexico in 1999 one of the longest strikes in the history of the university took place and was the site of a major conflict between civil society and the state. In Serbia in 2000 the universities were important sites of resistance to the state. In the twentieth century the university has been an important space in civil society where democratic values and citizenship were preserved in the face of what was often cultural and political totalitarianism. The university in the age of mass education has been a major site for the articulation of democratic and progressive values, for instance of racial equality, human rights, feminism and social democracy. The task of the university today is to continue this tradition into the age of technological and cultural citizenship. In organized modernity the university was important in shaping social citizenship; today it has the additional task of cultivating technological and cultural forms of citizenship.

Chapter 1 offers a theoretical foundation for some of the arguments that are developed in the course of the book. In it I attempt to locate my approach within the sociology of knowledge and the social theory of modernity. The main thesis advanced here concerns the distinction between knowledge as science and knowledge as culture. My argument is that the university is an institution of both knowledge and cultural reproduction.

Chapter 2 provides an overview of the university in the context of the rise and transformation of modernity. The main legacy is the Enlightenment's reshaping of the classical European idea of the university around a new understanding of knowledge and its role in defining the national state. In this chapter the modern discourse of the 'idea' of the university from Kant and Humboldt to Newman and Jaspers is discussed with respect to some of the main cognitive shifts in the idea of the university.

Chapter 3 deals with the emergence of the mass university in organized modernity, which is the model that has prevailed for much of the twentieth century. In this chapter I look at the university as an institution that exists between the state and capitalism. As an institution of social citizenship, the university is more than a provider of instrumental knowledge. These arguments are put forward through a reading of some of the classic conceptions of the university in the mid-twentieth century, such as the theories of the university of Parsons and Riesman.

Chapter 4 looks at what I call the transformative project, that is the transformation of the cultural project of modernity. My theme is the collapse of the older cultural cognitive models and the creation of new ones as a result of democratization. I argue that with the rise of an adversary culture in the 1960s the university ceased to be merely a transmitter of a received cultural tradition but a transformer. This is discussed with respect to the interpretations of the university of Touraine, Gadamer, Marcuse and Habermas.

Chapter 5 continues the theme of the university as the institutionalization of critique with an analysis of the role of intellectuals. I argue that universities do not simply reproduce social and cultural values but also problematize the cultural models of society. It is in this that the role of intellectuals can be discussed. Intellectuals are not just *reproducers* but also *transformers* of society's cognitive structures. The chapter offers a wide-ranging interpretation of the work of Gramsci, Mannheim, Benda, Bloom, Jacoby, Foucault, Said and Gouldner on intellectuals.

Chapter 6 concerns the work of Pierre Bourdieu on education and the university. By means of a reading of his work the aim of this chapter is to draw attention to the university as a set of social practices which serve as a medium of cultural classification. I argue that what is important in his work with respect to the university is his concern with the cognitive structure that lies behind the production of knowledge.

Chapter 7 examines the ways in which the university is moving from dependence on the state towards an embracing of the market. The main theme is that there is a new mode of knowledge production emerging in which the user is becoming more important than the producer in determining the nature of knowledge. The chapter offers an appraisal of the impact of this allegedly Mode 2 kind of knowledge and discusses the possibility that it might open the way to a technological citizenship.

Chapter 8 continues the theme of the previous chapter by focusing on the question of globalization and the restructuring of universities by academic capitalism. I argue that globalization is bringing about far-reaching change but this is not to be understood as the collapse of all aspects of national culture and the university is still largely a national institution. The persistence of national foundations for knowledge does not hinder the remarkable growth of global collaboration but makes it possible. Although the university is in danger of becoming dominated by global corporate capitalism, it is still an important site of democratization, citizenship and the cultivation of cosmopolitan virtues.

In Chapter 9 I critically examine some influential theories of the postmodern university: Lyotard, Bauman, Derrida and Readings. My aim is to assess the extent to which the thesis of the postmodern university and the paradigm of deconstructionism offers an alternative model to current developments encroaching the end of knowledge. Against deconstructionist approaches, I offer the argument that the university is less 'in ruins', to use Readings's metaphor, than a site of conflicts and is an essentially open institution.

Taking up the conclusion of the previous chapter, Chapter 10 explores some examples of the university as a new cultural battlefield. I argue that the new production of knowledge is not only a matter of market values, the arrival of a new technocorporate culture of managerialism and academic capitalism; it is also about conflicts over identity. The university was the space for the articulation of new kinds of cultural and political identity from the 1980s onwards. The older cultural models of society began to collapse and in the resulting fragmentation of meaning, social groups began to experiment with new models. I examine some of these, such as the culture wars around the curriculum, affirmative action and political correctness, the rise of cultural studies as a new discipline.

Finally, by way of conclusion, I offer an alternative scenario of the role of the university. I see this to be in essence a communicative role and one defined largely by reference to the growing salience of cultural and technological citizenship. The university is founded on the reflexive relationship of these wider cognitive structures to knowledge.

1

Knowledge and Cognition: The Sociology of Knowledge Reconsidered

The university as a site of knowledge production has always been a central institution in society and mirrors some of the great transformations of modernity in so far as these relate to knowledge, its production, organization, function and status in society. In a sense, the university is a microcosm of the broader society. It is reducible neither to power – the state, classes, technology, capitalism – nor to culture, be it that of the Christian religions, bourgeois culture, popular or elite culture; nor is it reducible to science and the academic cultures of knowledge. Rather, the university is an open space in which power, knowledge and culture collide. As a site of knowledge production, the university has been the point of conflict between power and culture. Knowledge is irreducible to either science, power or culture but has an 'imaginary' impulse beyond its concrete manifestations in social, epistemic and cultural structures. It is for this reason that the university as a site of knowledge production can be seen as an 'imaginary institution of society', to use the phrase of Cornelius Castoriadis (Castoriadis, 1987). As I argue in later chapters, this was not always the case, but to an extent the university since the 1970s has been one of the main locations in society where the 'radical imagination' has flourished. Indeed, this was the view of Alfred North Whitehead who, in an essay on universities and their functions, argued: 'The justification for a university is that it preserves the connection between knowledge and the zest of life, by uniting the young and the old in the imaginative consideration of learning. The university imparts information, but it imparts it imaginatively' (Whitehead, 1929: 139). The task of the university, Whitehead argued, was to enable people to construct an intellectual vision of a new world and weld together information and experience. It may be suggested, then, that an adequate view of the university must see it as being linked not only to the production of knowledge but also to the deeper level of experience. In this sense the university is a zone of mediation between knowledge as science (or academic knowledge) and cultural cognition.

In this chapter I am principally concerned with the question of knowledge as a social and cultural category and want to relate changes in knowledge to major social transformations in modernity. Taking this broader view of knowledge as embedded in, but at the same time transformative of, social and cultural structures, I shall attempt to outline a theory of cognitive shifts. In this view, a cognitive shift occurs when a change in knowledge production leads to changes in cultural and social structures: changes in the mode of knowledge bring about the articulation of new cultural models leading to institutional innovation. My aim is to demonstrate that in these shifts the function of the university changes, and that in the present period there is a cognitive shift occurring which is leading to the formation of a university based on what I call social interconnectivity.

I begin by placing these arguments and those which will be developed in subsequent chapters in the context of theoretical developments in epistemology and, more specifically, in the sociology of knowledge. In a second step I outline the idea of cognitive shifts in the context of a middle-range theory of modernity. In a third step I apply these ideas to the university in modernity. This approach is intended to provide a framework for the remainder of the book.

Rethinking the sociology of knowledge

The sociology of knowledge has its roots in classical French sociology, and has even deeper roots in late Enlightenment thinking. In the Enlightenment spirit of Condorcet and later of Saint-Simon, Auguste Comte conceived of the entire evolution of society in terms of the development of forms of knowledge of which the final stage would be the positivistic stage, by which he meant the coming of a society founded on knowledge. Inspired by Hegel, he developed a sociology that saw societies undergoing change accordingly as their systems of knowledge developed. His law of the 'three stages' describes the process by which societies progressed from the theological stage or traditional stage (when magical or pre-reflective kinds of knowledge were dominant) to the metaphysical or modern stage (characterized by rational and abstract knowledge such as conceptions of sovereignty and law) and finally to the positive or 'postmodern' stage (when modern experimental science becomes the dominant form of knowledge).

Another origin of the sociology of knowledge can be traced to the work of Emile Durkheim who saw knowledge as a social construction and related to the cultural system of meaning. Unlike Comte, Durkheim was more concerned with the cultural significance of knowledge as a cognitive structure and he did not see knowledge as the primary feature of modernity. He did not intend this to mean a complete identity between knowledge and society to the point that all knowledge claims are relativistic (Schmaus,

1994). Social knowledge for Durkheim was based on the observation of universal structures which could be uncovered by scientific knowledge. This peculiarly French positivistic tradition, which assumed the separation of science and culture, was taken up by his successor at the Sorbonne, Georges Gurvitch, who in a famous work first published in 1960, *The Social Framework of Knowledge* (Gurvitch, 1971), established the foundations of a systematic sociology of cognitive systems dealing with such forms of knowledge as knowledge of the external world, knowledge of the Other, political knowledge, technical knowledge and common-sense knowledge. While some of these early developments were greatly influenced by anthropology, with the work of Lucien Levy-Bruhl being of particular importance, the modern sociology of knowledge received a major impetus from Karl Mannheim who concerned himself with the social process of ideology and the limits and possibility of sociological analysis (Dant, 1991). Although Durkheim's work did suggest a broader concept of knowledge, such as the Comtean one, the sociology of knowledge in fact developed under Mannheim's influence and tended to reduce knowledge to the world of ideas, in particular ideologies associated with particular groups in society.

Before commenting further on Mannheim's influence I wish to allude to another, and older, classical tradition dealing with the confluence of epistemology and knowledge, namely the tradition begun by Hegel and taken up by Marx. The phenomenological constitution of knowledge was Hegel's central philosophical concept. In the Hegelian tradition, knowledge did not take the objective cognitive form it did in the French tradition from Comte to Durkheim. Rather than see knowledge as fixed systems of thought or as cultural models attached to social structures, Hegel saw knowledge as part of the self-constitution of society and the progressive forms it took were forms of self-consciousness. Knowledge and self-reflection were mutually entwined. This conception of knowledge was obscured in Marx's critique of Hegel and the consequent reduction of knowledge to ideology. Yet, it has remained an influential part of western Marxism and of critical theory and their notions of knowledge as consciousness-raising. The mainstream sociology of knowledge has tended to be regarded by Marxists as politically conservative, as is best represented in Adorno's critique of Mannheim or in Lukacs's revision of Marxism in the 1920s (Adorno, 1983). In one of the later expressions of western Marxism, Herbert Marcuse characterized all forms of knowledge as ideological (Marcuse, 1964). The possibility for a more nuanced understanding of knowledge was thus blocked in the Marxist tradition. Yet, the Marxist approach, with its Hegelian roots, contained the basic ideas for a constructivist sociology of knowledge. In this regard, of importance is the debate on theory and practice, which roughly corresponds to knowledge and action (Habermas, 1972).

Of these four classical conceptions – Comte, Hegelian-Marxism, Durkheim and Mannheim – there is no doubt that the latter was the most influential in shaping the dominant tradition in the sociology of knowledge. Mannheim established the foundations of a more rigorous sociology of knowledge as an analysis of how social groups construct systems of knowledge (Mannheim, 1936, 1952; Wolff, 1993; see also Chapter 5). Mannheim's approach was very influential in Europe, though not so in the United States where it was met with considerable resistance owing to its concern with the broader context of worldviews. Mannheim in fact had a greater impact on Marxist thinking – for instance on the work of Lukacs – than on American empirical sociology, not surprisingly given the concern of western Marxism from the 1920s with ideology; but since Mannheim gave no place to the dialectical moment the Marxist and Mannheimean approaches ultimately diverged. His ideas had a strong influence on Norbert Elias who brought the tradition forward, but in a new key, and there is some indication today of a more general rehabilitation of Mannheim's work. However, in the formative period of the sociology of knowledge, two quite separate approaches emerged, neither having much to do with the classical founder of the sociology of knowledge.

On the one side, there is the positivistically inclined tradition dealing with the more narrowly focused study of communication, public opinion and science and the sociology of social groups, such as the sociology of professions and intellectuals. In the United States, Robert Merton's approach, as represented in his influential 1938 study, *Science, Technology and Society in Seventeenth Century England*, offered an alternative to Mannheim's concern with ideas (Merton, 1970; see also Merton, 1973). Mannheim had excluded science itself from the domain of the sociology of knowledge. In effect, Merton reduced the sociology of knowledge to a more narrowly conceived empirical sociology of science within a broadly functionalist framework.

On the other side was the quite separate approach best associated with Peter Berger and Thomas Luckmann's well known book *The Social Construction of Reality* (Berger and Luckmann, 1967). In this tradition, which is rooted in the phenomenological sociology of Alfred Schutz, the sociology of knowledge is radicalized by a rejection of a focus on systems or bodies of knowledge, science, political ideologies, utopias and systems of ideas in favour of a more hermeneutic/phenomenological turn to common-sense knowledge (Schutz, 1967). In this rejection of Mannheimean sociology, Mertonian sociology of science and the American empirical sociology of knowledge, the cognitive dimension to knowledge, that is the basic cultural dimension which is necessary for the constitution or construction of all systems and bodies of knowledge, becomes the central concern of the sociology of knowledge. Schutz did not use the term the sociology of knowledge as such for his project, which also had resonances in the work of Piaget and Wittgenstein who wrote about the deeper cognitive and linguistic structures upon which all knowledge is based. This approach, as represented by Berger and Luckmann (1967), Cicourel (1973) and much of the ethnomethodological tradition, is characterized by its 'constructivist' stance with regard to knowledge as rooted in deeper cultural complexes and has laid the basis of much of the more recent constructivist sociology of knowledge, and the relatively new sub-discipline, social studies of science and

technology (Mendelsohn *et al.*, 1977; Stehr and Meja, 1984). Adopting constructivist theory, a whole variety of theorists – Bloor (1976), Knorr-Cetina
(1981), Gibbons *et al.*, 1984, Latour (1987), Woolgar (1988), Fuller (1993),
Nowotny (2000) – have produced influential works on the social production of technical knowledge and expertise. In the spirit of this constructivist
turn, the sociology of knowledge has also found its way into feminist epistemology (McCarthy, 1996) and the sociology of social movements (Eyerman
and Jamison, 1991) and has led to a reinterpretation of the history of
sociology (Strydom, 2000) and historical epistemologies of concept formation (Somers, 1996, 1999). Thus, whereas Mannheim focused on ideas and
later Merton more on knowledge as science (*Wissen*), Schutz, and following
from his lead, Berger and Luckmann, looked at the deeper cognitive construction of knowledge, that is knowledge as cognition (*Erkennen/Erkenntnis*).

From a different perspective, the sociology of postindustrial society, with
major contributions coming from Bell (1974), Touraine (1971a) and Castells
(1996) has produced studies on the role of knowledge and information in
contemporary society. According to the latest of these, we are now living in
what is in essence an information society, a society characterized by the
centrality of knowledge (Webster, 1995). One of the main challenges for
the sociology of knowledge is to link these analyses of the postindustrial or
information society to the constructivist sociology of knowledge. So far, no
explicit attempt has been made to do this, but some intimations can be
found in the social theory of modernity.

The social theory of modernity from Weber to Foucault, Bourdieu,
Touraine and Habermas has offered ways of linking knowledge and intellectual paradigms to major social transformations (Beck, 1992; Wagner,
1994; Delanty, 1999, 2000a). In particular, the work of Foucault (1980) on
knowledge has been pivotal in linking knowledge to historical epistemologies
and theories of power and discourse. According to Foucault, discourses are
all-inclusive language games which are 'productive' of knowledge and of
power. Discourse does not offer the possibility of communication, as it does
for Habermas for whom it contains unredeemed validity claims. For Foucault,
in contrast, discourse is a closed system of power and, in so far as power and
knowledge are co-extensive, knowledge does not have an emancipatory moment. The human actor is condemned to discourse and therefore to power,
which is coeval with the discourse, its rules and forms of knowledge. The
sociology of Bourdieu has not been too far removed from this approach to
knowledge as discourse. For Bourdieu, knowledge is embedded in cognitive
structures which are linked to the field of power and the struggle of social
groups for supremacy (Bourdieu, 1984; see also Chapter 6).

Other approaches in the philosophy of social science see the connection
between knowledge and power in different terms but are all agreed that
knowledge is shaped by deeper cognitive structures. The diverse approaches
of Kuhn (1970), on the one hand, and Apel (1980) and Habermas ([1968]
1978) on the other have opened up ways of seeing how social interests and
the wider cognitive structures of society enter into the world of science. In

the case of Kuhn, this was something threatening closed paradigms based on established forms of consensus on what constitutes a paradigm (Fuller, 2000). For Apel and Habermas, the recognition of social interests and cognitive structures within the scientific community is essential to the formation of a reflective and socially responsible 'scientific communication community', to use Apel's term (Delanty, 1997). In works such as his influential *Knowledge and Human Interests* published in 1969 (Habermas, 1978), Habermas's concern with 'knowledge' was not with knowledge as *Wissen* but knowledge as *Erkenntnis* (as cognition). In this context, mention must also be made of the work of Roberto Mangabeira Unger. In his *Knowledge and Politics*, Unger established the foundations of a radical theory of emancipatory knowledge rooted in a constructivist social theory (Unger, 1975). In these works a concept of knowledge as cognition is present, that is knowledge as a cognitively constructed system.

The concern with the broader context of knowledge is also present in American pragmatism, though there the focus was more with the relation of knowledge as science to public interests. This question of public role was also articulated within sociology by Robert Lynd, one of the leading figures in the Chicago School. His *Knowledge for What?* questioned the academization of social scientific knowledge (Lynd, 1939). The idea of knowledge as a public utility could be said to be central to the unwritten history of early American social theory. It was reflected in the writing of John Dewey (1930) and the Polish sociologist Florian Znaniecki (1968) in his *The Social Role of the Man of Knowledge*, first published in 1944. However, in the pragmatist tradition the concern with knowledge was largely confined to its social role rather than its cultural or cognitive dimension.

In sum, then, debates in the sociology of knowledge have established a conception of knowledge as linked to social and cultural structures. While views differ on the nature of this relationship and its political implications, the sociological approach to knowledge forces us to see knowledge as a socially constructed structure having a creative as well as an intellectual dimension. But knowledge is more than a social construction; it is also an open structure that admits of internal development. Indeed, this recognition of the openness of knowledge and of cognitive structures was the central point of much of Jean Piaget's work which had a huge impact on such social theorists as Habermas and Apel. This raises the question of learning mechanisms, to which I now turn.

Cognitive shifts and the social theory of modernity

I would like to begin by distinguishing among the mode of knowledge production, cultural models and the institutional framework. By a *mode of knowledge* I mean the production of knowledge as a set of discourses cutting across the institutional and the epistemological. Knowledge is not simply self-producing but occurs in a social and cultural context; it is a system of social relations and a category of cultural self-understanding and communication; or, as Foucault said, a system of power and a discursive practice (Foucault, 1980). Much of social life is based on knowledge: the production of food, technology, communication systems, security, the appropriation of nature, sport and consumption (Goldman, 1999). I am using the term knowledge, too, in the broader sense of a mechanism of collective learning, that is the accumulation of knowledge in groups, institutions and organizations. In this sense, then, knowledge refers to the cognitive structure of society in its cultural and institutional forms in so far as this relates to learning mechanisms. This concerns then the question of cultural models, the deeper cognitive basis of knowledge.

The concept of a *cultural model* refers to the interpretative models by which a society gains knowledge of itself and offers objective frames of reference for what Max Weber called value orientations and the social struggles for symbolic capital, to use Bourdieu's term. Cultural models, if we follow theorists as diverse as Weber, Castoriadis, Touraine and Habermas, are represented in major principles of rationality, imaginary significations, cultural value spheres, such as those of morality, religion and art, and historical narratives. The main cultural models of society are to be found in the cognitive, the normative and the aesthetic structures, but below these is what Bourdieu has called symbolic capital and also what an older sociology called values and norms (on Bourdieu see Chapter 6). Cultural models are thus broader than the mode of knowledge, for while including the cognitive they also entail aesthetic and moral structures. I shall be using the term to refer principally to the cognitive structures that define the basic conceptual structures of knowledge (see Holland and Quinn, 1991).

Finally, the *institutional framework* refers to the mode of production and the accumulation of wealth, the regulation of populations and social relations, and government. The institutional framework concerns social practices that make up the economic and political structures of society as well as the social institutions of the life world.

This three-fold distinction among knowledge, culture and society has the advantage that it gives a central role to the sociology of knowledge (and a basis for a sociological theorization of the university). In this view, knowledge is linked (largely through the institution of the university) to the cognitive complexes of culture and to social practices and institutional structures. The mainstream sociological approaches influenced by Mannheim and Merton tended to marginalize knowledge, reducing it to a body of ideas or ideology on the one side, or on the other, to science. Weber, for instance, was greatly interested in the role of knowledge but he subsumed it either under processes of intellectualization and instrumental rationalization – that is principles of rationality – or under the cognitive value sphere in the context of value pluralization and disenchantment. Durkheim conflated knowledge with culture and thus did not appreciate the constructivist tension between both. Marxists have, on the one side, reduced knowledge to an epiphenomenon of the mode of production and, on the other, reserved for it a quasi-essentialistic role as class consciousness. Mannheim reduced knowledge to the ideas of particular groups. Finally, in the classical tradition, Parsons recognized the importance of knowledge and the university as a subsystem in the zone of interpenetration lying between the cultural system and society. The 'university is the trustee of cognitive culture', argued Talcott Parsons and Gerald Platt in *The American University* (Parsons and Platt, 1973: 148). But the main weakness of the Parsonian theory was its inability to see how knowledge is contested, and its relation to culture and society is therefore prone to conflict.

This is precisely what Alain Touraine has remedied in his important book *The Self-production of Society*, published in 1973. In this work he distinguished between knowledge, the cultural model of society, and accumulation (Touraine, 1977). Taking up some of his ideas, though more from the perspective of the university than social movements, which was Touraine's concern in that work, I am stressing the importance of knowledge as a mode of social organization and as a 'social epistemology', that is as a cognitive structure that is always more than knowledge as science (Fuller, 1993, 1994). This approach recalls that of George Gurvitch who, in the *Social Frameworks of Knowledge*, distinguished among the mode of knowledge, cognitive systems and social frameworks (Gurvitch, 1971). However, in his approach, which was heavily influenced by Durkheim, there is no place for the internal development of cognitive systems or learning processes in society. The cognitive dimension to knowledge, and hence constructivism, is much more pronounced in the work of Touraine for whom the mode of knowledge and cultural models are two moments in the formation of modern society. Throughout this book I lean heavily on the distinction between knowledge as science (*Wissen*) and knowledge as a cognitive system (*Erkenntnis*), thereby allowing a theorization of the university as a mediatory site between these two levels of knowledge.

Such a theoretization of knowledge allows a perspective on *cognitive shifts* in modernity. By this is meant more than just changes in the mode of knowledge; it encompasses the wider transformation of culture and society. A cognitive shift entails a shift from the potential for learning that is contained on the level of knowledge to its socio-cultural appropriation on the level of cultural models and institutional innovation. A cognitive shift thus involves an evolutionary change in the cultural model and in the institutional framework. As such it is a contrast to a mere change in the mode of knowledge: for what is available on the level of knowledge may not penetrate into the cultural model of society, and if it does, it is also a further question as to whether it will be taken up in social structures in bringing about institutional innovation. Societies do not learn in the same way that individuals learn (Habermas, 1979; Strydom, 1987, 1992, 1993; Eder, 1999). Durkheim recognized this asymmetry between educational change and social change in the *Evolution of Educational Thought* but never followed up his conclusions (Durkheim, 1977).

Modern societies are learning societies in that a high degree of knowledge has been accumulated on the level of the mode of knowledge and much of it has become integral to the cultural model of society. Yet, as Klaus Eder has shown, this does not mean that society has availed of such collective learning, for learning does not always lead to evolution, that is change on the level of culture does not necessarily translate into social change (Eder, 1999). I am suggesting, then, that the idea of a cognitive shift refers to such major social transformations as those in which developments in *learning*, that is changes in the mode of knowledge, have led to the articulation of new cultural models and social *evolution* (in the sense of institutional evolution). This notion of a cognitve shift related to developments in learning and evolution has been explored by Santos (1995) who has introduced the idea of a 'paradigmatic shift' in law, science and politics by which knowledge as emancipation gains ascendancy over knowledge as regulation. The notion of a cognitive shift is similar in that it refers to the confluence of change in the mode of knowledge, cultural models and institutional frameworks.

It has occasionally occurred in history that the mode of knowledge has led to major social change, for instance in the early modern period from the Renaissance to the Reformation, which I shall call classical modernity. The mode of knowledge, which may be termed revolutionary knowledge, led to geographical, medical and astronomical discoveries, new techniques in painting, music and architecture, philosophical argument and religion. These changes in knowledge had major repercussions in the articulation of new cultural models and ultimately in the institutional framework of society, leading to the formation of modern nation states and modern forms of political authority. We can thus speak of a cognitive shift occurring in the period that culminated in the American and French Revolutions, which brought to a close the early modern period and constituted the first great crisis of modernity. In the early modern period cultural modernity emerged largely because of the great changes in the mode of knowledge that began with the New Learning in the Age of Discovery. With the French Revolution, classical modernity came to a close when its basic cultural model, the humanist idea of the unity of culture and the overall unity of culture and nature (which Toulmin (1992) has called the idea of a cosmopolis – the vision of a society as perfectly ordered as the laws of nature), became unsustainable. At about this time, too, the limits of its model of knowledge – revolutionary, emancipatory and humanist knowledge – was challenged by the post-Enlightenment era of nineteenth-century reform, historicism and positivism.

In the next period, liberal modernity, roughly from the French Revolution to the end of the nineteenth century, a new cultural model emerged around secularism and cultural differentiation. As a result of secularization and rationalization, the nineteenth century moved to a new cultural imaginary which was expressed in the ideal of autonomy in rights and in the pursuit of knowledge. Bourgeois or civil society replaced the court society, and in the mode of knowledge the unity of knowledge of classical modernity shifted to the neohumanist, positivist and Enlightenment aspiration towards the autonomy of knowledge. This was encapsulated in the philosophy of Hegel and Comte, and was present, too, in Kant who argued for the separation of the laws of nature and of morality. Although their conceptions of knowledge were very different, Hegel and Comte saw history in terms of the progressive self-constitution of humanity by forms of knowledge. In the modern period, the form of knowledge was held to be one leading to the self-legislation of knowledge. Liberal modernity ended in the mood of crisis that set in towards the end of the century with the *fin de siècle* and the culture of anxiety that surrounded the First World War, which marked the second crisis of modernity: the rejection of truth, autonomy and rationality.

The second crisis of modernity led to the decline of liberal modernity and the arrival of organized modernity which was to span the twentieth century, until its closure in the 1970s (Law, 1994; Wagner, 1994). In this period, which is one of institution building and nation state formation, we have the emergence of a new cultural model, the ideal of social integration, a development related to the replacement of bourgeois society by mass society. The mode of knowledge that prevailed over much of the twentieth century was one of differentiation, or specialization, within disciplinary boundaries administered by experts and which was part of wider processes of societal modernization (Wagner *et al.*, 1991a,b). This age of organized modernity has generally been held to come to a close in the 1960s and 1970s with the rise of developments associated with postmodernism, colonial liberation, the rise of new social movements and postmaterialist values, democratization, population growth and migration, ecological crisis and, more recently, globalization and complexity. In this period modernity enters its third and, for some, final crisis. The cultural model of integration has been challenged by new forms of exclusion and fragmentation; the mode of knowledge, the self-legitimation of expertise, has been challenged by the universal crisis of the risk society and processes of de-differentiation have undermined the logic of differentiation associated with modernization.

Now that this crisis is beginning to subside and give way to a new social formation, whose contours are as yet uncertain, we can speak of the emergence of a new mode of knowledge and a new cultural model within the context of a changing society. I return to this in later chapters, suggesting the notion of a cognitive shift in contemporary society analogous to that which appeared in early modern society. Briefly, it can be characterized as a movement towards social reflexivity and discursivity which comes with the opening up of new public spheres and the empowering of social actors by knowledge. Knowledge is neither a tool of domination, an ideology, nor a neutral category but is embedded in contemporary cultural models and in much of the institutional framework. In the sketch that follows I apply the idea of cognitive shifts and the social theory of modernity to the university as one of the most important sites of the articulation of the new mode of knowledge.

The university and the transformation of knowledge

In the early modern period, in classical modernity, the university was not central to the production of knowledge. In the Renaissance the university certainly played a role in shaping the New Learning but it was less important in the Enlightenment where the mode of knowledge was formed outside the academy. In this period, knowledge producers were mostly extra-institutional; they were men of letters, free-floating intellectuals and often members of the aristocratic orders or the reformed clergy. The mode of knowledge that emerged was one of revolutionary, emancipatory knowledge. It marked a turn to the subject as the measure of truth, in the sense that knowledge became something that was publicly available. The Renaissance, Reformation and the Enlightenment were all expressions of a preoccupation with the independence of knowledge from political and clerical authority. The rise of empirical method, on the one hand, and of modern rationalism on the other epitomized this trend away from dogmatism: the essence of inductive experimental science was that only that which could be subject to experimental verification was to count as knowledge; rationalism, in a similar way, declared that knowledge in its most certain form derives from the certainties of the mind. Although these epistemologies have become tainted as positivistic, it must be remembered that in their time they were emancipatory in their postulation of the democratic nature of knowledge as something available to any human being as opposed to the prerogative of an institutional authority. But as knowledge shifted away from the ancient authorities it came increasingly under the sway of the nascent absolutist state. A struggle for institutionalization emerged in classical modernity with the foundation of the royal academies and state-supported institutions of research from the mid-seventeenth century onwards and two forms of knowledge emerged, one institutionalized in the university and the academy, and the other in the extra-institutional in those public spaces in civil society that were the social basis of the Enlightenment. It has been the fate of history that the second form was to lose its epistemological relevance and many forms of knowledge, for instance sociology, had to choose with which side they would align themselves (Lepenies, 1988). In this period, too, the university shifted from the Church to the state in its basic allegiance, and as it did so it began to disconnect itself from society.

With the emergence of liberal modernity from the end of the eighteenth century, the university became more important as a knowledge producer, serving the nation state with professional elites and as a codifier of national culture. The neohumanist university, such as the Humboldtian university in Germany or the liberal arts college in the Anglo-Saxon world, was based on the idea of the autonomy of knowledge, a view of the university that received one of its most famous formulations in Kant's vision of the modern university as the protector of critical reason (Kant, 1979). This was a development of the Enlightenment ideal of knowledge and reflected, too, the broader humanist conception of knowledge, but differed from it in that it was heavily influenced by the new cultural model which was to dominate the nineteenth century: the differentiation of cultural spheres and the pursuit of truth. In a differentiated age, which Max Weber described as disenchanted in the sense of the irretrievable loss of an overarching principle of unity, knowledge becomes autonomous, an end in itself. In the neohumanist university this self-legislation of knowledge is reflected in the unity of teaching and research, which together serve the pursuit of truth, although the actual nature of this truth and the possibility of its attainment became increasingly obscure as the century progressed. Yet, the nineteenth century held on to the illusion of truth and the spiritual mission of knowledge. The differentiation of knowledge, for instance the emergence of hierarchies of knowledge and the separation of facts and values, did not challenge the still powerful ideal of truth. Natural theology was very influential in the universities in the second half of the nineteenth century (Reuben, 1996). Institutional secularism was not always mirrored in intellectual secularism, a reminder too that by far the most important source of Enlightenment ideas was the reformed Churches. In Catholic France, where the Enlightenment was more fiercely anti-clerical, the university was marginalized by the *Grandes écoles*, created by the post-revolutionary state, where the *Bildungs* ideal was totally absent. But France was the exception and the nineteenth-century conception of the university was on the whole dominated by the Kantian ideal of reason and the yet more influential von Humboldtian idea of culture. In Victorian England, literature served the function of philosophy in Germany; but there, too, the von Humboldtian idea was influential, as evidenced by Matthew Arnold, whose *Culture and Anarchy* transmitted the German tradition (Arnold, 1960). In the conservative English tradition, as in the German, from Arnold to Eliot and Leavis, the university was the custodian of culture which alone could provide spiritual leadership in an industrial age. Nevertheless, one qualification must be made. The radical, reformist zeal of many Victorians – from Bentham to Mill and Spencer – on the whole was suspicious of high culture as an end in itself, preferring a more utilitarian view of knowledge as leading to social and moral amelioration. Knowledge for the utilitarian cast of mind was not an end but a means to an end, the ends of happiness, social prosperity or peace.

In organized modernity, from the late nineteenth century and extending until the 1960s and 1970s, the founding ideals of liberal modernity are profoundly shaken. The ideas of *fin de siècle* destroyed the cultural model of liberal modernity and the older mode of knowledge collapsed with the emergence of a new one that was part of the new social order of mass society. Natural theology and the spiritual value of knowledge disappeared; logical positivism and disinterested inquiry became all-powerful. The new mode of knowledge demanded a far stricter separation of facts and values than before. It was one that stressed specialization and discipline-based knowledge within the confines of the national systems of governance above all else. The neohumanist integration of teaching and research became challenged by the new ideal of the research university and sharply defined disciplines. The twentieth century was the era of the expert, and professional society replaced the last remnants of Enlightenment humanism. The university acquired a new function in society: to supply a trained labour force. The teacher and the researcher acquired a new role: professional training. It is no longer a matter of the education of the whole person, as in the von Humboldtian ideal of *Bildung* or the ideal of pastoral care in the liberal arts college, but of *Ausbildung* – vocational training. The university affirmed the new cultural model of social integration in that it was an institution which serviced the economic needs of society, national prestige and defence as well as the production of the technological expertise. A famous expression of this was Clark Kerr's *The Uses of the University* (Kerr, 1963) but many other visions of the university from this period retained the older idea of autonomy, such as the work of Shils (1997) and Riesman (1998) for whom knowledge still had a moral role derived from the essential unity of the university.

Late modernity begins with the crisis of organized modernity from the 1960s onwards. This is best portrayed as a movement from crisis to transition in which a cognitive shift can be discerned. Some of the key aspects of this can be summarized as follows. There is a gradual disintegration of the older mode of knowledge based on disciplinary knowledge institutionalized within national frameworks and legitimated by the cultural models of modernization, specialization and routinization. First, knowledge which has historically been linked to the national state is now, under the impact of globalization, being produced by other institutions in society. Second, the structure of disciplinary knowledge within the academy was based on the supposition of two entirely different subject areas, external nature and human nature, the basis of the 'two cultures'. Today, nature has re-emerged as a new theme in natural and social science. As a construction, nature, like society, cannot be conceived in terms of the categories of modernity (Eder, 1996; Wallerstein *et al.*, 1996). Aside from this, there is a wider transformation within the disciplinary structure of knowledge within the university (Goodman and Fisher, 1995; Wallerstein *et al.*, 1996; Bender and Schorske, 1997). Third, new conceptions of democracy and citizenship are now emerging to challenge the older visions. Cultural and technological citizenship is centrally addressed to issues relating to knowledge (Delanty, 2000b). As a result of mass education, the media and technological developments in the postindustrial society, knowledge is more available than ever before and is at the same time more and more a functional necessity. But with this expansion in knowledge has come its growing contestability. Dissensus in politics and cultural values has penetrated the constitution of knowledge. Fourth, in places of debates on differences between the sciences, what is becoming more relevant is the question of the relationship between professional and other kinds of knowledge, such as lay knowledge. With the widespread de-legitimation of science and the culture of expertise this is becoming of central importance in the reorientation of knowledge, with major implications for the university. It is a question of the public relevance of professional knowledge.

I am suggesting that something like a cognitive shift is occurring today in the decline of the Enlightenment's 'republic of science'. With the rise of critical publics the demand for democratization has penetrated the heart of cognitive rationality in calls for the public accountability of science. This cognitive shift can be seen as a communicative one, but one that is challenged by a neoliberal understanding of the university. Once standing on the secure ground of the Enlightenment and the national state, the university now finds itself occupying the uncertain terrain of shifting forms of knowledge at precisely the time that the nation state is entering a period of decline. The age of Big Science, has suffered the fate of Big Government: its legitimation has gone but the reality is still with us. No longer protected from democracy, the logic of communicative rationality has entered the academy calling into question the old cognitive models of neutrality, universality and objectivity.

2

The University in the Age of Liberal Modernity: Between Cosmopolitanism and Nation State

In this chapter I deal with the rise and decline of the nineteenth-century university. The modern idea of the university derives from the Enlightenment which also bequeathed the notion that the university rests on an underlying *idea* which legitimates its mode of knowledge. This idea comes from the prevailing cultural models of the age: the unity of culture and the universality of cultural values. The nineteenth century adhered to the overriding belief in the possibility of truth and the spiritual mission of knowledge. Although the various national traditions differed in their attitude to the status and function of knowledge, there was widespread support for the view that the pursuit of knowledge is necessary for the well-being of society. The university was the dominant site for the production of knowledge, which was taken out of the margins of society and placed under the supervision of the state. But knowledge can never totally be institutionalized, and just as the prevailing cultural models of society enter into tension with institutional frameworks, so too does the mode of knowledge express a certain resistance to the state in its attempt to impose an epistemic regime on knowledge. This resistance is best exemplified in the tension between the national and the cosmopolitan faces of the university, to mention the most striking example. A related example, to be discussed in this chapter, is the nineteenth-century debate about secularism and the role of natural theology and the wider conflict between tradition and modernity. These conflicts can be more conceptually expressed in the terms of the sociology of knowledge discussed in the previous chapter as one of a tension between the mode of knowledge and cultural models. Epistemic shifts in knowledge and in cognitive structures have tended to be particularly pronounced in the institution of the university whose social practices have expressed not just the mode of knowledge but also the dominant and emergent cultural models of society.

The rise of the modern university

In medieval times, scholars in search of the truth came to the university giving it a cosmopolitan character. The medieval university was a place of 'universal knowledge'; it was tied to the universal ideology of Christendom and, in the beginning, it was an appendage to the monasteries but later became an ally of the secular rulers. The university, like the monastery, was a truly cosmopolitan institution in that it was not tied to a particular nation state but to a universal order. Universities did exist in the non-Christian world in this period, and several major universities flourished in the Muslim world. One of the largest universities in the medieval period was in Timbuktu, with over twenty-five thousand students in the fifteenth century. But the academic freedom and disciplinary specialization that was cultivated in the European universities was crucial. According to Randall Collins, European universities had a creative dynamism that was unique and which was based on their ongoing process of disciplinary specialization. 'Chinese, Greek, Islamic, Hindu and late Medieval Christian schools stagnated in scholasticisms; in each case their curricula became stuck in a set number of fields. The European university pattern, in contrast, has generated an ongoing stream of new specializations. It is the process of breaking off, and the resulting opportunities for new combinations of ideas, that drives creativity within the academic system' (Collins, 1998: 688).

In the great universities of the Middle Age – Paris, Oxford, Padua, Toledo, Bologna – scholars travelled from all over Europe to study and teach at these institutions giving them a cosmopolitan character (Wieruszowski, 1966; Cobban, 1975; Kittelson and Transue, 1984; Ferruolo, 1985; Rashdall, 1987). The universities, of which there were some fifty by 1500, were much more cosmopolitan in their membership than those of today: the ten thousand students at Bologna in the twelfth century came from all parts of Europe. With the fall of Constantinople to Islam in 1453, Greek scholars fled to the western universities. Their scholarship was to be crucial in the formation of the culture of the Renaissance and the gradual shift 'from humanism to the humanities' (Grafton and Jardie, 1986). Latin was the common tongue of European universities, and with its decline the university lost one of its most cosmopolitan features. Communication in a pre-print culture was extremely slow, and in the absence of academic technology, such as copying facilities, knowledge was frequently unreproducible, remaining the intellectual property of those privileged to have access to the great manuscripts of antiquity. Links between the university and the rest of society were few and those that did exist were mostly defined by the church. As anyone familiar with Umberto Eco's *The Name of the Rose* will recall, the mode of knowledge in the Middle Ages was one that had isolated itself from the rest of society. Because of limited technology of reproduction, knowledge, as Auguste Comte recognized even in his own time, was compelled to be 'metaphysical', that is not embodied in social reality.

Unlike the modern researcher, the medieval scholar could claim to be able to read everything written. It has been said, with some exaggeration, that Goethe was the last universalistic intellectual who could credibly claim to have read everything that had been written. Today, in contrast, most academics find it difficult to read everything published in their own field of enquiry alone and are often ignorant of the works of the classics, which are relegated to undergraduate courses. But the comparison cannot be taken too far, not least because most modern universities have no real ties with medieval universities and were products of industrialism, the majority being founded either in the three decades prior to the First World War or in the period following the Second World War. Moreover, the medieval university was pre-eminently a place of instruction not of teaching, living or research. The modes of knowledge that prevailed ranged from the doctrinal to the hermeneutical. Even in the case of the latter, the Enlightenment ideal of self-cultivation was absent: the knower was simply required to understand a text. It was a hermeneutic rather than a critical project. Enlightened knowledge, in contrast, was intended to be emancipatory with a unity of purpose between teaching and research, these being different ways in which knowledge could be created as opposed to merely being reproduced. Medieval universities were based on written forms of knowledge, unlike the early Greek preference for speech. By the time of Plato's Academy and later Aristotle's Lyceum there had already been some move away from the association of knowledge and speech. Knowledge ceased to be participation in the *polis*, signifying instead membership of an academy located on a higher plane of being (Gouldner, 1965). Speech became subordinated to the written word. Yet, even in this transition, teaching and learning retained their essential identity of purpose and knowledge was rooted in the cognitive models of the *polis*. This harmonious Greek model eventually collapsed with the rise of the Christian worldview and with it a new mode of knowledge.

The medieval conception of knowledge nevertheless retained the basic Aristotelian structure in its organization into the seven liberal arts (the three linguistic arts of the Trivium: grammar, rhetoric, dialectics, and the four mathematical arts of the Quadrivium: arithmetic, geometry, astronomy and music). But in the Aristotelian epistemic world there was no hierarchy, and the evolution of the modern European university from the medieval and Renaissance university can be seen as an attempt to impose a principle of hierarchical order on these seven arts. This was first to be theology and later to be philosophy. Theology was never central to the seven liberal arts which later evolved into modern disciplines such as philosophy, mathematics, literature, science, music.

At first the scholars were generally monks but later they were increasingly secular and became absorbed into the centralizing and absolutist state. With the rise of the territorial nation state from the seventeenth century onwards, the university became more and more nationalized and gradually lost its transnational, cosmopolitan character. With this went a decline in its ecclesiastical function: knowledge became a free-floating discourse to be used for domination or emancipation. In the early modern period there was a struggle for the institutionalization of knowledge in institutions such as the newly founded royal academies and in the universities, which began to become increasingly under the wing of the absolutist state. But the tension between the national and cosmopolitan dimensions of the university continued to contribute to the cultivation of its vibrant intellectual milieu and to guarantee that the university would be a site never totally dominated by any one power. It might even be suggested that the university was one of the few sites in society where culture was never fully dominated by power. Isolated in the academy, knowledge was detached from social struggles and made its peace with the state by offering to its cadres its degrees of distinction and accreditation. In this way the university was able to be a powerful actor in the social distribution of cultural capital.

As an institution the university owed its influence to the fact that it originated at a time when the moral and political power of the Church was in decline but when the modern state system had not yet fully emerged. A doctorate from the University of Paris was regarded as a doctorate from the Universal Church, remarked Durkheim (1977: 84). He also pointed out that this ambivalent position of the university between Church and state allowed it a certain autonomy. In 1259, the University of Paris, simply dissolved itself rather than submit to a papal decree (Durkheim, 1977: 89). With its background in the global culture of Christendom and an eye to the nascent national state with its centralizing and bureaucratic system of government, the university found itself in a powerful position and could monopolize the field of knowledge, which became tied to a system of social administration and the secularized ethos of Christianity. Even to this day the monastic origins of the university are evident in the cultural practices of the university (such as the conferring of degrees and honours, the role of ceremony, the belief in an underlying principle of harmony and the notion of faculties of knowledge), suggesting that the legitimation of knowledge is still tied to the legislating role of intellectuals. By the seventeenth century, the universal ideology gradually shifted from Christianity to modern experimental science and its rationalizing logic. The scientific revolution and the Reformation greatly facilitated this shift in the function of the university. European universities became established along with the rise of the city. As Thomas Bender argues, the city and the university share the cultural form of heterogeneity (Bender, 1988: 290; see also Bender, 1993). Like the European city in the Middle Ages, the university was a legally autonomous association and was capable of conferring a great many rights, exceptions and privileges on its members and on the political elite (Weber, 1958). Originally a guild organization, it became an autonomous, self-governing organization that was able to use the institution of knowledge to resist Church and state. This corporate order of the university as a guild gave to it its character as a 'republic of letters' or a 'republic of science'. While the cultural models of the age were very much shaped by the Church, the university remained a crucial actor in shaping the modern mode of knowledge: knowledge became a site to be inhabited by a knowledge producing and consuming elite. Unlike today, those who produced knowledge were also the chief consumers of knowledge.

The university became immensely important in the transition to modernity in western Europe, and the modern state quickly allied itself with it: it ceased to be dependent on private and clerical patronage and increasingly came under state patronage. It was by no means a progressive institution and in fact greatly facilitated the survival of religion under the conditions of secularism by transforming theology into a secular academic discipline. Both the Restoration government in England and the French Absolute state in the seventeenth century regarded the university, like the Royal Academy which was founded in this period, as important institutions in the administration of society (van den Dale, 1977). In England the Restoration government purged the universities of the radicals who had entered Cambridge and Oxford in the Civil War period. This was the beginning of the historic alliance of state and university (Wagner *et al.*, 1991a,b).

From the Enlightenment onwards the university developed under the auspices of the central and national state providing it with a system of knowledge, which was at the same time a system of power. One of the architects of the French Enlightenment, Condorcet, wrote the influential 'Report on the General Organization of Public Instruction', which was presented to the National Assembly in 1792 and promised a system of free elementary education to all citizens. The originator of the term 'social science', Condorcet believed in the emancipatory power of knowledge, in particular of higher knowledge, and believed the state should take responsibility for its provision (Baker, 1975; Heilbron, 1995; Kanuf, 1997: 48–9). This became, too, Napoleon's great design for a state-centred system of knowledge based on the technocratic and rationalistic values fostered by the Enlightenment. His plan was realized in the foundation of the *grandes écoles*, which in time overtook the older universities, many of which were closed down during the Revolution, as centres of useful knowledge. In no other country was the undermining of the medieval universities as great. With the fragmentation of the Sorbonne in the early 1970s the prestige of the university in France became even more seriously questioned (Nichols Clark, 1973). The exception being the survival of the Renaissance institution of the *Collège de France*. This institution remained exclusively a research institution but one which had a cognitive function. Napoleon's plan was to create modern research institutes, the *grandes écoles*, in order to confine teaching to the universities. This separation of teaching and research was more radical in France than in Germany or the Anglo-American tradition. However, according to Durkheim, the grouping of people for the pursuit of knowledge was the most important feature of the medieval universities and frequently there were universities in which the distinction between teacher and student did not exist, such as the medieval university of Bologna (Durkheim, 1977: 90–1).

As a result of the rise of positivism in the post-Revolutionary period, intellectual and expert cultures entered into conflict with each other. The intellectuals became isolated from the professionalized culture of experts, which was dominated by the natural sciences. Many intellectuals, especially in France, were forced to remain outside the university system and instead occupied the salons, which constituted the social basis of the Enlightenment. The university thus became the major institution for the nascent culture of experts. Nevertheless, while many intellectuals were distrustful of natural science's claim to the supremacy of knowledge, they shared the same belief in the self-legislating nature of knowledge that they inherited from the monastic orders of the Middle Ages: knowledge was their possession. Disdain for common knowledge eventually became the hallmark of the intellectual critique. However, it is important to recognize that most scientific knowledge was conducted outside the university. While the Renaissance was linked with the universities, the Enlightenment was not and most of the great philosophers of the Enlightenment era – Descartes, Bacon, Hobbes, Locke – worked outside the university. The incorporation of applied science into the university did not occur until the second half of the nineteenth century and it was to prove decisive for the national economies of the leading powers, Germany, France, Britain and the United States. But as Randall Collins argues, since the German academic revolution virtually all notable philosophers have been professors (Collins, 1998: 644). The Enlightenment thus becomes academized by a professionally organized knowledge elite.

In the period after the French Revolution, Enlightenment intellectuals began to debate the idea of the university whose great controversies reflected the major transformations of modernity itself, for instance reason and faith, modernity and tradition, facts and values. With the increasing importance of the philosophy faculty, which challenged the older faculties of medicine, theology and law, a space was created for reflection on the role of the university in society. These debates were particularly prevalent in Germany where the university preserved a strong connection with the tradition of humanistic knowledge and helped to shape German national identity. In this, the German university differed from the French university. This was not unconnected from the fact that Germany had not experienced the same centralizing trend towards a nation state, and the Enlightenment there placed a stronger emphasis on culture as *Bildung* (self-cultivation or the formation of the self) than on science and progress. The first major debate on the idea of the university as a centre for a liberal education was initiated by Kant in a plea to the king of Prussia to grant academic freedom to philosophers. His set of essays, *The Conflict of the Faculties*, was published in 1798 (Kant, 1979) and set the terms for a long debate on academic freedom and the idea of the western university (Rand, 1992).

Kant was influenced by the neohumanist idea of *Bildung*, but he was not romantically inclined and preferred to defend the role of the philosophy faculty against theology, law and medicine by an appeal to reason and the superiority of philosophy as a cognitive science. Rather than self-cultivation, as espoused by Humboldt, Kant advocated the critical power of reason as the justification of the university. In his view, the magistrates, doctors and ecclesiastics are in the service of the state and utility and not, like the philosophers, in the service of knowledge and truth. They are mere 'businessmen' and, since the university has no powers of its own, the state should keep these businessmen of knowledge in order. The philosophy faculty, he argues, 'must be conceived free and subject only to laws given by reason, not by government' (Kant, 1979: 43). The philosophy faculty is the 'lower faculty' in the hierarchy of faculties precisely because it is not in the service of the state as are the 'higher faculties' of law, medicine and theology. According to Kant, philosophy epitomizes modernity and the university should reflect this higher domain of knowledge: the 'conflict of the faculties' was ultimately a conflict between modernity and despotism, Enlightenment and ignorance. Philosophy differed from the other disciplines in that it was governed by nothing more than reason, and therefore was autonomous of social forces. This autonomy provided it with the status of a universality no other discipline could claim. Kant's defence of the university as a place in which truth is reflected upon had a great impact on the subsequent history of the university as an Enlightenment design and created the justification for academic freedom in terms of knowledge as an end: the university was the protector of the nation's cognitive structures, that is, its cultural models as well as its mode of knowledge. But we should not read into this debate a radical political commitment on Kant's part. He held quite strongly to the distinction between private and public reason, whereby the former included most of what we today would regard as public (Kant, 1996). Public reason in his sense was primarily argumentative academic discourse. Kant's thinking is a good example of the solution that modernity found to the need to reconcile the search for truth to the necessity for differentiated structures: the university is the site in society where truth can be pursued within a disciplinary structure of knowledge. As Friese and Wagner (1993) have demonstrated in their topography of academic practice, the emergence of the Enlightenment university was reflected in a new sense of academic space. This lofty mood of spatial separation from the social world was conveyed in the architectural designs of the modern university.

It is instructive to compare the French and the German conceptions of the university. The French Enlightenment concept of the university was reflected in Denis Diderot's 'Idea of a University', which he proposed to Catherine II of Russia in 1776 (McDonald, 1992; see also Diderot, 1971). This plan was very different from Kant's more humanistic emphasis on philosophy as the most autonomous faculty. It was in essence the difference between the technocratic modern idea of the university and the liberal idea of the university, both conceptions reflecting the two traditions in European modernity: the political tradition of the nation state and the *Kulturnation*; the intellectual traditions of rationalism and *Bildung*. However, we should not stress too heavily the differences: both were committed to the pursuit of autonomous knowledge, and in Germany, in the Kaiser Wilhelm Institutes, which preceded the modern day Max Planck Institutes, the natural sciences were quickly institutionalized by the rapidly industrializing state from the 1890s onwards. The situation was slightly different in England where the transition to political modernity occurred earlier, but where the arrival of cultural modernity developed more slowly. In contrast to the Enlightenment ideal of the republic of science, Oxbridge was shaped by the elitist tutorial system and anti-industrial values and was designed to produce gentlemen and clerics rather than scholars and technocrats. There, more than in Germany, the justification of the university precluded the experimental natural sciences. This began to change only in the second half of the nineteenth century when Oxford and Cambridge slowly adapted to modernity. The Scottish tradition, which had been influenced more strongly by Enlightenment values, was different and was closer to the continental tradition of research, and the resistance to the experimental natural sciences was not as great (Perkin, 1989: 17; see also Cambell and Skinner, 1982).

Nevertheless it was in Germany that the debate on the idea of the university began. The idealist philosophers Fichte, Schleiermacher, von Humboldt, Savigny and Hegel had all addressed themselves to the idea of the university in the context of the reform of the Prussian state at the beginning of the nineteenth century (Anrich, 1956; Müller, 1990). The themes in this debate, which began with Kant's *Dispute of the Faculties* in 1798, were the questions of the freedom of the sciences, the unity of knowledge and knowledge as education (in the more spiritual sense of *Bildung*). The concept emerged of a civil university (*bürgerliche Universität*) with the foundation of the University of Berlin in 1810. Wilhelm von Humboldt was the most influential advocate of the Kantian idea of the university and the idea of academic freedom and wrote a famous proposal to the Prussian king in 1809 which was subsequently incorporated into the constitution of the new university, the first truly modern university (Humboldt, 1970; Sorkin, 1983). His conception of the university was characterized by the need to combine teaching and research, which were separate in the previous centuries. The main thrust of his argument was against the subordination of the university to the state: the university is more than the mere training ground of civil servants but has a spiritual role to play in the cultivation of the character of the nation. Yet, the university needs the state to guarantee its autonomy. In return for this autonomy the university will provide the state with a moral and spiritual basis, becoming in effect a substitute for the Church. The German philosophers, influenced by postrevolutionary neohumanism and romanticism, reacted against the bourgeois utilitarian conception of knowledge that was emerging with the Enlightenment and saw the university as a kind of social utopia, a 'republic of letters', or 'republic of science' that would imitate the republic of the *polis* that modernity was seen as promising. In Fichte's more nationalistic view, the academics should be the new spiritual leaders of society, embodying the spirit of the nation as something that transcended the state. The professors constructed themselves as the representatives of the nation and in this way made themselves indispensable to the state for whom they were the 'interpreters' of the nation. This tradition in the German conception of the university as the link between nation and state remained a powerful ideal leading to the privileged position of the 'mandarins', the German professorate, in German society (Ringer, 1969; McClelland, 1980). The dominant German vision of the university was based on an understanding of knowledge as self-legislating, whereas in France and much of the rest of Europe and North America, where the rationalist Enlightenment had left its mark, knowledge was to be subordinate to society. Clearly this was a reflection of the different historical paths to modernity: the French path through state formation and the German through nationhood. The American university, however, was less committed to the state than to civil society and the training of the professional classes. The American university understood itself to be contributing to the making of a new nation rather than serving the state or expressing an already existing nation. In this tradition the nation was seen as resting upon civil society rather than a cultural identity (see Rothblatt and Wittrock, 1993).

The debate around the foundation of the University of Berlin in 1810 symbolized the spirit of modernity and its ideal that knowledge can be emancipatory but the pursuit of knowledge must be protected from the rest of society. It is to be noted that the Enlightenment model of university was developed in the context of the nationalization of knowledge: freedom and knowledge were one side of the coin; the other was nation and culture. Humboldt epitomized the two sides of the Enlightenment's model of the university in Germany. For him the university was not just the cradle of autonomous knowledge but also the custodian of the cognitive structure of the nation. It was not for nothing that the Prussian professors held the title of *Kulturträger* – the guardians of civilization or the custodians of culture. The idea of the university not only served the cognitive function of providing the state with functionally useful knowledge but was also an important transmitter of national heritage. In this sense, then, the Enlightenment model of the university was very different from the university of the Middle Ages. The difference was the shift from city to nation. The old universities of the Middle Ages were more akin to the autonomous cities. With the decline of the corporate orders of the Middle Ages and the tradition of the self-governing city, the university became allied with the state: in France it became allied with the centralist state; in Germany with the *Kulturnation*. In both cases there was an alliance with the state. In Germany, this was less direct: it provided Prussia with the means of preserving a German identity based on the intellect. Fichte believed that Germany could provide the world with spiritual leadership as opposed to military leadership (Collins, 1998: 647). The alliance with the state marks the birth of the modern university – the shift from the '*polis*' ideal to the ideal of the 'republic'. This move could be described as the move from knowledge as a closed and

harmonious system as symbolized by the *polis* to the differentiated and legis-
lative model of knowledge, whose political form was the modern republic
and whose cultural form was the nation.

Liberal modernity: the nineteenth century

The Enlightenment greatly influenced the nineteenth-century university
which was shaped around the modern nation state. Universities were
important in establishing the cultural foundations of national identity. With
the decline of Latin as a common language and the rise of the verna-
cular, the university was crucial in promoting national languages and in
codifying national literatures and geography. University departments were
important in collecting and defining ethnographic and cultural material
without which national cultural narratives, consciousness and national
imaginaries would not have been possible. The recruitment of professors
also changes in this period, with salaried professors replacing teachers paid
by fees. The older cosmopolitanism of the *peregrinatio academica* was abandoned in favour of a national academic elite, which was part of the consolidation of a wider national elite. This was particularly the case in Britain
where the entire national elite was educated at Oxford or Cambridge. As a
repository of national culture the university lost much of its cosmopolitanism.
It was only the formation of a national elite that was significant. The university also responded to the formation of bourgeois society and need for
cultural and educational institutions for the nascent middle class. As the
university gradually became open to the middle class as a result of secularization, industrialization and rationalization, its nationally specific character
intensified, since the middle class was the social basis of much of cultural
nationalism and of the rising urban professional society.

  The nineteenth-century university retained one link with the Enlightenment, and one which partly endures today: the belief that the university
rests on a founding *idea*. This notion is exemplified in one of the most
important debates on the idea of the university in the nineteenth century:
John Henry Newman's *The Idea of the University* (Newman, 1996). The debate around the foundation of the University of Dublin in the early 1850s
was in the tradition of the Enlightenment debate around the University of
Berlin, except that in this case it was a question of justifying the existence of
a theology faculty in a secular university. Only a few decades separated the
two events, but in this period, which had seen restoration and the rise of
modern conservatism, the intellectual, political and cultural gulf was enormous. If the Enlightenment had stood for the rule of knowledge, the liberation of humanity from tradition and ignorance, the historical experience
of the post-Enlightenment era subordinated knowledge to state formation.
But state formation was largely secular and provoked a reaction from those
who saw in liberal education a means of pursuing the cultural politics of
liberal Catholicism.

Cardinal Newman, an Anglican theologian who converted to Roman Catholicism and became the leader of English Roman Catholics, was invited to be rector of the new university in Dublin and gave a series of lectures in 1852 to provide a vision of the university and the concept of knowledge that it was to embody. The essential idea, set out in *The Idea of University*, was that the university is a place where 'universal knowledge' is pursued in teaching and in research. Newman's principal concern, however, was with teaching; research figured less in his model. As he put it in the preface, the university is 'a place of teaching universal knowledge'. The knowledge fostered by the university would make a humanist contribution to public culture and polite society. Newman's vision of the university was more in the English Oxford tradition than the Scottish or continental European, for instance his strong emphasis on the university as a *place* of pastoral care. In this he was very far from Humboldt and the German tradition in which the personal relationship between teacher and student was less strong. The German tradition was based on the authority of the professor as a representative of a discipline of knowledge. Newman's Oxford model, in contrast, was based less on the professor than on the tutor. This is presumably because he saw the purpose of education to be the transmission of a received body of knowledge and therefore not requiring basic research to produce new knowledge or the critical scrutiny of existing canons of thought. He differed, too, in seeing the university more as allied to the Church than as serving the state or as an institution that has a monopoly over accreditation. But like Humboldt, Newman stood for the idea of knowledge as an end in itself and his liberal humanist conception of the university became a framework for almost a century for university leaders seeking an alternative to the modern utilitarian model.

The English and German traditions, because of their specific models of the university, thus produced two distinctive ideas of the university, as reflected in the visions of Humboldt and Newman. The French university never produced an idea in the same way, presumably because of its professionalized function. It can also be speculated that because of the self-confidence of the republican state, the university in France was not in need of an idea that might point to an alternative model of leadership. The need for cultural and civic leadership was what was common to the Irish, American and German models. The main voice of cognitive as well as academic leadership that the English tradition produced – Newman's idea of the university – was the voice of a modernizing Catholicism and came from Dublin. Although he romanticized Oxford, his vision of the university, which was a modernizing one, was not that of the traditional ethos of Oxford.

Despite the similarities, an important difference between the Enlightenment model and Newman's conception was that Newman, a product of nineteenth-century secularism, wanted to adapt religion to the conditions of modernity: in the secular institution of the modern university theology could have an institutional existence as a cognitive science. This was Newman's ambition and one that epitomized the paradox of modern secularism: institutional secularism, the separation of Church and state, made possible the steady growth of religion as a private value system and as a cognitive system. Kant's defence of modernity in terms of the differentiation of reason into the spheres of the cognitive, the moral/practical and the aesthetic thus paradoxically served to facilitate the return of religion as theology, that is as an academic discipline. Newman's advocation of 'universal knowledge' was clearly derived from the Roman Catholic vision of the faith of the Universal Church reconciled to the conditions of modern secularism and the differentiation of cultural and institutional spheres. While he feared cultural relativism and critique the most, his greatest opponents were in fact the English liberal utilitarians.

The nineteenth century was by no means a century of piety, and Newman's vision did not go unopposed. University College London, for instance, founded by the English utilitarians such as Jeremy Bentham, specifically banned theology as a cognitive science and as a result it became known as one of the Godless colleges, which Newman sought to redeem with the help of the Catholics of Dublin who were also attracted to his modernizing and liberal Catholicism (O'Mahony and Delanty, 1998). The reformist idea of a university, which owed much to the newly reformed universities in Germany and Edinburgh, was inspired more by a belief in the public utility of knowledge than by the romantically imbued neohumanist conception of universal knowledge or an excessive concern with justifying the existence of a theology faculty (Young, 1992: 104). Newman himself was intent on undermining the Baconian conception of knowledge as a public utility. This tradition – which goes back to Francis Bacon's *The Advancement of Knowledge* (published in 1605) and is also to be found in John Locke's *Some Thoughts Concerning Education* of 1693 (Locke, 1968; Bacon, 1973) – sees the legitimation of knowledge to be in moral and social improvement: knowledge is to achieve a goal, not to express an already existing truth.

Newman's idea of the university was also challenged by Herbert Spencer and the ensuing debate brought rejoinders from other liberal reformers such as J. S. Mill and T. H. Huxley (see Sanderson, 1975: 115–38). Spencer opposed Newman on the grounds that the highest form of knowledge is not knowledge that is an end in itself but knowledge that is in some way useful to society. Spencer accordingly emphasized science in opposition to Newman's emphasis on the traditional humanities. The self-educated Mill, who had no need of a university as the protector of knowledge, differed from both Newman and Spencer in recognizing the importance of both the liberal and the modern idea of the university. While Mill tended to give primacy to the humanities, Huxley stressed science but did not exclude the humanities (Huxley, 1902). In the United States, where utilitarianism as a philosophical movement was not strong, a similar movement, known as pragmatism, began and was associated with the writings of Pierce, James and Dewey. This tradition tended to have a stronger commitment to the civic community than did the liberal tradition. Region and city were seen as more relevant to the identity of the university than was the state. In Britain, the rise of the civic universities, such as Manchester, Leeds, Liverpool, Birmingham and Nottingham, reflected the emergence of the rise of the professions and the need for vocational training (Armytage, 1955; Jones, 1988). These universities, closely linked to their city and regional locations, were endowed to create socially useful knowledge rather than to serve the nation or empire.

In England, the cultural discourse of tradition that lay behind Newman's vision of the university was also reflected in Matthew Arnold's work, *Culture and Anarchy*, originally published in 1869. This famous book gave a defence of culture as a force of stability in modern society, which for Arnold is always threatened by anarchy (Arnold, 1960; see also Sutherland, 1973). The only antidote to anarchy is culture, by which he meant the arts. His theory of culture and the university was much more influenced by German thinking than was Newman's whose ideas reflected the prevailing liberal Catholicism of the age. It was also an organic vision of culture that could be capable of providing moral and spiritual leadership and a contract to the other British tradition stressing the utility of knowledge. Echoes of this patrician idea of the university as the spiritual voice of culture were to be found in the writings of T. S. Eliot, *The Idea of a Christian Society* and F. R. Leavis in works such as *Education and the University* and *English Literature in Our Time and the University* (Eliot, 1940; Leavis, 1948, 1969).

One of the main battles of the century was fought on a different level of culture: natural theology. Julie Reuben has demonstrated the power of theology over science even until the end of the nineteenth century when morality was finally marginalized from science and the separation of fact and value finally accepted (Reuben, 1996). The controversy over the theory of evolution epitomized the attempt to reconcile all scientific explanations to Christian doctrine. Natural theology may be dead today, but the power of religion still remains. To this day, there are many American universities whose Protestant trustees forbid the teaching of evolution and others that require that science should not contradict the creationist myth.

At this point we can say that two models of the university are apparent: the liberal or neohumanist ideal and the modern ideal. The former was rooted in the predominantly German neohumanist idea of academic freedom and the pursuit of truth or knowledge as an end in itself; the latter, which was predominantly French, placed an emphasis on science but incorporated the idea of a liberal education. In reality, however, the two models existed together, especially in the United States after the period of reform of higher education began in the 1870s. It was not until the second part of the twentieth century that these two models became separated and the modern university increasingly moved away from the idea of knowledge as an end until it finally embraced the end of knowledge. The clash of these models was reflected in the wider clash of the 'two cultures', as described by C. P. Snow in Britain and earlier by Neokantianism in Germany. Bjorn Wittrock (1993) is correct to point out that the origin of today's universities is the late nineteenth century research-oriented universities and not those of the medieval era. The turn to research amounted to a new 'epistemic regime', he argues, under which a new cognitive and institutional system of knowledge emerged with the professional and specialized scientist replacing the broad-ranging generalist (Wittrock, 1993: 316). But this was primarily a development of the twentieth century and one related to industrialism which brought with it the need for new kinds of specialized knowledge, for industrial society was also professional society (Perkin, 1989).

That the university is founded on an idea and that there can be an idea of the university was rarely questioned in the nineteenth century whose driving animus was the idea of progress. A major exception to this was Nietzsche's anti-civilizational critique of the university. Behind the Humboldtian project, Nietzsche saw a homogenizing attempt to design an intellectual culture based on conformism and rules to an abstract authority. In his 'On the Future of our Educational Institutions', originally a series of lectures he gave in Basel in 1872, he attached the liberal and humanist idea of higher education (see Allen and Axiotis, 1998). Nietzsche saw the principle of autonomy in the Humboldtian model as a purely institutional one, substituting the state for the Church in its basic allegiance. Classical liberal ideals of education presuppose a faith in universality of knowledge and the rationality of the individual. It is these ideals that Nietzsche calls into question, arguing too that it is not just a question of finding an institutional space of autonomy for the protection of knowledge. With Nietzsche we have an early sense of the university as a site of cognitive resistance. The university does not simply reproduce knowledge or provide us with the necessary scientific means or an instrumentalizing mode of knowledge, rather it subverts the dominant cultural models of society.

The decline of liberal modernity

Both the Enlightenment and counter-Enlightenment theories of the university were based on the idea of knowledge as an end. Even though the French emphasized the utilitarian aspect of knowledge and the Germans the cultural dimension, neither questioned the university as the place where universal knowledge is pursued. One of the first intimations of a certain scepticism in this was evident in the thought of Max Weber, who wrote several newspaper articles on the university (Shils, 1973). Weber had always been interested in knowledge, which he regarded as a major vehicle of rationalization. One of his central aims was to understand how rationalistic thinking, such as that embodied in modern science, emerged primarily in the West. The rationalization of the world was also a process of increasing intellectualization which led to the disenchantment of culture and ultimately the loss of meaning. Weber departed from the Enlightenment in one major respect: he did not think that knowledge had a self-evidently emancipatory function. Indeed, he strenuously opposed the use of science for politics. Central to his thought was the irreconcilable conflict between the realms of science, politics, ethics and art.

In 1918, Weber gave his famous address, 'Science as a Vocation' (*Wissenschaft als Beruf*) in which he discussed the role of the university professor in the disenchanted age of modern rationalization (Weber, 1948: 131). Weber observes how the rationalization of the university in Germany is also its Americanization. 'This development, I am convinced, will engulf those disciplines in which the craftsman personally owns the tools, essentially the library, as is still the case to a large extent in my own field. This development corresponds entirely to what happened to the artisan of the past and is now fully under way'. Weber was writing about the disappearance of the old-style professor schooled in the neohumanist tradition and the rise of the instrumentally rationalized enterprise, a tendency he identifies with the United States. A second and related theme in Weber's lecture was the emptying of politics out of science. The conduct of science allows no room for politics, for science is the product of a rationalized world devoid of personality while politics still offers some scope for personality and the recovery of charisma. Yet, Weber seems unwilling to accept the American model: 'The American's conception of the teacher who faces him is: he sells me his knowledge and his methods for my father's money, just as the Greengrocer sells my mother cabbage ... no American would think of having his teacher sell him a *Weltanschauung*' (1948: 149–50). While berating those who seek in science moral leadership and intellectual direction, Weber is also unable to accept the American professionalization and instrumentalization of knowledge. His lecture ends on a note of resignation to meet the 'demands of the day' and the 'intellectual sacrifice' that science as a profession requires. He was unambivalent in his commitment to 'ethical neutrality' for he believed that cultural values could not be judged. Knowledge might gain some power over them if it confined itself to neutral analysis, but even then it will be limited. As he put it in an essay in 1908: 'The freedom of science exists in Germany within the limits of ecclesiastical and political acceptability. Outside these limits there is none' (Weber, 1973: 17).

The American model of the university differed from the continental European in one major respect. In America it had a much lesser relation to the state. Many of the American universities and colleges were private and in general a more utilitarian ethos prevailed concerning the role of knowledge. The American university, unlike the German university, did not see itself as a codifier of national identity. Indeed, in many of the colleges only an undergraduate education was provided. As in T. H. Huxley's address on the inauguration of Johns Hopkins University in 1876, the American university offers to deliver on the promise of a rational civil society and is not the expression of a pre-existing *Volk* as in the visions of the German idealists (Huxley, 1902). This is because, as Bill Readings pointed out, American civil society is structured by the trope of the promise or contract rather than on the basis of a single national ethnicity (Readings, 1996: 33–4). This argument is evidenced by the facts, for, according to Randall Collins, at the time of the American Revolution there were nine colleges in the colonies while in all of Europe, with a population fifty times larger, there were only about sixty colleges. In the nineteenth century the number in the United States had increased rapidly, with 250 by 1860 and twenty years later the number was 811 (Collins, 1979: 118). The liberal idea of the contract and the public utility of knowledge remained a powerful impetus in American higher education. With the exception of Scotland and utilitarian-inspired University College of London, the English model in Cambridge and Oxford was much more pastoral and paternalistic.

The American revised Humboldtian model of the university was scrutinized by another notable sociologist, Thorstein Veblen (1962). In 1918 he wrote an influential book, *The Higher Learning in America*, in which he broke with the liberal model in one respect: the university is a place of research to which teaching is subordinated. Veblen's critique of the modern American university addressed the decline of the liberal model and the rise of the modern twentieth century university. However Veblen held on to the Enlightenment humanistic understanding of knowledge as an end in itself. This transition was marked by the creation of the PhD, as an attempt to usurp the German liberal humanist tradition of knowledge as an end by institutionalizing a research culture. In Germany, Fritz Ringer described the decline of the Enlightenment model of the university in the period 1890–1933 into the sterile and elitist culture of the 'mandarins', the German professorate (Ringer, 1969). This was a reflection of the American tendency towards the professionalization of the academy, whereas on the continent the professorate had mostly been an extension of the civil service. Thus two different conceptions of the institutional context of the university emerged, the Anglo-American civic tradition and the continental European state-centred model. There is no doubt that the American tradition, reflected in the land-grant universities, believed its public commitment was to society and not to the state. Yet, underlying both of these traditions is a certain belief that academic freedom is rooted in citizenship, in the sense of a responsibility to the state, or at least in the public domain.

For Weber, science and politics were incompatible and it required a great intellectual sacrifice to recognize that science cannot offer a substitute for religion. Much later, Karl Jaspers asked the question again. In 1923, Jaspers published *The Idea of the University* in which he addressed the old question of academic freedom (Jaspers, 1960). This essay was revised in 1946 on the occasion of the reopening of the University of Heidelberg. In his view, the university is a place where teaching, research and cultural transmission takes place. In the Enlightenment tradition of Humboldt he speaks of the *Bildungsideal*, the 'education of the whole person', as the goal of the university that must be capable of offering a well-founded *Weltanschauung*. Academic freedom is the pursuit of truth: 'The university is the place where truth is sought unconditionally in all its forms' (Jaspers, 1960: 75). The Spanish philosopher José Ortega y Gasset in *Mission of the University* also expressed a very similar vision of the university whose functions consist of the transmission of culture, the teaching of the professions and the pursuit of scientific research (Ortega y Gasset, 1944).

Jasper's Enlightenment and humanistic defence of the liberal university can be seen as the beginning of a new European debate on the university and as a reaction to the foreboding vision of another great German philosopher: Martin Heidegger's famous address on assuming the rectorate of the University of Freiburg in 1933, 'The self-affirmation of the German university'. Jaspers, who opposed the Nazis, clearly thought that it was the duty of the university to be the custodian of *Kultur* and *Bildung*. However, in a curious way, Heidegger's speech, written at a time when his pro-Nazi sympathies were probably at their strongest, also reflected the primacy of knowledge and the need for spiritual leaders. The university, he argued, was the 'highest school of the German Volk' and requires its 'self-assertion', or a 'will', in order to fulfil the essence of knowledge, which for Heidegger is a form of metaphysical questioning: 'We understand the German university as the "high" school that, grounded in science, by means of science, educates and disciplines the leaders and guardians of the German people' (Heidegger, 1985: 471). This was one of the most controversial conceptions of the modern university. However, it only took to an extreme the nineteenth century and post-Enlightenment notion of the university as the protector of national culture. The destiny of the university was linked to the destiny of the state. Heidegger saw that task to be linked to the control of technology, for in his culturalist idea of the university knowledge speaks through the voice of the national community. Given Heidegger's political aspiration – which was to be nothing less than the official state philosopher – and his position as the Nazi-appointed rector of the University of Freiburg, this may appear to be a degeneration of the university, but in reality his notion of the university was not too far removed from the culturalist understanding of the university as the voice of tradition and the protector of the cognitive structure of the national community. The basis of this vision of the university was already in von Humboldt and the philosophy of the German idealists and fully endorsed by Jaspers, though in their conceptions the university is not fully in the service of either nation or state. It is in this sense that university as an institution of modernity contains within its consciousness the critique of modernity in the name of something prior to modernity.

The age of liberal modernity drew to a close in early decades of the twentieth century. The university became absorbed into industrial society. The cognitive structures that were to prevail over the twentieth century emerged in these decades, for instance the separation of facts and values, reason and faith, intellectuals and experts, the unity of nation and state, tradition and modernity. The university lost its Enlightenment right to judge values or to legislate over facts. The university became the enclave of the expert and with this came the retreat of the intellectual to the margins of society. It was upon these cognitive structures, the basic structures of the modern cultural models, that new modes of knowledge emerged. Although the university lost much of its older ethos and its ambivalent relationship to modernity, a new one was to be born: the embracing of democratic values in the wider society. In organized modernity, to be discussed in the following chapters, the university was both the enclave of the expert and the space in which a more democratic kind of citizenship could emerge. It was the site where cognitive structures and new structures in knowledge evolved along with the wider transformation in modernity.

3

The University in Organized Modernity: Capitalism, the State and Citizenship

The twentieth century was the era of the modern university. It was in this century that the research university and mass higher education as we know it today were created. Two-thirds of British universities were created after 1960; most of the remainder were founded in the three decades prior to the First World War. Despite having a history going back to the Enlightenment and often earlier to the Middle Ages, the university is a uniquely modern institution, more a product of organized modernity than of earlier modernities. No longer marginalized from the rest of society, the university has become central to a range of social, economic and political goals. In particular the university becomes crucial to the shaping of what has been called 'Big Science' (Price, 1963). According to John Kenneth Galbraith in a book that captures the spirit of organized modernity, *The New Industrial State*, the institutions of education, and in particular the university, have enormous power in the new kind of society and this could be used for political purposes if universities dared show their hand (Galbraith, 1967).

The university in the twentieth century emerged out of mass society and reflected the dominant cultural model of social integration based on citizenship as membership of a national community. The neohumanist or liberal model of the university was a product of bourgeois society; it was the expression of the alienation of culture from society and of the view that progress stems from the emancipatory power of knowledge. The modern university in the twentieth century was based less on culture as an autonomous domain and more on an ethos of integration. The belief in equality, rather than the pursuit of truth and progress, has been seen as central to its social mission in the past four decades. The mass university sought the dissemination of a received body of knowledge and cultural traditions. In more recent times this body of received ideas has been considerably challenged by developments in culture, politics and economy, but for much of the twentieth century the objective was to make knowledge available to a relatively uncritical society. Thus the relationship between the mode of knowledge and society is one of the transmission of new cognitive structures into institutional frameworks. But the mode of knowledge itself remains relatively autonomous of social determinants throughout the twentieth century. What occurs in organized modernity is the growing responsivness of the university to society accordingly as new cultural models emerge. In liberal modernity the university was a small institution and could legitimate itself by the traditional appeals to culture, but with the rise of the mass university and the growing demands of civil society this became more difficult and the legitimation of the university shifted from the humanities to the natural sciences. The university slowly moved to the centre of what was now a 'credential society' which required an institution devoted to accreditation (Collins, 1979). This was an inevitable consequence of the growing importance of the professions (Abbott, 1988; Perkin, 1989; Brint, 1994).

The twentieth-century university sought to reconcile the demands of differentiation and the pressure of integration. Liberal modernity was an age of differentiation, the growing separation of institutional and cultural spheres, specialization and rationalization. It was also an age that sought a principle of unity in culture and in society. It was an age of nation state building, but it was not until the twentieth century that the state took on the task of social integration. The university can be seen as akin to an incubator of organized modernity, for no other institution encapsulates the wider societal dynamics in culture and society. The cosmopolitanism of the nineteenth century inherited from the Enlightenment and Renaissance went into abeyance from the First World War when national lines of development became evident on many fronts. The university now becomes more tied to the nation state than before and its fate would be inexorably linked to it. Yet it retained a considerable degree of cosmopolitanism. The cosmopolitanism of the Anglo-American universities was owing in large measure to the influx of refugees from European totalitarianism from the 1930s onwards. The crisis that the university has entered at the end of the twentieth century is not unconnected with the more general crisis of the nation state and the institution of citizenship that emerged with organized modernity. As the link between state and university becomes uncertain, the evolving relationship of the university to capitalism is threatening the very identity of the institution as one based upon citizenship. In place of the dissemination of knowledge we are instead witnessing the spectre of the marketization of knowledge. To understand this we have to return to the period of organized modernity when the modern research university emerged along with the central state and mass society (Geiger, 1986, 1993; Kerr, 1991; Davis Graham and Diamond, 1996). In this period we witness the declining significance of the idea of the university. This may be owing to the fact that, as Margaret Bertilsson has argued, the larger the societal community, the less need there will be for an 'idea' (Bertilsson, 1992). The American university was thus in no need of a legitimating idea, unlike the Humboldtian university in early nineteenth-century Prussia where it clearly lay at the margins of the absolute state. And the French university never generated the level of debate that the German university did (Boudon, 1981).

In this chapter I outline how the mass university in the second half of the twentieth century emerged around the idea of citizenship. Despite the obvious elitism of academe, the university has been important in the shaping of the public culture of citizenship and democracy. More generally, we can say that in this period the university occupies a central position in society, standing as it does between culture and social structure, that is, the university as the principal site of the mode of knowledge production occupies a central location in the articulation of cultural values and shaping of social institutions which rest more and more on higher education. I take as points of reference the seminal works on higher education of Shils, Parsons and Kerr, for in many ways the twentieth century has been the American century and this is reflected strongly in the rise of the American university, one of the quintessentially American civic institutions.

The university and citizenship

The history of the university can be seen as the emancipation of the mode of knowledge from political and clerical authorities, a development of classical modernity and in particular of the Enlightenment, and its return to society. That was the great vision of Francis Bacon in *The Advancement of Learning* in 1605: knowledge is a public utility (Bacon, 1973). In modern thought, this was best represented in the writings of the American pragmatists (for instance, John Dewey) and earlier in the British utilitarians (for instance, Bentham and Mill) and Lockean epistemology. The Humboldtian ideal of *Bildung*, though liberal and far-reaching in its emancipatory promise, was not intended to achieve a social goal as such; it was primarily cultural. The university that it influenced was one cut off from the rest of society. The Humboldtian university was a product of bourgeois society and reflected the separation of culture from society; it was, in short, a university devoted to the protection of culture from society. The reception of Humboldt's ideas by the founders of University College London had a much stronger commitment to the public utility of knowledge. A stronger sense of the link with citizenship was the foundation of the London School of Economics and Political Science, created for the purpose of training social administrators for a future social welfare state.

However, the basic Humboldtian ideal, the formation of personality and the transmission of culture as a received body of values, remained a bulwark of the modern university and contributed to the formation of modern citizenship as participation in a national community. Although the overall model was one of the pursuit of truth for its own sake, one of its enduring characteristics was that in the university the personality of the 'whole person' can take shape. This is the true meaning of *Bildung*, which might be described as a kind of cultural citizenship as opposed to social citizenship. As a new idea of the university emerged in the twentieth century, the idea of *Bildung* has faded, though its resonances remain in the culture of individualism that scholarship necessarily brings. The modern university, a product of urbanization and industrialization, is an institution of mass education. What has been more important to it has been less *Bildung* than social citizenship: the dissemination of knowledge and the training and accreditation of the professions. The classical or liberal model of the university was based on the transmission of a received body of knowledge from teacher to student; the modern university instead seeks the dissemination of knowledge in society, thereby contributing to an educated citizenry. In that sense, then, it is true that the university has made a huge contribution to democracy, for citizenship is one of the most important dimensions of democracy.

Citizenship is one of the three central spheres of democracy. Democracy consists of (1) constitutionalism (i.e. the rule of law which restricts the domain of the state), (2) pluralism (the representation of social interests), and (3) citizenship (the participation of the public in the polity). Without citizenship, democracy is purely formalistic, confined to the institution of parliament and the negotiation of social interests. Citizenship entails the participation of the public in the affairs of the polity. As such it involves a relationship between rights and duties. But it is more than a passive condition; it is also active in that it is expressed in participation and identity.

According to T. H. Marshall, 'Citizenship is a status bestowed on those who are full members of a community. All who possess the status are equal with respect to the rights and duties with which the status is endowed' (Marshall, 1992: 18). In this classic work, first published in 1950, he argued that citizenship has developed from the acquisition of civic rights to political rights to social rights. Each of these sets of rights was an achievement of, respectively, the eighteenth century, the nineteenth century and the twentieth century (Turner, 1993). Civic rights emerged in the seventeenth century around the struggle for the freedom of the individual with respect to freedom of conscience, freedom of worship, freedom of speech, the right to enter contract and ownership of private property. Lying at the very core of citizenship right from the beginning was the recognition of the equality of all citizens in the eyes of the law. As a legal status consisting of rights, citizenship could be upheld by recourse to the courts of justice. Rights were thus ultimately secured by justice. This orientation to justice in the civic conception of rights means, according to Marshall, that citizenship is inescapably linked to the pursuit of equality, for in the eyes of the law all citizens are equal.

Although Marshall's theory has been severely criticized for its evolutionary model of citizenship as a passive quality, there is some truth in his general point that citizenship has moved from the market to the state in the twentieth century. Bourgeois society, in which civic and political rights initially arose, was ruled by the market. Indeed, many of the early civic rights upheld the market as the basis of citizenship. But by the twentieth century the state has assumed responsibility for citizenship as a social attribute. It is true that Marshall was not concerned with the relationship of citizenship to democracy and neglected, too, the radical dimension of democracy that is contained within citizenship, for citizenship, as I have argued, is more than a relationship of rights and duties; it also concerns participation and creation of identity. In so far as it involves an active dimension, citizenship can be antagonistic with respect to the state, as the arbiter of rights.

It is in this context that the university can be discussed. The university in the second half of the twentieth century can be seen as part of the development of social citizenship in society more broadly. In his wider social theory of the evolution of modern society, Parsons showed how the expansion of higher education was part of what he called the 'educational revolution', which for him is one of the three main revolutions that have shaped modernity, the others being the democratic and industrial revolutions. The educational revolution followed the democratic revolution which followed the industrial revolution, but whereas the latter coincided with bourgeois society, the educational revolution led to mass society and the dissolution of bourgeois society. Mass society – whether in the rise of popular culture and new kinds of consumption, the extension of the franchise, mass education, the welfare state – has been about the pursuit of equality. The principles of citizenship established equality as the basis of all legally definable rights, but until the twentieth century many of these rights were erected on the foundations of a society founded on extreme inequality. While not all movements towards democratization, in education, in health and in social welfare, were inspired by a desire to address the structural causes of inequality in so far as these derived from capitalism, it can hardly be denied that the century did see the progressive realization of social citizenship in much of the industrialized world. The educational revolution has been one of the great achievements of a century that was marked by two world wars and several genocides. The educational revolution led to the incorporation of the middle classes into education, and in the decades following the Second World War led to the massive incorporation of women into the workforce and into other areas of life from which they were previously excluded.

In this extension of social citizenship the university has played a pivotal role. It is clear that this has only been a very gradual process. In Britain in the 1960s the move to mass education that came with the Robbins Committee and the creation of such universities as Warwick, Lancaster, Essex, Sussex and York did not advance beyond an extension of the elite education, with no more than 8 per cent of the population participating in higher education. It was not until the mid-1980s that mass education as such began to be recognizable with more than 15 per cent participation, the threshold between elite and mass education (Scott, 1995: 5). Today the participation of the population in higher education in Britain is well above 30 per cent. In other western countries the degree of participation in higher education has been more extensive. In the past fifty years in the United States there has been a five-fold increase in the number of people with higher education. Access to higher education can now be said to be a central dimension to social inclusion in the western world.

The contribution of the university to social citizenship has been considerable. The university has provided a trained labour force to serve in the expanding and changing occupational system that the technologically dependent economies required. The university has also been central to the most important developments of the twentieth century, the enormous improvement in health care being one of the most striking. According to the World Bank, there is a clear correlation between the level of participation in higher education and economic development, the former of which is on average 51 per cent in the OECD countries, compared with 21 per cent in the middle-income countries and 6 per cent in lower-income countries (World Bank, 1994; Sadlak, 1998: 101). In the knowledge-based economies of today the link between education and wealth accumulation is yet more striking (Castells, 1996).

It was in the universities that the most important innovations were made in the twentieth century. The university has also provided the training of the legal profession which is central to the working of democracy. But the contribution of the university to democracy has been greater than providing training and accreditation for the professional occupations. This was one of Emile Durkheim's arguments about the nature of social integration in modern society. According to Durkheim in *The Division of Labour in Society*, in the transition from traditional to modern society, mechanical forms of integration (which are characterized by the collective consciousness with its strong focus on the group as the reference point for identity and a direct, or 'mechanical', relationship between values systems and social actors) are replaced by organic forms of solidarity (which are characterized by individualism and cooperation and are expressed in generalized norms as opposed to substantive values). Modern society involves the shift from social integration through religion and family to occupational groups and the interdependence of these groups and educational meritocracy. The cultural structures of modern society are restitutive as opposed to being repressive (as in traditional society) and provide individuals with possibilities for mutual cooperation and complementarity. It was his thesis that the possibility of an 'organic' civic morality could be nurtured by education which could be the basis of a new kind of social contract (Durkheim, 1960). In *The Evolution of Educational Thought* he stressed the importance of the teaching profession in the creation of a civic republican order (Durkheim, 1977). Durkheim's argument was that education as the most important part of civic citizenship is the principal means by which social integration can be achieved. This is because the state is unable to achieve alone what traditional cultural values can no longer provide: organic integration. Education, for Durkheim, could link the state more closely to the lives of individuals.

In one of his last essays, Edward Shils commented on the relationship of the university to values that are constitutive of liberal democracy:

> Universities, by their research and teaching, have greatly increased the stock, breadth, and depth of knowledge of nature and of man; have increased our knowledge of the history of human societies and civilizations and of the achievements of mankind in religion, art, literature, etc. They have, directly and indirectly, through the lower levels of the educational system, given to the citizens of liberal-democratic societies some knowledge of the history of their own societies and the ability to see themselves as participants in them. They have made human beings in modern liberal-democratic societies cognizant of the place of their civilization among the civilizations which appeared in world history.
>
> (Shils, 1997: 278–9)

What I interpret Shils to be saying is that the university has contributed to the articulation of the cultural models of society, in particular those that have carried with them the values of democracy and of citizenship. Without an institution devoted to the acquisition of knowledge in all its cultural forms, society would not have the capacity to reproduce the cultural narratives upon which memory depends. The university was important in defining the cultural identity of the nation state in its formative phase; it was inevitable that this would have wider ramifications for social identity, cultivating critical and reflective values in the population. At times in which democracy was threatened, the university was one of the few sites of resistance to reactionary ideas. But, on the whole, the university did not have an active relationship to the world outside in so far as this concerned citizenship. (In Chapter 4, I discuss a development towards a more active, political citizenship in the late 1960s.) In general, the contribution to citizenship that the university has made has been social, that is it has allowed the incorporation of increasing numbers of people into society. However, it has also provided the foundations of cultural and technological citizenship: cultural in so far as it has led to the preservation and dissemination of cultural traditions among the society as a whole, and technological as a contributor to professional society, the demands of the occupational system and the extension of equality of opportunity. However, in the period under discussion it is largely in the area of social citizenship that the gains were made (in later chapters I discuss the impact of the university on cultural and technological citizenship).

Western universities became centres of mass education at a time when the nation state had never been so strong and when the postwar economies were enjoying a period of boom. Indeed, the university was an important resource in national defence during the cold war. In this situation the university was able to steer a middle course between reliance on the state and serving the functional requirements of capitalism. It was inevitable that this delicate balance would not hold.

The Parsonian theory: the cognitive function of the university

Organized modernity led to a new mode of knowledge: knowledge contained within the boundaries of disciplines and controlled by experts. In liberal modernity the mode of knowledge within the university was still compatible with the Enlightenment's ideal of truth and the ultimate unity of culture. Social imperatives were relatively unimportant. Although the university was clearly allied to the national state and was important in the creation of national identity, it lay very much outside the institutional domain of civil society. The hierarchy of knowledge systems that existed in the Enlightenment tradition and continued in much of liberal modernity has lost any rationale in the age of specialization. Specialized knowledge is legitimated only by reference to itself and not by any transcendent criterion such as an *idea* of the university.

The history of the modern university has been the history of struggles of experts for their self-legitimation. The foundation of the American Association of University Professors in 1915 was to protect the university and its professors from control by the state. In many countries in this period, professors acquired the status of civil servants. In Germany, Bismarck regarded the professorate as a major ally of the state, a role the professorate was content with, for the autonomy that they were to receive enabled the university to protect the institution of academic freedom and academic self-governance. In Ireland after the foundation of the Free State in 1922, the university profession gained the right of tenure and the right to a permanent and unelected representation in the upper house. The Japanese Constitution, Article 23, guarantees academic freedom and many western European countries have given the professorate statutory tenure which effectively guarantees academic freedom. Although not all countries have had academic freedom guaranteed by the constitution, most have achieved some degree of autonomy from the very institution upon which they depend for their existence. In imperial Russia, professors also struggled to gain academic autonomy (Kassow, 1989). There, as in many countries, the professorate saw the students, who included revolutionary intellectuals, as an obstacle to their own objective to gain autonomy. The professorate were highly successful in constituting themselves a neutral ground between students – that is society – and the state. This trade-off between education and politics has mostly been beneficial for the university in protecting academic freedom from state interference, a fact of not minor importance in the return of academic censorship during the two world wars in the twentieth century. With the consolidation of a professionalized ethos in the early decades of the twentieth century the university increasingly lost is earlier reliance on a legitimating idea. In an age of specialization, knowledge loses its ability to define the cultural models.

One of the first casualities of specialization was the Humboldtian link between teaching and research. In the university that developed in the decades of mass higher education, which were also years of major scientific specialization, the spheres of teaching and research moved further and further apart. The demands of research and the rise in student numbers undermined the older tradition of the university at a time when an increasing number of graduates were entering the university for a career. As a result, co-option to an academic post became determined by research. With a large teaching programme to service, the Humboldtian link of an essentially moral relationship between teaching and research, education and personality, knowledge and culture was broken. Cognitive spheres (or faculties) become organized as disciplines which in turn become rationalized into university departments and a professorate emerges as distinct from the older institution of a single disciplinary chair. As a result, patronage becomes less significant as an organizer of knowledge and publicly available publication become the criterion of competence. In this way, too, knowledge becomes depersonalized, as well as denationalized. Having disenchanted knowledge, the university finally became itself a disenchanted institution.

Teaching, too, became rationalized and fragmented. The relationship between teacher and student, as Max Weber noted during his journey to the United States, had become a rationalized one for knowledge and had lost its higher function of spiritual enlightenment. The bureaucratization of the university is an inevitable product of growing complexity. But this bureaucratization must be seen as part of a deeper process of differentiation within modern society.

Parsons and Platt, in their magisterial study of the American university, noted that one of the most striking features of higher education was the separation of functions within the university, a differentiation that reflected wider societal differentiation (Parsons and Platt, 1973). The book, *The American University*, is a major attempt to apply Parsonian structural functionalism and the sociology of knowledge to higher education. For the authors, the university is the key institution of the 'fiduciary' (meaning trustworthiness) subsystem, which in their complex theoretical framework lies in the 'zone of interpenetration' between the cultural system and society. The function of the university is the production of the cognitive values of society. 'The primary focus of the university is the cognitive complex, which is grounded in the cultural system and institutionalized in the structure of modern society. Higher education in general and the university in particular represent institutionalized concerns with cognitive matters. On the cultural side, it is concerned with the cognitive subsystem of the cultural system, on the social side, it is with the fiduciary system' (Parsons and Platt, 1973: 33). In other words, the university is an institution – that is, a set of functions – that exists in both the domains of culture and of society. It is interesting to note that Parsons and Platt in this work, which can be regarded as the most theoretically sophisticated study of the university ever undertaken, do not see a conflict between these two functions. Influenced by functional theory and a liberal political ideology which predisposed them towards a largely harmonious view of society, they saw a complementarity, or unity, in these functions and believed that the university did not have to compromise its role as the 'trustee of cognitive culture'.

The central theme of their work might be said to be the question of the extent to which the university is forced to service the needs of other parts of society. The unity of the university for Parsons is not the unity of a legitim-ating idea but the functional unity of its structures with respect to the societal community. The two principal features of the American university are: '(1) that it, and with it the institutionalized cognitive complex, has become a differentiated part of a complex society and (2) that it has become upgraded in prestige and influence within the society to the point that some commentators describe it as the central institution in the society' (Parsons and Platt, 1973: 103). They refer in this context to the work of Daniel Bell (1966) for whom the university is a central part of the postindustrial society, which depends to a great extent on the production of knowledge. The key concept for Parsons and Platt is 'interpenetration', the proccess by which one subsystem affects another: the university is forced to occupy a zone between culture and society, and therefore must be cut across these systems. But the imperatives of differentiation do not preclude the possibility of an overall integration. This complementarity between differentiation and the possibil-ity of integration is the central and unifying theme in Parsons's entire sociology of modernity (Parsons, 1974). It was his firm conviction that there is an overall unity of function in the core components of modern society. In the Parsonain framework this unity of purpose – which had a spiritual dimension to it, as became apparent in his final and mysterious work, *Action Theory and the Human Condition* (Parsons, 1979) – is reflected in the univer-sity's interpenetration into the domains of culture and society. Indeed, the very term 'cognitive rationality' embodies both a cultural (cognitive) and a social (rationality) dimension, as Parsons and Platt point out (1973: 38).

The academic profession is that group primarily concerned with the cog-nitive complex that is institutionalized in the graduate schools and research activities of the university. It deals with the advancement, perpetuation and transmission of knowledge. However, the university is too multifunctional to be merely a place where universal knowledge is pursued but is neverthe-less more fiduciary than technocratic or instrumental in that it differs from the corporation in being primarily a place of learning and research (Parsons and Platt, 1973: 148). The centre of gravity of academic professionalism is located in the graduate schools of the arts and sciences and in the research complex, not in purely professional training.

In this way, for Parsons and Platt, the university is still connected to the non-cognitive structures of the cultural system, but is autonomous from the moral community at large. The complexity of interrelationships that char-acterize the university prevents it from being the moral arbiter of society: the modern university cannot function as the 'Prince's conscience', as in the early modern university (Parsons and Platt, 1973: 47–50). Its main fiduciary functions are: (1) research, (2) professional training, (3) general education, and (4) cultural development. Of particular importance is the growing significance of professional training, which they see as a response to the demands of the economic system which creates the need for a public system of accreditation. These functions are related to the different institutions within the university: research is concentrated in the graduate schools, professional training in the professional schools, and teaching in the colleges. Cultural development is not underpinned by a specific domain within the university but is located within society where professors can gain influence in the public domain either as intellectuals or as professionals. While Parsons and Platt argue that the primary core value of the university is cognitive rationality, they recognize that the university is increasingly becoming a certifier of professional competence within the occupational order. In Parsons's words: 'the university became the primary trustee of that phase of the cultural heritage of modern societies that was important for the grounding of professional competence' (Parsons, 1979: 91).

In Parsons and Platt's framework, intellectuals, who have access to the mass media, are also important in their contribution to the 'general definition of the situation', with respect to the human condition as a whole and the status of the social sciences. The university, they argue, makes a major contribution to public knowledge which is central to modern society. The public, unlike professional knowledge producers, is concerned less with the problem of explanation than with the problem of meaning (Parsons and Platt, 1973: 279–82). In his final work, *Action Theory and the Human Condition*, Parsons returned to this question of human meaning and social action. It remained his firm belief that the 'cognitive complex' was rooted in the cultural system itself. This allowed him 'to challenge the notion that the basic American cultural heritage, specifically that aspect of it relevant to the normative order, has been as materialistic as has so frequently been alleged' (Parsons, 1979: 120). In this he remained thoroughly Weberian, but went far beyond Weber in his conviction that the cognitive complex as a result of its interpenetration has supplanted the economic complex.

In sum, then, the two main lines on interpenetration, according to Parsons and Platt, are those of institutionalization (the interpenetration of the mode of knowledge into the social system) and socialization, the moral/cultural dimension of values and meaning. It was perhaps an expression of the self-confidence of the American liberal ideology that the university in the age of mass society could retain the primary function of cognitive rationality and at the same time aspire to being the central institution in society. This vision remained central to many great American conceptions of the liberating role of knowledge. In his famous work, *The Coming of the Postindustrial Society*, Daniel Bell defended the relevance of the traditional and the modern functions of the university (Bell, 1974). The function of the university, he argues, 'is to relate to each other the modes of conscious inquiry: historical consciousness, which is the encounter with a tradition that can be tested against the present; methodological consciousness, which makes explicit the conceptual grounds of inquiry and its philosophical presuppositions; and individual self-consciousness which makes one aware of the sources of one's prejudgements, and allows one to re-create one's values through the disciplined study of the society' (Bell, 1974: 423). In this, Bell has identified an important feature of the university: it is one of the few locations in society where so many modes of knowledge are concentrated. Whatever unity is possible in the face of such specialization and differentiation consists precisely of this concentration of functions.

The 1970s marked the decline of the idea of the university as the citadel of knowledge as an end. In contrast to Parsons's liberal endorsement of the American university, another sociologist, the more conservative Robert Nisbet, in *The Degradation of the Academic Dogma*, wrote of the decline of the idea of the American university from community to the crass world of professionalism (Nisbet, 1971). He laments the degeneration of the university from the elevated and lofty world of *universitas* into the profane world of the corporation. For an early generation the commitment to the pursuit of knowledge was akin to the priestly vocation; now, he complains, universities speak of 'hiring' personnel whereas they once preferred the more elevated 'appointing' of professors (1971: 102–3). Nisbet's idea of a university rests on the connection between community and *universitas*, a community of scholars seeking knowledge as an end. Parsons's position was a more realistic assessment of the situation of the university in the context of societal differentiation. It was a thoroughly modern understanding of the university as part of the project of citizenship.

Parsons and Platt's work on the American university never received the attention it deserved and did not succeed in overshadowing the more widely read and influential but superficial book by Clark Kerr, *The Uses of the University*, published in 1963. Kerr, who served as president of the University of California at a time when this university grew to become the biggest university complex in the world, gave expression to a vision of the modern university not too far removed from the Parsonian model. In what had been a series of lectures at Harvard University, Kerr's book became a benchmark in the history of the idea of the university. In effect, however, he announced the end of the idea of the university. Rather than a founding or guiding idea, he spoke of what he called 'multiversity', a term that in effect debunked the very idea of a 'university'. The university has become a whole series of communities which bear no resemblance to Newman's unitary community which has become an illusion, he announced. 'The modern American university', he went on to say, 'is not Oxford nor is it Berlin; it is a new type of institution in the world' (Kerr, 1963: 1–2). As Newman was fighting the ghost of Bacon, Kerr was fighting the ghosts of Newman and von Humboldt whose beautiful world has been shattered by the democratic, industrial and scientific revolutions of the twentieth century. Like Parsons, he argued that the modern university has a plurality of functions and should be described as a 'multiversity':

'The Idea of Multiversity' has no bard to sing its praises; no prophet to proclaim its vision; no guardian to protect its sanctity. It has its critics,

its detractors, its transgressors. It has its barkers selling its wares to all
who listen – and many do. But it also has its reality rooted in the logic
of history. It has an imperative rather than a reasoned choice among
elegant alternatives.

(Kerr, 1963: 6)

But there are clear differences between Parsons and Kerr. Parsons, while
arguing for the reality of pluralism, specialization and differentiation as the
chief characteristics of modernity, insisted on the existence of an overall
unity of function in society as a whole and its individual institutions. Kerr
would appear to reduce the university to its actual functions, or its 'uses'. In
fact, he is quite adamant that the 'idea' of the university has been replaced
by its 'uses'. Kerr gave expression to the emergence, which was particularly
apparent at Harvard, of institutional pluralism (Rothblatt, 1997b: 30). According to Rothblatt, the American departure from the European tradition
was most evident at Harvard but was characteristic of American higher
education in general. For instance, the early turn to course credits designed
to increase flexibility in the curriculum, the creation of electives which
replaced common degree programmes, these developments had the effect
of allowing new subjects to enter the teaching programme, which could not
be done with programmes based on a single discipline. Rothblatt sums up
the American path succinctly: 'while in Europe the "problem" of adapting
the university structure to an urban, technological, professional civilization
was often viewed intellectually as finding the correct "idea" of a university,
in the United States a single "idea" of a university was increasingly impossible' (Rothblatt, 1997b: 33). Pluralism was better suited to the federal and
local structures of American society. The different historical experience was
important in this. Kerr points out that in the United States the land grant
universities (i.e. the state universities) combined studies of agriculture and
engineering which in Germany were relegated to the *Techniche Hochschulen*
(the polytechnics). This meant that in the United States the children of
farmers and workers could enter the universities (Kerr, 1963: 14). For Kerr
this all meant that the American university had become more and more
involved in society to the extent that, as the city degenerates, the campus
can take over the civic mission of culture (Kerr, 1963: 115).

Social change and the university

The two synthetic visions of the modern university which were the focus of
this chapter – those of Parsons and Kerr – expressed in different ways the
decline of the idea of the liberal university under the conditions of mass
education in what was now a mass, industrial society. But these were by
no means pessimistic visions. On the contrary, they saw pluralism within
the academy and in society as enabling integration. The fact that, in the
modern university, knowledge has a social utility is not seen as a threat to
the autonomy of the university. The university is seen as responding to

outside forces, such as those of the market and the stratification system, but is not in danger of losing its own identity. Of course, this was the age of Big Science and Big Government and driven by the cold war and the organization of capitalism along Fordist lines. The modern university in organized modernity was protected by the state, which relied heavily on it for its ability to define the national mission and to legitimate government policy. Heavily funded and responsive to market forces, the university was able to steer a middle course between state and market forces. But the age of academic capitalism is far away: the university while participating in the capitalist order retains its own ethos of cognitive rationality and remains committed to citizenship.

A general conclusion can be drawn with respect to social change and the situation of the university. Taking the domains of knowledge, culture and the social order, first we can say that the university is coming increasingly to occupy a position in all these domains; it is not just a knowledge producer, but is also important in shaping and transmitting culture, and is coming to be a central actor in society. Second, the main social change that we need to note is that because of different rates of change the university has been most affected by changes in the mode of knowledge and changes in the social order. Cultural models in this period were relatively static and did not undergo dramatic change until the 1970s. This is the subject of the following chapter.

In this chapter I have tried to show that the university becomes interpenetrated, to use Parsons's term, into the cultural and social systems. This was the beginning of one of the most important developments in the history of the university. With respect to culture, this is not new: as was argued in the previous chapter, the university has been related to culture since the nineteenth century. The Enlightenment university was one based on reason, as reflected in the work of Kant, and the nineteenth-century university in the visions of Humboldt and Arnold, in their different ways, expressed the turn to culture. The university was the custodian of national, secular Christian and bourgeois culture. It did not interrogate or transform this culture, but constructed and reproduced it within the cloistered citadel of academe. Thus, the interpenetration of the mode of knowledge into the cultural system in the decades of the expansion of higher education was largely a part of a conservative movement. The transformative project had yet to come.

The main change that occurred in this period and which was revolutionary, or rather part of a revolution in societal structures, was the completion of the educational revolution, identified by Parsons as one of the three central revolutions in the modern project. The interpenetration of the mode of knowledge into the social system leading to changes in the occupational order and the stratification system in the direction of greater equality, the meritocratic allocation of social recourses, and an ethic of personal achievement was a major change for the university which previously had been isolated from the intrusion of social forces. It was a period marked, above all, by the tremendous strengthening of industrial capitalism and of social democracy. It was also the apogee of the university which became for the first time a part of the *social* project of modernity. Today, in the twenty-first century, there is the danger that this social project may be at an end, with the university embracing the values of the marketplace. It is clear that this project was deeply connected with social democracy, for the age of the expansion of higher education was also the era of social democracy and of Big Government.

In the following chapter I look first at the major crisis in the modern university: the rise of the transformative project and the wider crisis in cultural modernity that this entails. In subsequent chapters, I move on to look at the crisis of the social project of the university in late modernity.

4

The Transformative Project:
Democracy, the Counter-culture
and Communication

The modern university, I have argued, was a product of the social project of organized modernity. In becoming tied to citizenship and social goals, the university lost its earlier isolated position as a purely cultural institution devoted to knowledge and became more organic, part of a functioning totality. Its older faculties, now organized internally as departments, were connected up with a whole range of societal functions. This transformation of the mode of knowledge within the university in the direction of greater specialization was related to major social transformations within society as a whole. The two world wars, the cold war, the growth of industrial capitalism and the consolidation of nation states in a growing international society led to a very different kind of society from the one that existed in liberal modernity. As far as the university is concerned, it was one that required a more educated population and the greater participation of the middle class in education. But the values and wider cultural models of this society had not greatly changed, at least not to the same extent as social and economic models had. The *social* project of organized modernity had created an entirely new scenario for the university but the university was still immersed in the *cultural* project of an earlier modernity.

The cultural ethos of the university, like the cultural models of society for much of the twentieth century, had remained very much in the mould of the nineteenth century. These were the cultural models of male, bourgeois, Christian, classical European culture. In the United States the unreformed university system was a bastion of the Anglo-Protestant values of the professional middle classes, 'defending their holds against the ethnic and lower-class intruders' (Collins: 1979: 127). The incorporation of the middle class into the previously elite-dominated spheres in politics, culture and economy was far-reaching but the class system in what was still an industrial age and male dominated had remained intact. Until the last three decades of the twentieth century, the ethos of the university was not far removed from the

older tradition of liberal education; it was one of personal discipline, political orthodoxy, and bourgeois privatism. Scholarly inquiry, if not an end in
itself, was a preparation for a professional career or a place in the marriage
market. Politics had no role to play in an institution that was modelled on
Christian and bourgeois privatism. As Parsons commented, academic freedom 'is closely related to the rights of privacy enjoyed, for example, by the
family and (subject to very broad restrictions) the rights of parents to have
the main voice in the bringing up of their children' (1979: 108). The role
of the university was not to criticize or transform culture and morality but
to pass on relatively intact a received tradition to future generations. Clearly
this was an inherently conservative function. The constitutive social movements of modernity – the Renaissance, the Reformation, the Enlightenment, socialism – all derived from outside the university which remained
largely oblivious to radical thought (Wuthnow, 1989). As Fuller points out,
'they were all eventually co-opted by the university, which in turn made the
movements its own, by chanelling their dynamic energy into the university's
processes of disciplinization' (Fuller, 1999a: 50). Radical thought has generally come from the margins of society, from intellectuals who have gone
beyond the conventional ways of thinking. As Durkheim observed in his
history of educational thought: 'the evolution of education always lags very
substantially behind the general evolution of society as a whole' (1977: 164).
He noted how, for instance, 'a great scientific movement was to be born in
the sixteenth century and to be developed throughout the seventeenth and
eighteenth centuries without making the slightest impact on the university
before the beginning of the nineteenth' (1977: 1964). In liberal and organized modernity the university provided a legitimation of the dominant social
values of society, but in late modernity the university came gradually to
incorporate voices from the margins of society.

It was inevitable that the cultural mould of the university would be broken
once cultural models in society underwent transformation. This transformation of the cultural project of modernity is the subject of this chapter. In
the late 1960s and 1970s, as a result of cultural revolution in the western
world, the university underwent a major change in its cultural and political
self-understanding. Indeed, the university was a major contributor to political and cultural unrest. In this chapter and the next we look at the cultural
and political challenge to organized modernity that came from revolutionary
cultural currents in society. Our theme is the collapse of the older cultural
cognitive models and the creation of new ones. I shall be arguing that these
changes did not so much attack the mode of knowledge and the institutional
context of the university as lead to a new cultural ethos for the university
which had to accept the politicization of knowledge and its public role in
society. In short, the university was forced to become a political actor in
society and therefore was no longer able to seek refuge in the remnants of
cultural modernity that had survived the transition to mass society. However,
as I argue in this chapter, the university managed to remain embedded in
a cultural project and its fate was not entirely shaped by the functional

demands placed upon it. The essence of this new cultural project which reinvigorated the older idea of the university was one of democratic pluralism, for the university, once a bastion of elite culture, was to become one of the most important sites for the preservation and articulation of democratic values. With the rise of an adversary culture in the 1960s the university ceased to be merely a transmitter of a received cultural tradition but a transformer. We can therefore speak of the university as a central institution in the transformative project of modernity.

The crisis of organized modernity: culture and politics

In no country was the incongruity between the cultural and the social projects of modernity more apparent than in Germany, the country where the history of the university was inseparable from the history of the German nation and where the first genuinely modern university was founded on Enlightenment principles. The German universities had encapsulated the spirit of the Enlightenment and the spiritual mission of modern culture which, in Germany, was believed, at least by the idealist philosophers and by much of the late nineteenth-century professorate, to be of sufficient power that it could offer the foundations of a modern national state, which had not yet existed in Germany. But this mandarin culture once it acquired political influence and a constitutional guarantee retreated from its political responsibilities, seeking instead professional power. This is the theme of Fritz Ringer's famous study of the German professorate, *The Decline of the German Mandarins* (Ringer, 1969). He outlines how this group acquired social influence in the nascent nineteenth century Prussian state, becoming a national elite, but descended into professional privatism and into an inner cultural world from the turn of the century. It was not the point of Ringer's work but it can be argued, furthermore, that the political and moral impotence of the neohumanist culture of the German university finally became apparent in its complicity with, or at least failure to resist, the Nazis. The separation of politics from culture demanded by Max Weber, when taken to the extreme, ultimately destroyed German culture.

The Humboldtian model of culture was in essence one of morality and had the effect of bequeathing a cultural tradition of extreme political indifference. With its origins in German romanticism, the neohumanist notion of *Bildung* as a spiritual and moral education reflected the German romantic tradition's turning of its back on politics. The aim of *Bildung* was the formation of personality, the construction of the bourgeois self, through the acquisition of cultural knowledge. In this tradition, culture existed as an autonomous and fixed set of values that had to be internalized by the student for the shaping of a biographical narrative. The professor was the interpreter of this stable and enduring body of received wisdom. Knowledge did not have a critical function, as it had for Kant, but a conservative function of transmitting an already established cultural tradition. In one way or another this model of liberal education was the basis of most western universities until quite recently.

Cultural revolution in the western world from the 1960s onwards shattered the cultural framework which carried liberal education (Lipset, 1967). In this period the university became less a transmitter of culture than its transformer. According to Norman Birnbaum in *The Crisis of Industrial Society*, the university came to represent the crisis of industrial culture and held out the hope that industrial culture can be humanized by a 'new technological humanism' to which the universities can contribute (Birnbaum, 1969: 156–8). In Germany this was particularly pronounced, for there denazification was a project led by the universities. What is striking about the revolutionary decades was the emergence of a clash within culture which loses the relative homogeneity that it inherited from the previous century. New cultural voices emerge: the women's movement, black and ethic cultures, nationalist liberation movements, Marxism and the postmodern avant-garde which sought to relink art and politics. As a result of the Vietnam War and the civil rights movement, the American university became a major political site, a factor enhanced by the academization of Marxism. Politics had now entered the previously privatized domain of culture which lost its connection with morality. The social project of organized modernity, discussed in the previous chapter, was responsible for creating the opportunity structures for much of the radicalization of universities. The extension of higher education to wider segments of society had the inevitable effect of opening the academy to social and political discontent. The intrusion of this cognitive factor – the openness of the political – into the university destabilized its previously apolitical ethos in bourgeois privatism.

In the previous chapter I remarked that with the movement towards mass education in the twentieth century the university became an important institution in society for the development of citizenship. This was owing to the social responsibilities of the university to certify intellectual and professional competence as well as to its commitment to progressively extend higher education to wider segments of society. In these ways, something like a civic and a cultural citizenship were cultivated by the university in the age of mass society. But there was also the more radical component to citizenship that was fostered by the university. Universities were crucial sites for the preservation of democratic values and public discourse. This was particularly the case in the United States in the 1950s when, in the McCarthy era, political conservatism and censorship greatly compromised the democratic values of the society (Lazerfeld and Theliens, 1958; Hofstadter, 1963). Despite political censure, universities preserved a culture of critique and resistance to intolerance which was to be the public basis of much of the radical developments of the early 1970s. As Richard Lowenthal, writes: 'the western university has been one of the basic institutions which made the growth of an open and more dynamic society possible in the West' (1975: 80). Thus, there is, he argues, a historical link between the freedom of science and learning and the other basic freedoms of an open society. This was reiterated by the sociologist Immanuel Wallerstein in 1969 who argued that the university could offer not just cultural direction but also political direction (Wallerstein, 1969). Of course the notion of the freedom of science and political liberty was central to the work of Popper for whom the epistemic structure of scientific knowledge – which is uncertain, revisable and refutable – is linked by its antidogmaticism to the 'open society' of liberal democracy (Popper, 1945).

In the 1960s and 1970s the counter-cultural impulse stemmed largely from the students, a contrast to the other great period of academic revolution – the 1790s and the opening decade of the nineteenth century – when it came from the professors. This is illustrated, for example, in a famous incident at Warwick University in 1970 and became the subject of the book edited by E. P. Thompson, *Warwick University Ltd*, when students, protesting about the lack of accountability in the university, occupied the administration and gained access to controversial information relating to what E. P. Thompson later called the 'industrial–intellectual oligarchy' (Thompson, 1970).

The 1960s and 1970s can more broadly be seen as a time of deconstruction, to take the term that came to epitomize the contemporary developments in philosophy and which was to have so much impact on the self-understanding of the human sciences for the remainder of the century. What was deconstructed was the established wisdom, fixed cultural identities and the traditional values of the bourgeois epoch of modernity. This included the very self that was the basis of the notion of *Bildung*. The radicals in the universities and the students made alliances with the workers in an attempt to forge a coalition between the life of the mind and labour. In a book entitled *Culture in the Plural*, published in 1974, Michel de Certeau discussed the embracing of democratic popular culture by the university: 'The relation of culture to society has been transformed: culture is no longer reserved for a given mileau; it no longer belongs to certain professional specialities (teachers or liberal professions); nor is it any longer a stable entity defined by universally received codes' (de Certeau, 1997: 41). He believed that the introduction of popular culture into the university was leading to the birth of the student worker and the wider abolition of the social divisions of labour. Although this socialism of the intellect and of labour was not to last, the politicization of the university was irreversible. Even in the postrevolutionary period of the 1980s, when neoliberalism and managerialism penetrated the universities, the university had become a site of cultural plurality. Although this was often to become a token political correctness, the university had been destined to become one of the major sites of cultural deconstruction. Its capacity to engage in sustained political critique may have been limited, but a more indirect, mediated politics of contestation, subversion and irony continued to be central to the identity of the university in the age of advanced capitalism. If the revolutionary politics of academic communism associated with May 1968 in Paris failed, what succeeded was a cultural politics. This is most apparent in the civil rights movement in the United States and in feminism. Without the democratic space afforded by the university these developments would not have been able to gain the momentum they did. The university must be seen as an incubator, not a prime originator, of cultural change. It responded to the transformation of cultural models in a way that led to their further cognitive development.

It is, then, in this sense that the university cultivated a democratic citizenship. This kind of citizenship differed from the older tradition of citizenship described by T. H. Marshall and briefly recounted in the previous chapter. It consisted in the progressive unfolding of rights – civic, political and social – granted by the state to citizens in order to compensate for the inequalities of social class. But the Marshallian understanding of citizenship was a passive kind of citizenship in which citizens were simply the recipients of rights bestowed by an increasingly benevolent state to alleviate the vicissitudes of capitalism. Active citizenship, as participation in the political community, entails a break from this, essentially privatistic kind of citizenship, bringing citizenship closer to democracy. My argument is that universities, once bastions of Christian piety, bourgeois privatism and class privilege, became, with the rise of the adversarial culture, crucial sites of citizenship in this more active mode. As they became more and more drawn into the social order and as the clash of culture and politics became unavoidable, the university opened its arms to democracy. The promise of a cultural democracy remains one of the most important legitimations of the universities.

The new German debate on the university: Habermas, Gadamer and Schelsky

The German debate on the university was renewed in a series of interventions by leading German social theorists from the 1960s to the reform of the German university system in the early 1970s. It can be seen from this debate how different the conception of the university had become since the time of Humboldt and the idealist philosophers. In a curious way, however, the lines of division were between those who, like Jaspers, Gadamer and Schelsky, stood for a renewal of the Humboldtian conception of the university and those, who like Jürgen Habermas, stood more in the Kantian tradition, now allied with Hegelian Marxism, of the university as a site of critique. In all cases there is a defence of the university as a social and cultural institution that is based on a legitimating idea, in the sense of a cognitive principle.

The German debate emerged with the reopening of the University of Heidelberg in 1945 when Karl Jaspers gave an address, 'The Renewal of the University', which he based on the theme of his book *The Idea of the University*, originally published in 1923 and reprinted in 1946. However, the debate of the 1960s on the reform of the German university system frequently referred to the revised edition of the book published in 1961 (an earlier edited version appeared in English in 1960). In an age that had yet to experience social protest, Jaspers believed something in the old German tradition still offered the present a model and that this lay in the fact of the university resting on an idea. Jaspers chose to ignore the differentiation of knowledge as a threat to the viability of this idea and the fact that there might be many ideas attached to many different cultural forms of life. His defence of the idea of the university was one of the last bourgeois humanistic visions.

In a lecture given at the Free University of Berlin in 1967, 'The University in a Democracy: Democratization of the University', Jürgen Habermas (1971a; see also Habermas, 1969) reopened the old German question of the idea of the university. His perspective was radically different from the conservative and liberal positions of earlier intellectuals such as Jaspers who had not fully reconciled tradition and modernity. Habermas attacked those who try to reduce the university either to a site of instrumental knowledge or to the culture of humanism. In other words, for Habermas the university was not defined by either organized or liberal modernity. In his view the task of the university was to provide a political education by shaping a political consciousness among its students: 'For too long the consciousness that took shape at German universities was apolitical. It was a singular mixture of inwardness, deriving from the culture of humanism, and of loyalty to state authority' (Habermas, 1971a). In the context of the growing radicalness and unrest of the late 1960s he feared the university would be absorbed into the role of merely producing and transmitting technical knowledge and providing society with a technically skilled labour force. Habermas emphasized the role of the university as an interpreter of a society's self-understanding and not just passing on its heritage in an unmediated manner: 'it belongs to the tasks of the university to transmit, interpret, and develop the cultural tradition of the society' (Habermas, 1971a: 2). To interpret is also to critically transform, and it is in this function of enhancing the capacity of a society to develop its communicative action that the university has a major public role to play. Essential to that task, in Habermas's estimation, was the need for the university to critically reflect on its own presuppositions and to embark on radical democratization. After 1945, the German university was given the task of preparing society for the political order of democracy, and many chairs were established in social and political science. The problem as Habermas saw it was that 'the university was inserted into democratic society with a certain political extension of its traditional understanding, *but otherwise just as it was*' (Habermas, 1971a: 5). What had remained unchanged and which was an impediment to its new task was a certain immobilism which derived from its unreformed self-governing autonomy. Thus to many professors the reforms that were soon to be enforced on the university appeared too much like the capitulation of the university to technology. Habermas believed that the reform of the

German university was compatible with some of the goals of German idealism, such as the emphasis on self-reflection. The university had two choices open to it: it must embrace either democracy or the values of capitalism and technology: 'The link between our postwar democracy and the traditional university – a link that seems almost attractive – is coming to an end. Two tendencies are competing with each other. Either increasing productivity is the sole basis of a reform that smoothly integrates the depoliticized university into the system of social labor and at the same time inconspicuously cuts its ties to the political, public realm. Or the university asserts itself within the democratic system. Today, however, this seems possible in only one way: although it has misleading implications, it can be called the democratization of the university' (Habermas, 1971a: 5–6). In practical terms this amounted to a university no longer run by professors but by students, junior academics and non-professors. The democratization of the university also entailed the ending of the dualism of academic hierarchy and the administration of departments.

Many intellectuals of the left were also conscious, too, that the German humanistic tradition failed to offer a resistance to the descent into fascism and as a result it had lost the moral role that Jaspers thought it might retain. In this stance, Habermas was not too far removed from Hans-Georg Gadamer's writings on the university and knowledge. Although Gadamer's position differed from Habermas's, and both took up an antagonistic position in the 1960s on the question of the theory of hermeneutics, with Habermas defending a critical approach and Gadamer a historicist, relativisitic position, the two theorists moved in a more complementary direction in later years. One of Germany's leading philosophers and former student of Martin Heidegger, Gadamer advocated a hermeneutic conception of the university. In a series on essays and interviews, Gadamer defends the Humboldtian ideal of education as a hermeneutic undertaking (Gadamer, 1992). In line with his hermeneutical philosophy, elaborated in his major work of 1960, *Truth and Method,* he sees the university as a place of interpretation, not just of training (Gadamer, 1979). Though often associated with a conservative view on society, Gadamer is not defending the Humboldtian understanding of education as merely the transmission of culture, for the act of interpretation is also a transformative process. Moreover, he repudiates the political legacy of Heidegger and his pro-fascist vision of the university as 'national self-determination' (Heidegger, 1985). The university is a hermeneutically inclined institution, aimed at self-interpretation. But to interpret is also to see things differently, and in this cultural dialogue tradition undergoes a creative renewal, for every age sees the documents of history in a new light. His concern is less with advocating policies for the reform of the university than with an analysis of the meaning of education for the modern age. What is interesting and important in his writings is that *Bildung* can still be relevant to modernity, less as a personal ethic as was the case for the idealist philosophers who remained within the confines of the philosophy of consciousness than as a creative appropriation of language, experience and cultural tradition. It might be mentioned, too, that Gadamer, as rector of the University of Leipzig from 1947 to 1957, struggled to both preserve and renew the old humanistic tradition, discredited by compliance and silence in the fascist period, in the communist regime of the German Democratic Republic where censorship made academic autonomy difficult. In various addresses and essays, Gadamer defended the essential unity of teaching and research as advocated by von Humboldt. All research for Gadamer is interwoven and the significance that the natural sciences have for humanity only reinforces the overall unity of science and society. In a world of specialization, differentiation and rationalization the university is, he says, one of the few 'free spaces' where unity is still possible. It might be suggested that what Gadamer is pointing to is the idea that the unity of knowledge – learning and research – is to be found in the occupation of a particular kind of space, the open space of the university. This unity is not based on an underlying idea or structure but emerges from the experience of openness.

Gadamer followed Humboldt in using the expression 'solitude and freedom' to describe the university. This phrase was also the title of a widely read book in Germany in those years, *Einsamkeit und Freiheit*. In this book by one of Germany's most well known sociologists, Helmut Schelsky, a sociologist of education and political culture in Adenaur's Germany, the Humboldtian tradition was affirmed once again (Schelsky, 1963). However, Schelsky does not seek to appeal to the discipline of philosophy for a point of unity, as Jaspers in fact attempted; instead he finds the unity of science within the differentiated structure of the sciences, in the natural, human and social sciences. Schelsky demonstrated the unrealistic idea of an overarching and transcendent point of unity. Unity is instead to be found in the 'solitude and freedom' of science and scholarship, an argument that is reminiscent of Weber's remarks on the intellectual sacrifice of science. In a way, this also bears out Gadamer's argument and might be said to be a kind of unity that is not found in a particular discipline.

At this point we can return to Habermas. Two decades after his essay on the university and in the context of the sexcentenary celebrations of the founding of the University of Heidelberg, Habermas returned to this debate, defending in a seminal article the contribution of the university to the public sphere (Habermas, 1992). Arguing against the systems theory of Niklas Luhmann (1987, 1990, 1995) for whom the university was a mere organization without a moral function, he claimed that despite the functionalizing of the university, knowledge even in a decentred society preserves a connection with the life-world and cultural reproduction. His main argument was that the critical appropriation of the idea of the university has remained unrealized. In his view, the older Enlightenment ideal has still some relevance today but must be realized under the conditions of something like a 'communication community', a concept also proposed by the philosopher of social science Karl-Otto Apel (Apel, 1980). The university, as a site of intense communication, captures the essence of Habermas's position. What is peculiar to the university is that it is a 'bundle institution'. The universities are still rooted in the life-world through the bundling of functions, he argues, such as the research process, general education, cultural self-understanding, the formation of public opinion, the training of future specialists: 'As long as this complex has not been completely torn apart, the idea of the university cannot be completely dead' (Habermas, 1992: 107–8). However, he makes clear that the university no longer has the power of reconciliation that the Prussian reformers and idealist philosophers once believed possible, for this would be to overburden the university with demands incompatible with the reality of complexity and specialization. The university has lost the power to offer the social world a vision of totality and thus a vision of emancipation. This is clearly the idealist illusion and is open to all the objections that Marx levelled against Hegel. For Habermas the university stands in the balance between the cultural weight of its neohumanist heritage and the pressure of power and money. In short, it is located between the social and cultural structures of the life-world and the instrumentalized imperatives of the 'system' of money and power.

The older debates on the idea of the university all assumed that the unity of the university was to be found in science and scholarship itself, in other words cognitive rationality. The problem can therefore be stated as:

> But if science can no longer be used to anchor ideas in this way, because the multiplicity of the disciplines no longer leaves room for the totalizing power of either an all-encompassing philosophical fundamental science or even a reflective form of material critique of science and scholarship that would emerge from the disciplines themselves, on what could an integrative self-understanding of the corporative body of the university be based?
>
> (Habermas, 1992: 123)

The answer Habermas gives is communication. Citing with approval the early Enlightenment philosopher Schliermacher, the founder of modern hermeneutics, and who wrote that knowledge is inseparably connected with communication, Habermas argues that, 'in the last analysis it is the communicative forms of scientific and scholarly argumentation that hold university learning processes in their various functions together' (Habermas, 1992: 124). In a lecture given in New York in 1967, Habermas pointed out that students have been major social actors in democratization (Habermas, 1971b). The older conception of the university emphasized too much the professorate as the protector of the cultural and moral values of society, but students were central to moral and political change at many times in the history of industrial society. They played a revolutionary role in nineteenth-century Russia, in China in the 1920s and 1930s, and in Cuba in the 1950s. In 1956 the revolts in Budapest and Warsaw were set off by student protests. Many dictatorships were overthrown by students in Southeast Asia and Latin America, and in much of the world where democracy has been poorly developed students have exercised strong political pressure. In particular, in the non-western world, the university has been an agent of social change: 'It generates both new, technologically exploitable knowledge and the consciousness of modernity, with all of its practical consequences' (Habermas, 1971b: 13).

Habermas's concept of the university as the site of critical and transformative action rooted in communication reflects the revolutionary spirit of the 1960s and the years of university reform of the 1970s. His essay offers a way of steering a middle course between the extremes of the neohumanist model of knowledge as rooted in the life-world and the nascent technocratic model of knowledge as shaped by the social system according to the media of power and money. As is also evident in his other work from that period, *Knowledge and Human Interests* (Habermas, [1968] 1978), knowledge is a differentiated structure and is linked to society by its inseparable connection with cognitively specific human interests. But what links all the sciences together is not scientific rationality as such but the embeddedness of science in communication, for despite extensive differentiation and specialization the mode of knowledge production within universities has not become totally detached from the cognitive horizon of the life-world and to that extent it contains within it a connection with communication. This communication community is different from everyday communication, but it is nevertheless a form of communication: 'The egalitarian and universalistic content of its forms of argumentation expresses only the norms of scientific and scholarly activity, not those of society as a whole. But they share emphatically in the communicative rationality in whose forms modern society, that is, societies which are not fixed once and for all and which have no guiding images, must reach an understanding about themselves' (Habermas, 1987: 125).

In his social theory of modernity – in works such as *The Theory of Communicative Action*, first published in 1981 (Habermas, 1984, 1987) and earlier in *The Structural Transformation of the Public Sphere*, first published in 1962 (Habermas, 1989) – he elaborated the theoretical basis of a view of modernity as the increase in the potentiality of communication and sites of contestation. Habermas sees modern society as the expansion of communicative forms of action which serve as points of resistance against the instrumentalizing forces of the market, bureaucracy and the state. This perspective on modernity, as the unfolding of processes of communication, allows for a more transformative theory of modernity as the permanent contestation of legitimation.

What I think emerges from the whole debate is that the continuity with the cultural project of the neohumanist, liberal university can be maintained only at the cost of abandoning the privatism upon which it was historically based. In this chapter I am arguing that one of the main developments in the modern university was the collapse of the separation of the private and public dimensions of the university. The break-up of this dichotomy is one of the most striking features of the legacy of the late 1960s when the cultural assumptions of bourgeois society were shaken. What was once a politically neutral territory suddenly became a place of intense political activity. In my view the ideas of Gadamer and Habermas capture the transformative project of modern culture crystallized in the institution of the university. Culture is not a prepolitical unity as in the von Humboldt vision of the university but a site of contestation. Gadamer's hermeneutic theory of the university as a place of interpretation and Habermas's theory of communication express in different ways the fact that under the conditions of an advanced modernity the unity of culture is possible only as a communicative process. It does not rest on a particular discipline or social structure but on the essential interconnectivity of all forms of knowledge and on the interconnectivity of knowledge and the cognitive structures of the life-world.

I believe that there is some justification for Gadamer and Habermas's insistence that despite the reality of specialization and rationalization, the university is still linked more with the life-world than with the bureaucratic spheres of money and power. To that extent it is still meaningful to speak of the idea of the university. But this 'idea' must not be seen as a totalizing cultural principle and, above all, the idea of the university does not necessarily derive from the university itself. As Habermas intimated, a 'new life can be breathed into the idea of the university only outside its walls' (Habermas, 1992: 108). Some further thoughts on this are now warranted.

The rise of student revolt: Marcuse, Touraine and Riesman

Herbert Marcuse brought critical social theory on to a new level in the 1960s. His entire writings were preoccupied with the fate of revolution in the advanced industrial society and in particular of the role of universities in the revolutionary project. It was his belief – and which led him to become the most famous American intellectual of the left in the 1960s – that the revolutionary actor was no longer the proletarian but the younger members of the middle class, in particular the students. The university thus becomes the vanguard of western Marxism. In *Reason and Revolution* (Marcuse, 1941) he prepared the philosophical foundations for a new Marxism based on a rereading of Hegel, whose great lesson was that knowledge was a striving after what does not yet exist but whose possibility is contained in the 'system of needs' of the present. In *Eros and Civilization* (1955) Marcuse added Freud to the project of Hegelian Marxism in order to show how political revolution also had to be sexual revolution and that the 'system of needs' must be broadened to include new human needs relating to culture and the psyche. Capitalist society, in his view, required sexual repression because it requires the postponement of gratification necessary to maintain the work ethic. The impulse for social revolution comes from the repression of eros. Revolution now becomes human revolution, the struggle to release the forces of life over death and repression. In this work the proletariat is no longer a revolutionary movement. In *One-dimensional Man* (1964) a pessimistic turn becomes evident in his thought, for he now sees the potentially liberating forces of eros as trapped in the consumerism of advanced capitalism which forces all of culture to be affirmative and ideological. Despite his pessimistic tone, this work was to be the inspiration of much of student radicalism in the late 1960s and that something like what he called a 'Great Refusal' might be possible against technology and capitalism. In *An Essay on Liberation* (1969) Marcuse, inspired by the students revolts of the previous years, new militant movements, the emergence of radical art and the civil rights movement, restates his belief that the university might be a site of social revolution. In his later writings, such as his final work *Aesthetic Dimension* (1979), Marcuse eventually abandoned the idea of social revolution as a real possibility, seeing instead the revolutionary dream contained in the writing of Hegel, Marx and Freud as preserved only in high art that could maintain its distance from society. Marcuse was certainly an important writer, although his theory of revolution did not endure and universities, while once places of rebellion, ceased to be central to the counter-culture whose animus declined in the 1980s as a result of cultural fragmentation, the institutionalization of the radical generation and a new kind of politics, which Christopher Lasch has described as one of psychic survival (Lasch, 1979, 1985).

Another leading text on the university from this period was Alain Touraine's *The May Movement: Revolt and Reform*, which dealt with the impact of the students' movement on the university (Touraine, 1971b). Touraine had already written his first major work, *The Sociology of Action* (1965), in which he established the foundations of a new sociology based on social movements. In these years he also outlined the theory of the postindustrial society. In *Post-industrial Society* (1971a) he argued that advanced industrial society had become a 'programmed society' and had entered its postindustrial phase. In this kind of society services are becoming more important than industrial labour in terms of employment and the shaping of biographies. The idea of action as the fundamental component of society and the notion of postindustrialism provided the foundations for a theory of the university.

For Touraine in this early work, written at a time of intense political involvement, the university is an institution located between bourgeois class power and the demands of the postindustrial society for knowledge. In the 'postindustrial society', knowledge is the key to the new struggles. This means that the university as the institution producing knowledge can ally itself with either knowledge or capital. This dichotomy is not unlike Habermas's dualism of life-world and system and, like Habermas, Touraine wants to defend the link between the mode of knowledge produced in the university and the wider context of knowledge embedded in the cognitive structures of cultural models and social practices. The postindustrial society offers the possibility of a new system of needs, to use Marcuse's Hegelian terms, and there is much that is similar between the writings of Marcuse and Touraine, both seeing the possibility of a major challenge to power residing in students as the most progressive actor within the middle class. But Touraine, like Marcuse, was eventually forced to reconsider the possibility of social revolution as a real possibility.

In Touraine's view, the university was failing to respond to the new kind of society that was emerging. He saw the students' movement emerging to fulfil this responsibility. However, he argues, it soon became apparent that the students' movement was too political and offensive, it did not force the university to reflect on its role in society, thereby opening up new possibilities. These possibilities consist in recognizing the connection between knowledge and power:

> Science is not itself democratic but there exists a possible alliance of producers and democracy against power. Science needs liberty to innovate and criticize dogmatism, just as democracy needs science to destroy the self-interested deceits of those who identify their power with reason.
>
> (Touraine, 1971b: 338)

The university need not be the instrument of the state but could become more allied with society. The new role for the university will be to facilitate reflection on society, for the 'progress of knowledge is inseparable from the critical self-reflection of society on itself, on its intellectual operations as well as on its social and political organization' (Touraine, 1971b: 332). The university thus exists between politics and knowledge: just as there is no pure or autonomous knowledge, neither is there pure politics. 'The university was and is, simultaneously, an instrument to reinforce the dominant scientific creation and a relatively independent center of criticism and cultural change' (Touraine, 1971b: 334). Knowledge and politics are mediated in the cultural model of society. In this way Touraine is able to criticize both the conservatism of the university and the offensive politics of the students.

From this point onwards Touraine tended to be wary that modernity might be able to produce a social actor capable of transforming society. In his subsequent writings, *The Self-production of Society* (1977), *The Voice and the Eye* (1981) and *The Return of the Actor* (1988), he explored the idea of social movements as transformative agents. But in these writings it was never clear whether a social movement corresponded to a particular social actor, and in his later work of the 1990s, such as *Critique of Modernity* (1995) that possibility appears to be finally abandoned.

It might be said, then, that the politicization of higher education has led to the fundamental restructuring of the university. The political animus of adversary culture eventually went into decline and the university ceased to be a political actor, but its internal politicization remained to become an irreversible part of its legacy. In this context I would like to conclude by a brief mention of Riesman's writing on the university.

David Riesman is widely recognized to be one of the leading sociologists of American higher education. His reputation was established with the publication in 1950 of *The Lonely Crowd*, which was to become one of the most widely read sociology books ever written. In another major work on higher education, *The Academic Revolution*, David Riesman and Christopher Jencks (1968) did not write about social revolution but the rise and expansion of the academic profession whose pre-eminence coincided with the student movement. It is not surprising, then, that Riesman regarded this work as a study in counter-revolution. After almost a century of ascendancy, the academic profession attained the height of its power in the 1960s. In a later book, *On Higher Education: The Academic Enterprise in an Era of Rising Student Consumerism*, first published in 1980, Riesman told of a new story: the 'decline of faculty dominance' (Riesman, 1998). It was a work on the impact of student revolt and cultural change on the university, the inevitable result being the decline in the power of the academic profession. The earlier period was one in which tenured professors dominated university policy and when students and administrators were relatively silent. The students were subdued and administrators were subservient to the professorate. From a later period, Riesman reflects on the massive turn to student power that came with the counter-culture of the 1960s: 'The counter-culture – unlike, for instance, students protests against the Vietnam war or other particular social evils – has not been an ephemeral movement, but rather one that has profoundly changed our whole society' (Riesman, 1998: 6). He speaks of the rise of 'student consumerism', a key factor in the transformation of higher education. This is manifest in increasing student influence in governance, admissions policy and on the determination of the curriculum. The adversary culture brought politics into the curriculum as well as into the governance of the university.

In sum, we can say that after the critiques of Habermas, Marcuse and Touraine, the Enlightenment idea of academic freedom can no longer be upheld as before: academic freedom is no longer legitimated by the 'republic of science' but by the need for society to have a zone of engagement between power and knowledge, politics and culture. The university has entered the transformative project of modernity. The legacy of the adversary culture was not revolt but the opening up of the university to new cognitive structures, such as the values of demoracy which now penetrate the mode of knowledge. I have tried to show that the adversary culture forced the university to enter the wider transformation of cultural models and to take up a public role in advancing democratic values. Thus, as the mode of knowledge was beginning to change as a result of the functional imperatives of mass education, the requirements of the postindustrial society and the growing specialization of science, the cultural models of society also began to shift in this period. In the next chapter we look at a further dimension of the opening of the university to the transformative project, namely the role of intellectuals as the key agents of change.

5

The Institutionalization of Critique: Intellectuals, the Public Sphere and the University

In the previous chapter I argued that the university has been one of the most important institutions in society which contributed to the cultivation of democratic values. In this sense the university cannot be separated from civil society. Parsons gives as one of the four functions of the university the role of contributing to the cultural self-understanding of society. This particular function is not rooted in a specific academic role of contributing to cognitive rationality as such but is to be found in participation in public life. The academic as a professional – as expert, professional trainer or teacher – operates within the relatively closed world of scientific specialization. Yet the pursuit of knowledge has a public role other than the servicing of socially useful knowledge tasks. It contributes to citizenship and to the transmission of cultural values in the wider society.

In this chapter I wish to discuss one dimension of this public role of universities. Universities do not simply reproduce social and cultural values but they also problematize the cultural models of society. It is in this the role of intellectuals can be discussed. Intellectuals are not just *reproducers* but *transformers* of society's cultural models. In the previous chapter I looked at this question of the transformative project of the university from the perspective of student radicalism. Protest and revolt in the campus were critical in the articulation of democratic values. With the decline of the adversary culture in the late 1970s the transformative project lost a good deal of its animus, although remaining a powerful force not least because many of its objectives were in fact met, but in the wider society and as a result of reform within the university. In this chapter I am arguing that intellectuals and intellectual culture are vital to the existence of universities. Exactly what is an intellectual and to what extent do intellectuals contribute to the transformation of cognitive structures is my theme.

I begin by looking at the Mannheim and Gramsci's theory of intellectuals, then I discuss the conservative critique of intellectuals which opposes the politicization of culture. Next I deal with Gouldner's theory of the New Class and finally I look at some attempts to relink politics to culture.

Mannheim and Gramsci on intellectuals and modernity

Karl Mannheim and Antonio Gramsci, in two classic but quite different works, have shaped the terms of debate on intellectuals in modernity. In *Ideology and Utopia*, a foundational work in the sociology of knowledge, Mannheim made the problem of knowledge central to modernity: 'The emergence of the problem of the multiplicity of thought-styles which have appeared in the course of scientific development and the perceptibility of collective unconsciousness motives hitherto hidden, is only one aspect of the prevalence of the intellectual restiveness which characterizes our age' (Mannheim, 1936: 30). Modernity for Mannheim was an age when no one cognitive or cultural framework attains dominance and, as a result, modernity is perpetually in crisis. He believed intellectuals were both the cause of as well as the solution to this situation, for intellectuals can express a vision of the world which other groups cannot because of their social location. 'In every society there are social groups whose special task it is to provide an interpretation of the world for that society. We call these the "intelligentsia"' (Mannheim, 1936: 9). In fairly static, traditional societies intellectuals were linked to dominant institutions, such as the Church, and were 'scholastic' in that they were relatively separate from everyday life. Universities contained such kinds of intellectuals, such as the genteel scholar, the man of letters. But with modernity, according to Mannheim, the ability of these groups to hold a monopoly over knowledge declines and culture separates from everyday life and as it does so it crystallizes into many competing frames of reference:

> From a sociological point of view the decisive fact of the modern times, in contrast with the situation during the Middle Ages, is that this mono-poly of knowledge of the ecclesiastical interpretation of the world which was held by the priestly caste is broken, and in the place of a closed and thoroughly organized stratum of intellectuals, a free intelligentsia has arisen. Its chief characteristic is that it is increasingly recruited from constantly varying social strata and life-situations, and that its mode of thought is no longer subject to regulation by a caste-like organization.
>
> (Mannheim, 1936: 10)

What collapses with this shift is the illusion that there is only one way of thinking:

> The almost unanimously accepted world-view which had been artificially maintained fell apart the moment the socially monopolistic position of its producers was destroyed. With the liberation of the intellectuals

from rigorous organization of the church, other ways of interpreting the world were increasingly recognized.

(Mannheim, 1936: 11)

Mannheim goes on to describe this as the 'profound disquiet of the present day' and out of which there emerged fundamentally new modes of thought and ones which lack any overall unity.

For Mannheim, the modern intellectual is a free agent. The famous term that Mannheim used, the 'socially unattached intelligentsia', which in fact was first used by Alfred Weber, suggested that the intellectual in modernity can rise above their social position and gain a vision of totality (Mannheim, 1936: 137). What unites intellectuals is education, and it was Mannheim's conviction that education could allow society to overcome its deep divisions of class and nationality. By means of education the intellectual can resist the prevailing *Weltanschauung* and the conditions of the immediate social situation. Mannheim goes so far as to say that the modern bourgeoisie had a double social origin: one in its ownership of capital and one in its possession of education, a division traditionally approximating the property-owning class and the educated class. It was clear that Mannheim saw the redemption of modernity to lie in the latter from whom the modern mind derives all its uniqueness. Intellectuals have created the modern mind which is dynamic, in constant flux and perpetually confronted by new problems, he argues. But their distinctive character is that they are unattached and therefore they can transform the conflict of interests into a conflict of ideas:

> This ability to attach themselves to classes to which they originally did not belong, was possible for intellectuals because they could adapt themselves to any viewpoint and because they and they alone were in a position to choose their affiliation while those who were immediately bound by class affiliations were only in rare exceptions able to transcend the boundaries of the class outlook.
>
> (Mannheim, 1936: 141)

Thus what characterizes intellectuals is their cosmopolitanism which comes with their education.

Mannheim's great faith in intellectuals was shared by his contemporary on the left, the Italian communist Antonio Gramsci. But while the former saw intellectuals as unattached, the latter was unambivalent on the possibility of attached intellectuals becoming influential and gaining political pre-eminence. According to Gramsci in his *Prison Notebooks*, written, when he was a prisoner of the fascists between 1929 and 1935, every nascent social group seeks to create an ideological framework in which to anchor its aspirations. Intellectuals give these social groups a certain homogeneity and a means of articulating a self-consciousness. He distinguished between traditional and organic intellectuals. The former – priests, lawyers, teachers, doctors – are like Mannheim's traditional intellectuals, tied as they are to a predominantly premodern, rural way of life but one that they are separate from by virtue of their social status. Their narratives are ones of uninterrupted historical continuity and a conservative endorsement of the social and political order with which they identify. However, Gramsci associates them with a quality that Mannheim reserved for modern intellectuals: they are autonomous and independent of the dominant social group though they have a politico-social function (Gramsci, 1971: 7, 14–15). Modern intellectuals, which he calls organic intellectuals, in contrast to both traditional intellectuals and also to Mannheim's characterization of modern intellectuals as unattached, are socially connected in complex ways. They are products of an urban world and do not have a direct relationship to the state in the way that traditional intellectuals were connected with the system of domination. What is the criterion of the distinctiveness of the intellectual, asks Gramsci: 'The most widespread error of method seems to me that of having looked for this criterion of distinction in the intrinsic nature of intellectual activities, rather than in the ensemble of the system of relations in which these activities (and therefore the intellectual groups who personify them) have their place within the general complex of social relations' (Gramsci, 1971: 8). The organic intellectual that comes with modernity is shaped by an active participation with the real world, 'as constructor, organizer, "permanent persuader" and not just a simple orator', he argues. The rise of a new social group involves the conquest of the discursive space previously occupied by traditional intellectuals and the creation of its own organic intellectuals. One of the most important sites of this conquest is education:

> The enormous development of activity and organization of education in the broad sense in the societies that emerged from the medieval world is an index of the importance assumed in the modern world by intellectual functions and categories. Parallel with the attempt to deepen and to broaden the 'intellectuality' of each individual, there has also been an attempt to multiply and narrow the various specializations. This can be seen from the educational institutions at all levels, up to and including the organisms that exist to promote so-called 'high culture' in all fields of science and technology. School is the instrument through which intellectuals of various levels are elaborated.
>
> (Gramsci, 1971: 10)

One of his more general philosophical-political arguments was that all groups, from reactionary conservatives to communists, seek to articulate a hegemonic project and that they do this with the aid of organic intellectuals who are crucial for the shaping of hegemony, by which Gramsci means a world-view or comprehensive ideology. Organic intellectuals have more oppositional potentialities than traditional intellectuals.

Mannheim and Gramsci offered two different visions of the modern intellectual, as unattached and as attached to a social group seeking political power or social influence. But for both it was clear that modernity unleashes cultural and cognitive frameworks from fixed structures and from the control of dominant elites. That intellectuals could play a key role in the articulation of a new social and political order was something that Mannheim and Gramsci recognized. Thus, though they wrote from different political persuasions – Mannheim from the liberal left and Gramsci from the communist left – they profoundly shaped the understanding of the intellectual as a central figure in the articulation of cultural models and in the social shaping of a new mode of knowledge. Gramsci stressed the idea of the intellectual as critical and politically motivated; Mannheim emphasized the cognitive orientation of the intellectual as someone who seeks to understand the cultural codes of modernity from a point beyond the immediacy of everyday life. For both thinkers the intellectual was a political being since intellectual activity had an unavoidable transformative nature.

Traditional intellectuals and conservative critique: from Benda to Bloom

From the liberal and communist controversy on the meaning and function of the intellectual in modernity, we now turn to the conservative critique. A whole range of European and American authors from the 1920s to the 1980s have heavily criticized the idea of the committed intellectual, be it Mannheim's free-floating intellectual, Gramsci's organic intellectual or Sartre's total intellectual (Sartre, 1967). John Carey paints a picture of modern intellectuals as contemptuous of the masses (Carey, 1992). His subject, however, is the English literary intelligentsia and their distaste for modern mass culture, a distaste that was matched by their distaste for politics.

One of the classic critiques of the political seduction of the intellectual was Julien Benda's book *The Treason of the Intellectuals*, originally published in French as *La Trahison des Clercs* in 1928 (Benda, 1969). Benda used a medieval meaning of clerk – the opposite of layman – rather than its modern meaning of office worker to highlight his thesis. The true meaning of an intellectual is like that of the ecclesiastical 'clerk in holy orders' who has a transcendent mission beyond the mundane world of the layman. The 'treason of the intellectuals' is their betrayal of culture for politics. For Benda the embracing of politics by intellectuals was a disaster for modern Europe since the release of knowledge from its elevated position beyond the social and the political provided tremendous legitimation for dangerous political projects. He was responding to the situation in Europe since the late nineteenth century when many intellectuals, one by one, found in the current situation a political embodiment of their cultural designs: 'Our age is indeed the age of the intellectual organization of political hatreds. It will be one of its chief claims to notice in the moral history of humanity' (Benda, 1969: 27). He deplored the patriotic fanaticism that this produced and feared the implications of mixing art with politics. Benda was defending not the traditional intellectual, as described by Mannheim and Gramsci, but the traditional humanistic ideal of culture as autonomous and separated from politics: 'the "clerks" who indulged in this fanaticism betrayed their duty, which is precisely to set up a corporation whose sole cult is that of justice and of truth, in opposition to the peoples and the injustice to which they are condemned by their religions of this earth' (Benda, 1969: 57). Benda believed that this traditional humanistic idea of the intellectual might contain a critique of the social world but only at the price of surrendering a political commitment.

This conservative critique of the political engagement of the intellectual was also to be found in the writings of Benda's Spanish contemporary, José Ortega y Gasset who, in books such as *The Revolt of the Masses*, sees the modern age as one in which the masses threaten the prevailing order in which authority is established by the elites and their intellectuals (Ortega y Gasset, 1932). He feared the political domination of the masses and the loss of cultural leadership by an intellectual elite. This concern with culture as a source of leadership received its most famous statement in the work of the English germanophile Matthew Arnold, whose *Culture and Anarchy* (published in 1869) argued for intellectual leadership by an elite capable of defending society against the false promises of politics and thus separate political modernity from cultural modernity (Arnold, 1960).

In more recent times this conservative defence of high culture found a powerful voice in Allan Bloom's controversial work *The Closing of the American Mind* (Bloom, 1987). Bloom's well known thesis was that modern America was facing a profound intellectual crisis because 'higher education has failed democracy and impoverished the souls of today's students'. He blamed this on the politicization of the curriculum and the erosion of the distinction between high and low culture. It is also a crisis in liberal education: 'the crisis of liberal education is a reflection of a crisis at the peaks of learning, an incoherence and incompatibility among the first principles with which we interpret the world, an intellectual crisis of the greatest magnitude, which constitutes the crisis of our civilization' (Bloom, 1987: 346). For Bloom, part of the solution lies in restoring the tradition of the 'great books', in which a vision of truth can be found. He bemoans the embracing of relativism as a positive fact. Recognizing its place in the cultivation of tolerance, he sees relativism as having been taken too far, and to the point that it has led to a rejection that something can be learned from history and to a rejection that there might be a shared public culture.

In this interpretation the intellectual has a social responsibility but this responsibility must not be compromised by an over-commitment to a political mission. The social responsibility of the intellectual is to culture not to politics.

Gouldner on the New Class and universities

As we have seen in the previous discussion it is not easy to define the precise sense of an intellectual. Intellectuals are those social actors who transmit ideas, but where the border between cultural ideas and political ideologies lies is not clear. What is culture to one may be politics to another and ideas can be emancipatory or they can be affirmative with respect to a system of power. In the latter sense we might use the term ideology to refer to ideas that tend to legitimate a system of power, but the world of ideas is broader and, to follow Mannheim, often has a utopian aspiration and one in tension with an existing order. This ambivalence has led some, such as Alvin Gouldner, to distinguish between intellectuals and the intelligentsia. The former are interested in emancipatory and critical knowledge, and as such they are mostly political and frequently contribute to revolutionary leadership. The intelligentsia, in contrast, is a group whose interests are more technical. The intelligentsia can be revolutionary too in the sense of disrupting social solitarities. Yet both, according to Gouldner, have a social mission beyond the status quo, one emancipatory and one technocratic: 'Revolutionary intellectuals are the medium of an ancient morality; accommodative intelligentsia are the medium of a new amorality' (Gouldner, 1979: 48). Gouldner argues that the intelligentsia tend to remain within the established ways of cognitive thinking and although their primary allegiance is to science and technology they are politically ambiguous. The rise of the intelligentsia is part of the consolidation of professionalism, which Parsons regarded as one of the distinctive features of modern society, and not capitalism. Intellectuals, in contrast, are more transgressive and do not seek the normalization that the intelligentsia desire. In short, one is more concerned with the means of influence and power and the other with political emancipation.

In this famous book *The Future of Intellectuals and the Rise of the New Class*, Gouldner advanced the thesis that intellectuals and the intelligentsia together formed a New Class, a new elite that has emerged in postindustrial society. Since it is composed of two overlapping elements (it is, he says, 'a contradictory class') it cannot be said to be either emancipatory or reducible to old class interests. In an argument that anticipates the sociology of Pierre Bourdieu, he says the New Class is a 'cultural bourgeoisie' that is not under the hegemony of the old class, for both the professions and the radical intellectuals are in revolt against the old class ties and seek the appropriation of a different kind of capital, namely cultural capital. Gouldner described his analysis as a version of left-wing Hegelianism:

> It is left Hegelianism in that it holds that knowledge and knowledge systems are important in shaping social outcomes, but, far from seeing these as disembodied eternal essences, views them as the ideology of special social classes; and while ready to believe that knowledge is one of the best hopes we have for a humane social reconstruction, also sees our knowledge systems as historically shaped forces that embody limit and, indeed, pathologies.
>
> (Gouldner, 1979: 5)

This led to a view of knowledge producers as socially located and with a very open agenda, being neither positive nor negative. As Lyotard argued in a book published in French the same year and which has become the canonical work in postmodern social theory, *The Postmodern Condition: A Report on Knowledge*, knowledge has lost its emancipatory promise for it has ceased to be a meta-narrative, having entered the social fabric and economic production in many ways (Lyotard, 1984). Despite the decline of modernist knowledge and the rise of the New Class – or, in Lyotard's term, the postmodern condition – knowledge can still be emancipatory but in a more restrictive sense. Both Gouldner and Lyotard, writing from the left, believed that knowledge can be politically committed but some of the illusions of the old left must be discarded. Gouldner argues that despite its morally ambigious nature, the New Class is a 'flawed universal class,' but still the best option for the left: 'The New Class is elitist and self-seeking and uses its special knowledge to advance its own interests and power, and to control its own work situation. Yet the New Class may also be the best card that history has presently given us to play' (Gouldner, 1979: 7). The New Class is based on a paradox in that it is both emancipatory and elitist but its discourse contains within a critique of the established forms of domination and at the same time an escape from domination and from tradition: 'The paradox of the New Class is that it is both emancipatory *and* elitist. It subverts all establishments, social limits, and privileges, including its own. The New Class bears a culture of critical and careful discourse which is an historically emancipatory rationality' (Gouldner, 1979: 85).

One of the striking features of the New Class is that, as a kind of 'cultural bourgeoisie', it has control over education and through this means it is in contest with the old class. The school is the major alienation from the old class, but the decisive break is in higher education: 'Colleges and universities are the finishing schools of the New Class' resistance to the old class' (Gouldner, 1979: 44). Gouldner is not unaware that education serves the function of the reproduction of the social order, as Marxists such as Louis Althusser argued. But education, in particular higher education, is more than just the 'ideological state apparatuses', as Althusser said (Althusser, 1971). Gouldner recognizes that academization often converts social crises into technical puzzle-solving, designed to protect the dominant paradigms and societal frameworks from critical scrutiny and subversion. As he points out: 'Obsequious professors may teach the advanced course in social cowardice, and specialists transmit skills required by bureaucracies. But Ronald Reagan did not set out to curb the University of California because it was the servant of capitalism' (Gouldner, 1979: 44–5). The university is a contradictory place in which the New Class may seek alliances with business or with apolitical culture or with political subversion. In a far-reaching assessment, Gouldner writes of the university as, like the New Class itself, internally differentiated:

> To understand modern universities and colleges we need an openness to contradiction. For universities both reproduce *and* subvert the larger society. We must distinguish between the functions universities

publicly *promise* to perform – the social goods they are chartered to produce – and certain of their actual consequences which, while commonly unintended, are no less real: the production of dissent, deviance, and the cultivation of an authority-subverting culture of critical discourse.

(Gouldner, 1979: 45)

Cultural capital, unlike moneyed capital, is not as tightly controlled and in education it is not dependent on the private sector. Gouldner's thesis is that the New Class, which is much more contradictory than the old class, does not control cultural capital such as knowledge. He believes that there is enough empirical evidence to suggest that, in particular, in higher education power is loosened not tightened. Higher education thus becomes a major 'cosmopolitanizing influence' in modern society. In it there is a shift from causal to reflexive speech and a discourse emerges in which claims and utterances may not be justified by reference to a speaker's social status. As a result, all authority referring claims are potentially problematic (Gouldner, 1979: 3). As he put it elsewhere:

The university's central problem is its failure as a community in which rational discourse about social worlds is possible. This was partly because rational discourse as such ceased to be its dominant value and was superseded by a quest for knowledge products and information products that could be sold for funding, prestige and power – rewards bestowed by the state and the larger society that is bent upon subverting rational discourse about itself.

(Gouldner, 1973: 79)

In sum, he argues that universities foster a 'culture of critical discourse', cosmopolitanism and reflexivity. This view is in line with the arguments of Habermas and Touraine, discussed in the previous chapter, though Gouldner distinguishes his position from Habermas's in that he believes the New Class offers the possibility of a more direct kind of political critique than what he takes to be Habermas's moral and cultural critique.

Whether this is a correct interpretation of Habermas need not concern us since the issue in the present context concerns the substantive question of the role of the intellectual. Gouldner points to the existence of two kinds of intellectual who together form the New Class. This line of argument has been reflected in several studies, such as the well known work by the Hungarian exiles, George Konrad and Ivan Szelenyi, *The Intellectuals on the Road to Class Power*, published in 1979 after being smuggled out of Hungary. They argue that intellectuals have become more important in modern society and constitute more an elite than a class. Their concern is with the intelligentsia rather than intellectuals in general and they see the intelligentsia as a source of domination in a society that requires rational knowledge: 'The society of rational distribution which came into being in the aftermath of the Bolsheviks' triumph created a new value-system for intellectual activity and for knowledge in general. It encompassed the direction of society, social planning as an ideology guided by the activity of technical experts' (Konrad and Szelenyi, 1979: 21). In their analysis, intellectual knowledge becomes free of traditional ties and this freedom becomes a new source of domination especially under communism.

It seems to me sensible to differentiate intellectuals from experts, the latter being what in essence constitutes the intelligentsia, in Gouldner's use of the term. Gouldner has been heavily criticized for this emphasis on the intellectuals as a New Class. The New Class, it is often held, is closer to an elite than a class (Bottomore, 1964; Eisenstadt, 1966; Etzioni-Halevy, 1985). Daniel Bell in *The Coming of the Postindustrial Society* also used a similar designation, the Knowledge Class (Bell, 1974). For Bell, the Knowledge Class, in essence the intelligentsia, is composed of the scientific, the technological, the administrative and the cultural. The cultural includes intellectuals in the narrow sense of the term: political and public intellectuals as opposed to experts. There is little doubt that this overall concept of the New Class or the Knowledge Class has given rise to too much confusion. Intellectuals need to be distinguished from the broader category of the New Class since they are more adversarial. In sum, it seems important to separate intellectuals from experts. As Eva Etzioni-Halevy argues, the term 'intellectual' came into widespread use in France during the Dreyfus trial of 1894 and was used by the political right to refer to those who opposed the trial, most of whom were educated (Etzioni-Halevy, 1985: 1). Since then the term has retained its association with critical, even radical opposition by those who possess a certain amount of cultural capital. However, what remains of importance in Gouldner's analysis is the contradictory nature of knowledge in general, that knowledge is not appropriated entirely by any one elite and is spread throughout society by the extension of the Knowledge Class into the middle class.

A general point emerges from this: the production of knowledge in late modern society is not independent of social interests and cultural models. As we have seen in the previous chapter, the university begins to lose its ability exclusively to define the field of knowledge and becomes more and more drawn into debates about the cognitive structure of society. Within the university no single discipline is dominant, and with the growing power of intellectuals within and outside the university, the ability of any one group to achieve lasting hegemony is limited. What occurs is the opening up of discourses in which debates occur about the epistemic/cognitive foundations of society.

In search of public intellectuals

Let us now consider the work of a number of theorists who have written about the, essentially political, critical intellectual in modern society. One of the most influential conceptions of the modern intellectual is clearly that of Michel Foucault who has himself encapsulated the very idea of the

intellectual. The political function of the intellectual for Foucault is primarily somebody who subverts the dominant orders of discourse (Foucault,
1977). He is less concerned with the intelligentsia which would fall under
the aegis of 'governmentality' whereas intellectuals operate in the inter-
stices of discourses. They are not connected with major social movements
or even necessarily social groups of any kind but seek the transformation of
established discourses. For Foucault, knowledge and power are interwoven
and therefore the point of intellectual intervention is to open up knowledge to new political strategies. While his entire vision of modernity was a
pessimistic one that saw oppressive institutions dominating subjectivity, his
later thinking addressed possibilities for emancipation. The intellectual was
central to such politics because modern society depended more and more
on knowledge. Intellectuals had a role in establishing the rules of these
discursive structures and therefore they could be active in deconstructing
them. It is in this sense that Foucault's theory is useful in understanding the
relationship between knowledge and cognitive structures: in his approach
these are united within the framework of discourses. However, in Foucault's
writings we do not get a sense of the public intellectual, as we do, for
instance, in Richard Sennett's *The Fall of Public Man*, who might be capable
of crossing discourses in society. Sennett (1978) associates the intellectual
with the public realm and notes the decline of public life in modern times.
The chief feature of this public realm is precisely the fact of a multiplicity of
discourses.

The preoccupation with public life has been central to American conceptions of the intellectual, who appears to have moved from the left to the
right in recent years, as the career of Daniel Bell demonstrates (Brick,
1986). In a widely read book, *The Last Intellectuals: American Culture in the Age
of Academe*, Russell Jacoby (1987) has complained about the decline of the
public intellectual. His diagnosis of the ills of academe runs counter to
Allan Bloom's for whom public life has been precisely the source of the
major problems of intellectual life. According to Jacoby, the university has
corrupted the mission of the intellectual. It has made the public intellectual
into an expert. Jacoby's ideal is the free-floating intellectual celebrated by
Karl Mannheim. But the problem as he sees it is that this category which
has been derided by both the right and the left – by the right for stray-
ing from pure culture and by the left for not being sufficiently politically
committed – has become a career intellectual. With the professionalization
of academe, the public intellectual goes into decline. Mannheim's vision
remains for him the ideal conception of the vocation of the intellectual.
However, there appears little hope in this vision of the intellectual becoming a reality simply because most intellectuals have become attached (in the
sense of being institutionalized) to the corporate organizations, such as
newspapers and above all universities.

The intellectual today is far from being marginalized, which is the principal characteristic of the intellectual according to Edward Said in his Reith
Lectures (Said, 1994). 'There is a danger that the figure of the intellectual

might disappear in a mass of details and that the intellectual might become only another professional, or a figure in a social trend' (Said, 1994: 8). Said's intellectual is politically radical and is epitomized by the marginalized exile. The university is not the primary location of the public intellectual for critics such as Jacoby and Said. The jargon and career-ridden nature of academe is antithetical to public enlightenment in much the same way as the political parties are detrimental to independent thought. From a slightly different perspective, Tony Judt, in a major and controversial work on the decline of the French public intellectuals, *Past Imperfect: French Intellectuals 1944–1956*, documents the replacement of the public and politically inclined intellectual with the academic, who is more responsible but who also has become reinvented by a largely non-French and international academic culture. The older French intellectuals of the postwar years – Malraux, Camus, Sartre, Merleu-Ponty – became the master thinkers of a later period, but a time which was quite separate from theirs and in which there has been an exaggeration of their importance: 'Left to their own devices, intellectuals are thus better placed to retain their local influence if they can point to the imprimatur of quality that comes with institutional attachment and disciplinary conventions. The correspondence between the decline of the great public intellectuals and the resurrection of the professors is thus no mere coincidence' (Judt, 1992: 297). For Judt the problem is not the replacement of the intellectual with the professor but the reinvention of the latter as a French intellectual. It is foreigners, particularly the English-speaking world, that sustains the myth of the French intellectual: 'The late-lamented French Intellectual is alive and well and living everywhere . . . except in Paris' (Judt, 1992: 299). These French intellectuals – Foucault and Derrida – have been quite detached from the political and social context of France, he argues. But Judt's main thesis is that the political category of the intellectual may have to be discarded as one no longer appropriate to the current situation. However, his characterization of intellectuals borders on confusing it with the intelligentsia: 'it is incontrovertible that modern tyranny not only gave the intelligentsia a privileged place but was in certain important respects a tyranny *of* the intelligentsia. Where the tyrant embodies reason, the role of the intellectual becomes vital in the transmission of that reason to the people in whose name it is applied' (Judt, 1992: 317–18). Judt thus demands a fundamental questioning of the role of the twentieth century intellectual as the bearer of a truth.

The relatively conservative position of Judt concerning the academic appropriation of the intellectual would appear to be echoed in many other works on the relation of intellectuals to academia (Ross, 1989; Fink *et al.*, 1996). Paul Bove sees academic culture enriched by the intellectuals who have not compromised their political aspirations (Bove, 1986). Many see critical possibilities preserved in academe, for instance in literature, philosophy, sociology and history. Thus the academic institution of criticism can, according to Michael Walzer, offer a better means of achieving the goal of public commitment (Walzer, 1987, 1988).

Rejecting the republican concept of civil society that underlies some of these arguments for a stronger sense of democratic society, Thomas Bender does not see a tension between the academy and the polity (Bender, 1993). This dichotomy has been asserted by too many critics and one of its strongest formulations was in Hannah Arendt's essay 'Truth and Politics', which distinguished academic knowledge from political knowledge (Arendt, 1967). Bender's argument is that the 'unreflective acceptance of this distinction hampers our ability to rethink the dilemma of the relation of expertise and democracy' (Bender, 1993: 128). In a collection of historical essays he tried to reconnect this lost tradition, which he associated with American philosophers such as John Dewey. There is a lost historical tradition, he argues, which did not polarize intellectual and professional cultures. The publicly committed intellectual culture and a professional culture of expertise were once linked. For Bender, the city was an important focus of attachment for both intellectuals and professionals. This can be called 'civic professionalism' as opposed to 'disciplinary professionalism':

> The former pattern has a historic association with the commercial city and the Florentine tradition of civic humanism, while the latter coincides with the emergence of industrial and corporate capitalism. During the course of the nineteenth century in America, civic professionalism declined in significance and even the traditional professions of law, medicine, and the ministry began to associate themselves with the model provided by the rising disciplinary professions.
>
> (Bender, 1993: 6)

The cosmopolitanism of the early professions in this civic sense of the term did not compromise their attachment to a locality, the city and thus to what might be called 'local knowledge' (Geertz, 1983). But the city and the civic professionalism did not endure and the preservation of intellectual life itself ceased to be of significance. Disciplinary specialization took over and isolated the intellectual commitment to city and democracy. We need to recover this older tie between the two worlds, Bender argues: 'Communities of discourse supply collective concepts, mechanisms for exclusion and appropriation, and give institutional force to the paradigms that guide the creative intellect' (Bender, 1993: 31).

The discussion of intellectuals in this chapter has highlighted a number of different perspectives. A central issue has been the relationship between professional and intellectual cultures. Intellectuals have been seen as constituting a political or cultural critique of their own and they have been seen as forming an elite, even a class, of their own, often compromising their autonomy by being part of an intelligentsia. However, what is clear is that intellectuals in the narrow sense of critical thinkers are essential to public life. Views will differ as to whether their proper location is outside the walls of the academy or within it, but there is no denying the fact that universities are the primary sites of intellectuals. This may mean that they cannot be unattached, but the chances are that they will be more unattached than those who are not protected by academic autonomy. Although profession-alism and career objectives may have diluted, the potency of the radical critique, the 'tenured radical', has nonetheless more autonomy than most other social actors, such as contract workers within the university itself. Intellectuals will continue to be important. Many critics have argued in recent works on intellectuals – Boggs (1993), Eyerman (1994) and Collins (1998) – that intellectuals have been important cosmopolitan actors who have emerged at decisive points in history and have been pivotal in shaping the cognitive terms of cultural self-understanding and societal innovation. As Jeffrey Goldfarb says in *Civility and Subversion*, intellectuals contribute to democracy by helping societies to talk about problems. They contribute to civility in public life and to promoting the subversion of common sense. He is surely correct when he says 'much of America's public life is now found in the universities, overshadowing the traditional public spaces of cities. As painting, music, and theater have found their place in American univer-sities, so has intellectual life' (Goldfarb, 1998: 125). I believe Jacoby's objec-tions are misplaced since there is no reason why universities cannot harbour intellectuals and why this cannot be compatible with the other roles of the academy. It is indeed true that the greatest danger is that the university as the last refuge of the intellectual will not give sufficient space to this import-ant role. As I have argued in earlier chapters, there are four academic roles – professional researchers, professional trainers, teachers, and intellectuals – and the danger is that the latter two will be overshadowed by the first two. Many academics can, and have to, perform these roles. The question remains how the interconnections can best be established. I believe it makes sense to characterize as one of the main functions of the university the institu-tionalization of critique which complements the functions of research and education.

6

Academic Power and Cultural Capital: Bourdieu on Knowledge and the University

Pierre Bourdieu can be placed alongside Parsons and Habermas as one of the most important theorists of the modern university. Author and co-author of numerous books on the university and education, Bourdieu offers a challenging account of the institution of knowledge in modern societies. It is an account which differs in many respects from some of the other major conceptions of the university in seeing the university as a set of social practices which serve as a medium of cultural classification which allows power to circulate within and across institutional contexts. It is this concern with the cognitive structure of society that is of particular interest in his work on the university. In fact, he has relatively little to say on the university as a producer of knowledge. It would appear that the cognitive question is more central to his concerns, that is the role of the university in defining, and being defined by, the dominant cultural models embodied in the various kinds of cultural capital that circulate in society. However, as we shall see, he ultimately subordinates this cognitive question to a theory of power.

It was the basis of Parsons's theory of the university that there is a functional link between knowledge and citizenship. For Habermas, too, knowledge is rooted in socially shaped interests and the university can have an emancipatory function if it is articulated in communicative contexts. In contrast, the sociology of Bourdieu offers quite a different approach to the university, which he sees as a self-preserving institution in which different kinds of power are produced, circulated and reproduced. The university is primarily an autonomous site in which different orders of power clash as their holders struggle for self-reproduction. Although Parsons and Habermas differed theoretically and politically, they both saw the university as being connected to society through links such as those of citizenship and communication. For Parsons these links were primarily functional with respect to the working of society and cognitive structures, and for Habermas they had an emancipatory potential in enhancing the self-understanding of society. It is this kind of interconnectivity between the university and society that Bourdieu questions.

Sharing with Foucault the view that knowledge is power, Bourdieu maintains that knowledge is not primarily emancipatory but is socially located in contexts of power which are in essence classificatory, or cognitive, systems in which symbolic capital circulates. His concern is to reveal these contexts of power in order that knowledge might be reflexively reconstituted. In the context of the theoretical perspective afforded by the constructivist sociology of knowledge outlined in Chapter 1, it can be stated at this juncture that the importance of Bourdieu's theory of the university resides in his cognitive approach to cultural reproduction. His sociology of knowledge offers an important perspective on the cognitive structures that shape, limit and influence the production and circulation of knowledge in society.

This chapter begins by outlining Bourdieu's early theory of education as a form of social reproduction, discussing, too, his central theoretical concepts. It then looks at his account of the fields of power within the university and, finally, discusses the broader sociology of knowledge and reflexivity that informs his work.

Education as social reproduction

Bourdieu's sociology departs from the conventional view that education reduces social inequality leading to the development of social citizenship. His work maintains that education, and particularly higher education, serves to reproduce inequality as much as to reduce it. This is because it is the primary rationale of educational institutions to reproduce selection to social status, the means of influence and economic power. Educational institutions do not directly reproduce relations of inequality. Education is a means of legitimating the unequal distribution of social resources by means of a differential access to cultural capital.

In an influential work, *Reproduction in Education, Society and Culture*, Bourdieu and Jean-Claude Passeron developed a social theory of education as part of a sociology of power and 'symbolic violence' (Bourdieu and Passeron, 1977; see also Young, 1971). Education, while not being a tool of class power or of state hegemony, serves to reinforce power in society by providing a mechanism of transmission, or 'reproduction' to use the term of Bourdieu and Passeron. Education reproduces power by processes of imposition and inculcation which establish 'symbolic violence', that is the symbolic order of a particular group whose interests are reproduced by means of a culturally mediated structure of power. In this view, dominant groups surrender the power of selection to an academic institution which serves the interests of the dominant groups: 'In ever more completely delegating the power of selection to the academic institution, the privileged classes are able to appear to be surrendering to a perfectly neutral authority the power of transmitting power from one generation to another, and thus to be renouncing the arbitrary privilege of the hereditary transmission of privileges' (Bourdieu and Passeron, 1977: 167). The meritocratic ideology of education thus disguises the reality of social stratification into the economic, cultural and geographical separation of classes. This is what constitutes symbolic violence. In fact, for Bourdieu all of culture is symbolic violence since it involves the imposition of dominant groups or classes. In other words, culture, while being autonomous on one level, is also arbitrary and bears within it the violence of power, that is the power to impose classifications. Symbolic power nevertheless does not happen without some compliance by social actors. It must have a resonance in a habitus, in a form of life: 'Symbolic violence is that particular form of constraint than can only be implemented with the active complicity – which does not mean that it is conscious and voluntary – of those who submit to it and are determined only insofar as they deprive themselves of the possibility of a freedom founded on the awakening of consciousness' (Bourdieu, 1996a: 4).

Culture is arbitrary in that it is not based on a natural order but on symbolic violence:

> In any given social formation the cultural arbitrary which the power relations between the groups or classes making up that social formation put into the dominant position within the system of cultural arbitraries is the one which most fully, though not always indirectly, expresses the objective interests (material and symbolic) of the dominant groups.
>
> (Bourdieu and Passeron, 1977: 9)

All of culture is based on a fundamental condition of 'misrecognition' (*méconnaissance*), a French term Bourdieu employs to mean something like false consciousness, that is, the cognitive ability of the dominant culture to disguise the social conditions of its existence by falsely giving itself the status of something natural and therefore legitimacy: 'In any given social formation, legitimate culture, i.e. the culture endowed with the dominant legitimacy, is nothing other than the dominant cultural arbitrary insofar as it is misrecognized in its objective truth as a cultural arbitrary and as the dominant cultural arbitrary' (Bourdieu and Passeron, 1977: 23). Education is the means that modern society has devised for the transmission of cultural capital, which can be seen as the cognitive structures that are constitutive of the dominant cultural models in society.

In this view, education, and in particular higher education, is concerned with the consolidation of the mechanisms of selection, legitimation and accreditation. It is a central tenet of Bourdieu's sociology that culture exists as a cognitive system by which it offers groups the means of imposing and maintaining classifications. This is what constitutes cultural capital, one of Bourdieu's central concepts. For Bourdieu there are two kinds of capital: symbolic capital and material capital. The former refers to cultural resources, such as status, prestige and various kinds of cultural distinctiveness, while the latter concerns largely economic resources such as inherited wealth, income and property. This also includes education, knowledge and artistic reputation. Bourdieu refers to symbolic and material capital also as, respectively, cultural capital and economic capital. Symbolic capital is primarily cognitive; it is power that is recognized as having a value in itself and as such it exists in being perceived by social actors. In this sense, the cognitive dimension of symbolic capital is less a form of consciousness than it is a cultural disposition. It is unclear whether the symbolic level is separate from the cognitive level. These are best seen as separate, with the cognitive more basic that the symbolic. However, and it is one of Bourdieu's main arguments, beneath the cultural level frequently is the other face of power, economic power: 'Symbolic power, a subordinate power, is transformed, i.e. misrecognizable, transfigured and legitimated form of the other forms of power' (Bourdieu, 1991c: 170).

Thus it is the category of power that lies at the centre of Bourdieu's sociology. Power is manifest in the struggles of groups to reproduce either material or symbolic capital. These contests take place in particular fields – the fields of power – which can be seen as the social spaces of power. In modern society there are more and more fields of power and these also are independent of each other. However, what links them is that they are sites in which social actors contend for reproducing either symbolic or material capital.

His sociology is principally concerned with the analysis of symbolic capital, such as the various kinds of cultural reproduction in education and knowledge. This view of culture clearly departs from the Parsonian notion of a shared normative system, since culture, in being pervaded by power, is forced to be a site of contestation. This kind of contestation also differs from the discursive notion of culture in Habermas since it is based on the supposition that classificatory systems, although they are interrelated, are incommensurable and that fields of power are sites of struggle involving irreducible forms of capital. Symbolic or cultural capital has a cognitive component to it for it ultimately exists in the ability to make classifications with which certain, privileged definitions of reality are imposed against competing definitions. Culture for Bourdieu is about the making of distinctions, as is suggested by the title of his major work on aesthetic taste, *Distinction: A Social Critique of the Judgement of Taste* (Bourdieu, 1984) or his work on the museum-visiting public and its cultural dispositions (Bourdieu and Darbel, 1991). Where others have seen culture as a means of social integration or of legitimation, Bourdieu sees symbolic systems of difference and exclusion. It is a question not of legitimation but of the construction of group identities and the constitution of their social locations. In all his writings on culture he seeks to explore this question of the making of distinctions for it is this that precedes the act of legitimation. Education, too, becomes a means of making group distinctions through accreditation, selection, hierarchy. That is because Bourdieu sees society in terms of how group distinctions are maintained by reference to cognitive structures inscribed in all social practices. In *Distinction* two basic facts stand out: the close relationship between cultural practices (as measured by opinions) to educational capital (as measured by qualifications) and to social origin (as measured by father's occupation) (Bourdieu, 1984: 13). The basis of many of these distinctions is distance from economic necessity: 'Objective distance from necessity and from those trapped within it combines with a conscious distance which doubles freedom by exhibiting it. As the objective distance from necessity grows, lifestyle increasingly becomes the product of what Weber calls a 'stylization of life', a systematic commitment which orients and organizes the most diverse practices' (Bourdieu, 1984: 55–6).

Cultural capital is a resource of other kinds of power, as well as being a form of power in itself, the power of symbolic violence – the power to impose classifications (Bourdieu, 1991a). Cultural capital is more than a cognitive cultural structure, it is also a disposition defining particular kinds of habitus. In general, cultural capital can refer to the objective, classificatory structures of society; it can refer to institutional structures such as schools and universities as well as specific cultural objects, such as art; or it can refer to socio-cultural predispositions. Thus a major form of inequality in modern society is unequal access to cultural capital in the sense of education. Education is a pertinent example of how cultural reproduction is more than a self-perpetuating structure or the product of an agency, or intentionality. Rejecting the functionalist and the Marxist approaches, Bourdieu combines a perspective on structure and agency (Bourdieu, 1977, 1990a). Seeing action as strategic and practical, on the one side, and, on the other, structure as a set of dispositions and constraints which constitute what he calls the 'habitus', he is able to see something like education as a dynamic field of struggles. The idea of the field of power is important. It expresses the sense by which forms of capital – economic and cultural – are produced and reproduced by social actors who struggle to impose their definition of reality. Fields are social spaces in which cultural, economic and political structures interact. The fields of power Bourdieu is particularly interested in are the intellectual field and the field of cultural production (Bourdieu, 1993). It is important to see this notion of fields in terms of struggles over power. The basis of fields of power is dissensus, not consensus.

Education, then, is a field in which the wider conflicts and sources of inequality in society are manifest. The idea of inequality – in economic capital – the pursuit of distinction – in cultural capital – is very pronounced in education. The expansion of education has not led to greater social equality, according to Bourdieu and Passeron (1977, 1979). This, too, is one of the themes in Bourdieu's major work, *Homo Academicus* (Bourdieu, 1988) and in *The State Nobility* (Bourdieu, 1996a). Participation in French higher education is predominantly middle and upper-middle class. Education is a form of cultural capital which can lead to economic capital but it is also something that is inherently a source of power in its own right. This kind of power is becoming more significant accordingly as cultural fields become more and more autonomous of the state and of particular social groups such as classes. Education becomes a cultural field in which society selects individuals for positions of power and allocates status and prestige. Schools and universities are primarily institutions of selection. It is this functional selectivity that connects the university to society. Since education is then primarily a form of social differentiation it is inherently stratified.

The fields of power within the university

Much of Bourdieu's analysis of education centres on the internal structure of power within the university. Power in society is refracted through the prism of the university, which produces different kinds of power but which are linked to the reproduction of power in society. Demonstrating this highly mediated link is the central aim of *Homo Academicus* and the *State Nobility*.

Although Bourdieu's main studies on higher education are based on research conducted in the late 1960s and 1970s and are specific to the French context, they provide a striking account of some general trends in the transformation of higher education. One in particular of these trends might be mentioned: the struggle between three kinds of symbolic capital that is fought out in the university. These are academic power, scientific power and intellectual power. Academic power refers to the power of control over the administration of academic resources and the means of career influence. It is the power to preside over credentials and allocate status and as such it is a socially codified power. Scientific power is in essence the power that comes from research reputations based on scholarly publications. It is a matter of prestige deriving directly from knowledge as opposed to the status of honorific position. Intellectual power (or intellectual renown) comes from the ability to influence public opinion. It can derive from either academic power or scientific power but it is more likely to stem from the latter. In France this is represented by membership of the Académie Française, writing reviews in the influential weeklies, or in publishing a book with a publisher read by the educated middle classes (Bourdieu, 1988: 78–9). The university can be examined as a site of struggle between these three fields of power and where different kinds of cultural capital collide.

In *The State Nobility* Bourdieu (1996a) shows how higher education reflects the inequalities in society by an internal system of stratification. The *grandes écoles* hold a higher position than the universities. Within these elite schools, from which the state and economy draws its leading members, Bourdieu shows how traditional cultural capital is concentrated in the Ecole *Normale Supérieure* which recruits its members from the educated middle class while the *Hautes Etudes Commerciales* draw from the bourgeoisie and the *Ecole Nationale d'Administration* recruits from the wealthy middle class. These elite institutions in which the higher echelons of the professions are formed thus reveal a connection with a particular kind of class habitus. The cultural capital that they produce grant those who possess it access to other kinds of power as well as enhanced cultural capital. The universities, on the other hand, recruit their members from a broader social spectrum. This conflict between the *grandes écoles* and the universities reflects a fundamental conflict in French higher education.

Bourdieu's analysis of this divide is based on the uniquely French context and does not easily translate into other national systems of higher education. There is nothing in the German system that approximates to it although a comparison can be made in Britain with the privileged status of an Oxbridge education or in the United States with the prestigious private universities. The *grandes écoles* thus constitute a 'state nobility', a professional status group whose power rests on their educational credentials, in other words on cultural capital. Notwithstanding this, Loic Wacquant argues that Bourdieu offers an analytical approach that can have a wider relevance beyond the French context:

> Distinguishing the (specific) empirical findings from the (general) theoretical model contained in *The State Nobility* suggests an agenda for a comparative, genetic and structural sociology of national fields of power that would, for each society, catalog efficient forms of capital, specify the social and historical determinants of their degrees of differentiation, distance, and antagonism, and evaluate the part played by the system of elite schools (or functionally equivalent institutions) in regulating the relations they entertain.
>
> (Wacquant, 1996: xv)

There is no doubt that one of Bourdieu's main arguments is of wider relevance to understanding the dynamics behind higher education. For instance, his conceptualization of the conflict between 'two principles of hierarchization': 'the social hierarchy, corresponding to the capital inherited and the economic and political capital held, is in opposition to the specific, properly cultural hierarchy, corresponding to the capital of scientific authority or intellectual renown' (Bourdieu, 1988: 48). This opposition, which is related to the opposition between economic power and cultural power, is played out in many different situations. Membership by academics of prestigious political and economic bodies are examples of economic capital and the principle of social hierarchy which offers a means of stratifying the various faculties.

One of his conclusions in *Homo Academicus* is that professors of law and medicine tended to be allied with social power and thus opposed to political activity. However, of the politically active academics in the events of May 1968, the professors in the natural sciences were often closer to the left than professors in the humanities and social sciences. This is because those who are distant from social power – economic capital – and strong on scientific capital, as opposed to academic capital, tend to have left-wing political views. Thus many professors who possessed only scientific capital tended to be supportive of the left while those who were allied in any way with social power were more inclined to the right. He found that many social science and humanities professors, influential in their academic capital, were politically conservative. His analysis in *Homo Academicus* also reveals that professors strong in academic capital are more likely to come from lower down the class structure than those who possess primarily scientific capital. This is because of the security of the upper middle class for whom material gain is less attractive than the status that comes from research reputations. In this way, Bourdieu has given an ironic twist to Kant's account of the 'conflict of the faculties': instead of battles over different orders of reason (i.e. knowledge and rationality) it is a question of conflicts over different kinds of symbolic capital (i.e. of cognitive or cultural models).

In this sociological analysis the state, and much of the economic order, has come to rest on professionals who have become essential for the reproduction of power in society. Indeed, the situation at the beginning of the twenty-first century concerning the professions is very different from that of the previous century when the professions constituted themselves against the state; today the growing power of the professions is precisely because of the state's need for expertise. From this need new status cultures has arisen. The changing role of the professions is reflected in the decline of the traditional power of the *Ecole Normale Supérieure* and the rise in the status of the administrative and economic schools, *Hautes Etudes Commerciales* and *Ecole Nationale d'Administration*. Many forces have shaped this decomposition of the older scholastic capital of intellectual knowledge. Technical knowledge is supplanting scholarly knowledge not just in economic but also in symbolic capital. In an increasingly visual as opposed to print culture, the ability to influence public opinion is also coming more and more to rest on access to the mass media than on scholarly discourse. Yet, academic power is the overriding kind of power to be found in the scholarly milieu.

It is Bourdieu's argument that *homo academicus* is a product of the field of academic power, the power to control and classify knowledge, and thereby restrict the academic field. It is from this field that the whole scholarly discourse and institution is 'consecrated', that is ordained legitimate. 'Academic capital is obtained and maintained by holding a position enabling domination of other positions and their holders, such as all the institutions entrusted with controlling access to the corps' (Bourdieu, 1988: 84). Academic power consists in the capacity to influence expectations and objective probabilities, for instance by limiting the world of possible competitors (1988: 89). In his analysis, academic power has been associated with the 'canonical disciplines, such as literature, classics and philosophy' and constitutes a kind of 'social magistrature', a defender and codifier of national culture. The idea of 'academic forms of classification' in Bourdieu's analysis is inspired by the 'primitive forms of classification' that Durkheim and Mauss wrote about (Bourdieu, 1996a: 30). Academic power is a cognitive machine that organizes cognitive structures, disciplines and social space. One of its main functions is 'consecration', that is creating symbolic boundaries in social space and legitimating those who inhabit them. For Bourdieu,

one of the striking features of the university is the power of the professorate. Where Ringer (1969) wrote about the decline of the 'mandarins',
Bourdieu sees only the ascendancy of the professorate and its formation as
a 'state nobility'. It is the power of consecration, the ability to define and
legitimate a field of power, that has made the professorate a state nobility:
'While there is probably no leading group that has accumulated more insurance – property titles, academic titles, and, sometimes, noble titles –
than the great state nobility, there is no group that has to provide as much
insurance either, especially in the area of competence and devotion to the
universal' (Bourdieu, 1996a: 382). This analysis does not take account of
the phenomenon described by Riesman, the decline of professorial power
in face of a nascent manageralism (Riesman, 1996). Most of Bourdieu's
research on higher education is derived from work done in the period of
professorial self-governance, that is prior to 1968, and is based on the no
longer tenable assumption of the university as isolated from direct contact
with material capital.

Bourdieu's sociology of the university, in accordance with this theory of
fields of power, is a strongly relational one. This entails the view that the
university is constituted in the system of relations, such as those between
the different kinds of power. As he puts it: 'The structure of the university field is only, at any moment in time, the state of the power relations
between the agents or, more precisely, between the powers they wield in
their own right and above all through the institutions to which they belong;
positions held in this structure are what motivate strategies aiming to transform it, or to preserve it by modifying or maintaining the relative forces of
the different kinds of capital' (Bourdieu, 1988: 128).

His approach is one that sees the university as a relatively autonomous
institution in society. In it power is refracted in the different kinds of cultural power specific to the university. Reproduction in society is coming
more and more to rest on cultural reproduction. 'The structure of the
university field reflects the structure of the field of power, while its own
activity of selection and indoctrination contributes to the reproduction of
that structure' (Bourdieu, 1988: 41). Culturally mediated forms of power
are becoming more and more important in modern society, according to
Bourdieu. These spaces are also written into the very structure of language,
which in the final analysis is the basis of all kinds of symbolic power.

Although it is allied to particular kinds of power in the wider society,
the struggles within the educational field are not significantly shaped by
the extra-institutional context. This is particularly vivid in *Homo Academicus*
which offers a structural taxonomy of the May 1968 crisis. Unlike the work
of Riesman in the United States or Touraine in France or Habermas in
Germany, Bourdieu ignored the wider social context, preferring to see the
crisis as deriving from problems within French higher education. David
Swartz has commented: 'The focus of his analysis – and the methodological
point he wishes to score – is on how external factors are filtered through
and mediated by the internal logic of cultural fields such as the French

university' (1997: 215). That is, for Bourdieu the most important factors are to be found *within* the university system. It is presumably for this reason that he ignores the international political environment and the social movements surrounding the university revolts of May 1968.

What comes across strongly from Bourdieu's analysis of the university is the inescapability of power and consequently of the limits of protest, as is apparent in this analysis of May 1968. Power circulates primarily within a system, such as the university, but does not escape the system except in the highly mediated forms of cultural capital. Cultural capital thus serves as a medium of exchange between the various fields of power. But within these fields, the structure of power is tightly defined. Consequently, the university does not really have a capacity to transform society since it is forced to be an agent of reproduction. Social actors are primarily motivated by the desire to augment either cultural or economic capital. In the case of the former, which is particularly evident in the case of higher education, this is largely seen by Bourdieu to be the pursuit of distinction by the aid of classificatory systems, which are frequently incommensurable, as he demonstrated in his analysis of academic discourse – the language and cognitive apparatus of teachers and students belong to different orders of discourse (Bourdieu *et al.*, 1992). In general for Bourdieu, the communicative content of the university is reduced to strategies designed to maximize cultural capital. As a result he tends too readily to dismiss the transformative potential of university as a public space never entirely inhabited by power. Yet, it is clear, as I discuss in the next section, that he has a notion of the reflexive transformation of knowledge. However, this is largely confined to a restrictive intellectual stratum and is apparently unavailable to the mass university.

Reflexivity, the scholastic fallacy and intellectuals

One of Bourdieu's central tenets is that: 'Any position adopted toward the social world orders and organizes itself from a certain position in the world, that is to say from the standpoint of the preservation and augmentation of the power associated with this position' (Bourdieu, 1988: 13). The scholastic fallacy is the failure to see this connection (Bourdieu, 1997). In his writings on academics, intellectuals, writers, artists and other producers of cultural capital he wants to demonstrate that all cultural discourse is shaped by its relation to a certain position in the world. Cultural producers are not a free-floating intellegentsia but are power-producing agents. By demonstrating their social positioning and their strategies in particular fields of power a certain reflexivity may be possible by culture producers, allowing for the possibility of critical interventions. Since power is symbolically reproduced in modern societies, those involved in cultural reproduction occupy a crucial political position.

Bourdieu is a left-wing intellectual who is sceptical of the claims of intellectuals to be authentic political critics of society. He sees intellectuals as having power-vested interests of their own and which are connected with their cultural capital. In modernity there are more and more fields of power for intellectuals to operate in because modern society creates mass publics. Cultural reproduction involves a relationship between intellectuals and these mass audiences. But this situation also entails dangers for cultural reproduction. As Simmel recognized in his work on cultural production in modern society, intellectual creation can become ossified in structures that have lost their relationship to subjectivity (Frisby and Featherstone, 1997). In Bourdieu's terms, the field of power is where social actors strive to possess cultural capital in one of its forms. In this situation, intellectuals are as much part of the established order as opposed to it. For instance, in a study on Heidegger's political commitment, Bourdieu shows how the intellectual field can be inclined towards the extreme right (Bourdieu, 1991b). However, in general, intellectuals tend to be critical of the status quo. The pursuit of cultural capital in isolation from the pursuit of other kinds of capital such as economic capital or, in the case of university professors, the pursuit of academic capital, is likely to encourage a critical attitude towards the status quo. Although Bourdieu sees intellectuals and academics as primarily engaged in augmenting their cultural capital rather than in aspiring to a primarily political goal or serving the disinterested cause of culture or knowledge for its own sake, it is his view that intellectuals can play an emancipatory role in the critique of ideology and power. But this critique can never escape the field of power. The recognition of this is the basis of a reflexive kind of political practice.

All of intellectual creation is an expression of the 'scholastic view', the point of view of the *skholè*. This is the context-bound vision of the academic space whose condition is freedom from determination and it is a precondition of all knowledge. Bourdieu's sociology is based on the assumption that all scholarly, intellectual work is restricted by the fact that the academic must withdraw from the world in order to study it. 'This is a fundamental epistemological question since it bears on the epistemic posture itself, on the presuppositions inscribed in the fact of thinking the world, of retiring from the world and action in the world in order to think that action' (Bourdieu, 1998a: 129). The distancing that this involves is both the weakness and the strength of scholarly knowledge. Its weakness is that knowledge is forced to be separate from its object and its strength is that knowledge can be reflexively constituted. Knowledge is possible only because those who pursue it are free from social constraints. But this means that disinterestness is not possible since the scholastic situation is interested in reproducing itself and the luxury of the *skholè*.

One of the main themes of Bourdieu's sociology concerns the limits and possibility of the autonomy of artistic or scholarly discourses. The autonomization of art and academic discourse must be explained as a field of competition for a monopoly on particular forms of cultural capital. In

The Rules of Art, Bourdieu (1996b) documented the autonomization of the artistic and literary field as a struggle to establish different kinds of cultural capital, such as the movement towards 'art for art'. As a market emerged in the nineteenth century for symbolic goods, artistic creation differentiated into various paths, for instance one shaped by the popular market and one by high art. The detachment of the latter was not independent of the accumulation of cultural capital by writers and artists who could afford to reject the social world and economic capital which was associated with popular art. Bourdieu's general thesis is that the degree of autonomy of a field is related to the amount of cultural capital accumulated. This antagonism between economic and cultural capital is central to the formation of the intellectual field and the different kinds of habitus that operate within. Thus all struggles for autonomy are related to the struggles within a field of power to augment capital, be it economic or cultural.

Bourdieu nevertheless believes the intellectual world can create a 'free exchange', despite the fact that it is itself pervaded by power. His position would appear to be that the intellectual field must resist forms of power that are foreign to it. In a dialogue with Hans Haacke, Bourdieu says: 'The intellectual world is a site of often fierce struggles and the independence and autonomy of intellectuals are ceaselessly threatened by all sorts of external forces, the most formidable of which today is no doubt journalism' (Bourdieu and Haacke, 1995: 28). The greatest threats to intellectual autonomy come from journalism and television (Bourdieu, 1998b). These fields lack the autonomy that is necessary for critical thought to be possible. 'The distance between professional cultural producers (or their products) and ordinary consumers (readers, listeners, or viewers, and voters as well) relates to the autonomy of the field in question and varies according to field' (Bourdieu, 1998b: 76). The journalistic and televisual fields are shaped by the market and by politics, not by an autonomous field such as that of the intellectual field. He is sceptical that this can easily be reversed by intellectuals who will have to find other means of expression. It took several centuries, for instance, for the scientists, artists and writers to gain the autonomy of their fields with respect to the religious, economic and political fields and it is therefore unlikely that this can simply be achieved in a short time by intellectuals today (Bourdieu, 1998c: 76).

For Bourdieu, the challenge for intellectuals is to protect their hard-won autonomy: 'it is especially urgent today that intellectuals mobilize and create a veritable *Internationale of intellectuals* committed to defending the autonomy of the universes of cultural production or, to parody a language now out of fashion, the ownership by cultural producers of their instruments of production and circulation (and hence of evaluation and consecration)' (Bourdieu, 1998a: 344). In resisting power, sociology has a central role to play and which it can play only if it accepts its historicity, that is the fact that like all forms of knowledge it is context bound, and engages in a radical doubt. Thus reflexivity is linked to scepticism, the subject of a major philosophical work, *Pascalian Meditations* (Bourdieu, 1999). For Bourdieu, culture entails a certain resistance to other kinds of power and it is this tension between the cultural and the social that is being deployed by the critical intellectual. Sociology is an example of an intellectual field that is particularly suitable for putting itself into question, a precondition of the reflexivity of knowledge (Bourdieu and Wacquant, 1992). It is a sociology that renders itself reflexive through self-objectification.

Despite all his critique of intellectuals and the intermeshing of culture and power, Bourdieu is clearly on the side of culture producers:

> Cultural producers hold a specific power, the properly symbolic power of showing things and making people believe in them, of revealing, in an explicit, objectified way the more or less confused, vague, unformulated, even unformulable experiences of the natural world and the social world, and of thereby bringing them into existence. They may put this power at the service of the dominant. They may also, in the logic of their struggle with the field of power, put their power at the service of the dominated in the social field taken as a whole.
>
> (Bourdieu, 1990b: 146)

Although his work on the university is not directly relevant to the debate on the idea of the university, his theoretical approach offers a useful perspective on how modes of knowledge are intertwined with social practices and cognitive structures. The university as a producer of knowledge is deeply embedded in the production of cultural capital. The social practices that constitute the university do not amount to an essential 'idea' of the university which transcends power. Since power is symbolically produced and maintained by cultural models, the university occupies a crucial position. It can be seen as a medium of exchange, or interconnectivity, between other kinds of capital, as well as being a major dispenser of cultural capital. Although his earlier work on education and the university suggests that the university lacks a capacity to transform society, being concerned merely with maintaining existing distinctions, there is much to indicate a broader view of cultural capital being reflexively transformed by the producers of culture.

7

The University and the New Production of Knowledge: From the Producer to the User

The philosopher of science Paul Feyerabend's attacks on Big Science (Feyerabend, 1975, 1978) have a contemporary relevance. His 'anarchist' theory of knowledge declared that scientific knowledge is no different from other kinds of knowledge, such as religious knowledge and lay knowledge, and consequently that scientific knowledge should not be given privileged treatment. His opposition to the state's support for Big Science – large-scale and nationally funded research – is now becoming a reality with the withdrawal of the state as the primary financier of knowledge and the emergence of new knowledge producers. At the moment it is difficult to say exactly what kind of a political economy of knowledge is emerging, but if we follow some recent sociological accounts of knowledge production we can point to the contours of new cognitive and institutional configurations that have major implications for the university.

The theories under consideration in this chapter offer a very different view of the university from Bourdieu's theory discussed in the previous chapter. Where, for Bourdieu, the university is a central organ of the state and the professorate serves as a 'state nobility', crucial actors in the field of academic power and the guardians of much of the nation's symbolic capital, current developments suggest the decline in the older forms of symbolic capital and the dominance of economic capital. Bourdieu's model of higher education is located within the contours of a kind of knowledge production that was secured by the national state and isolated from the immediacy of economic imperatives. It is precisely this vision of the university that is in question in much of recent literature which sees symbolic capital as being undermined by all-pervasive economic capital and a nascent managerialism (Halsey, 1992). A view is emerging of the transformation of higher education by market and technological forces which the state is powerless to prevent. Reflexivity is now supposedly integral to the production of knowledge, not opposed to it or, as in Bourdieu, to a relationship between knowledge and cognitive structures.

In recent years, developments in the sociology of knowledge and the sociology of science have greatly added to our understanding of the changing forms of the social production of knowledge. In this chapter I am principally concerned with one such approach, namely the theory of the 'new production of knowledge'. The next chapter continues this theme with a review of the developments related to the arrival of 'academic capitalism', to use the term of Slaughter and Leslie (1997) in the context of globalization. This chapter deals with the broader context of the new production of knowledge.

According to many commentators, the production of knowledge entered a new phase in the latter part of the twentieth century. In the most well known version of this thesis, the new production of knowledge can be called Mode 2, that is, a form of knowledge production characterized by reflexivity, transdisciplinarity and heterogeneity (Gibbons *et al.*, 1984). One of the major implications of this theory is that the university will no longer dominate the field of knowledge production as it did for much of the modern age and accordingly will go into decline. This chapter concentrates on this particular characterization of knowledge in the context of implications for the university. The essence of this theory of knowledge is that, as a result of changes in the relation of the state to economy and as a result of changes in the relation of technology to economy, the ethos of knowledge is radically different from what it was in the Enlightenment period. Knowledge is seen as more democratic because knowledge users are increasingly becoming involved in the actual production of knowledge, thereby making knowledge more relevant to concrete applications. In this chapter I argue that these developments are leading less to the end of the Enlightenment's conception of knowledge than to a major transformation of it. Stressing as much the continuities as the discontinuities, I argue for an approach that recognizes the contemporary relevance of some of the features of the older model of knowledge. In this view the university can become an important mediator between producers and users of knowledge and thereby contribute to citizenship. As knowledge production moves out of the university, and accordingly as a whole range of knowledge users outside the university become increasingly involved in determining the nature of knowledge, the university is forced to occupy the ground of reflexivity. However, rather than client-determined reflexivity, an alternative reflexivity can be seen to consist of public reflexivity. In this sense, the relationship between producers and users of knowledge is less direct than in the thesis of Gibbons *et al.*

In sum, then, my approach in this chapter is to offer a modified view of the thesis that there is a new mode of knowledge production in contemporary society. Broadly in agreement with Gibbons *et al.* that there has been a shift to the user in the production of knowledge, my approach differs from their more affirmative stance in that I see this shift to be one in which a client model of the user predominates and that therefore there is not a greater democratization in knowledge production. I also depart from their assumption that the older model of knowledge was primarily the discipline-

and paradigm-based Mode 1. In this way, as will become more fully apparent in later chapters, my approach also differs from the negative scenario of the postmodern university.

The end of knowledge?

I begin by pointing to new developments in the production of knowledge. Three general developments can be identified.

The first development relates centrally to the changing role of the state. It has been widely recognized in recent years that there has been a shift from government to governance with the displacement of national government by new regulatory policies (Rhodes, 1996). The national state has entered a crisis as a result of the increasing primacy of the post-Fordist economy and transnational financial capital with the result that the nation state is no longer the primary site of economic management and integration. Processes of globalization in economic organization, communications and policy regimes have challenged the sovereignty of the nation state, which has responded with a variety of strategies that include a shift towards governance: the displacement downwards of economic and social organization. The implications of these developments for the production of knowledge are far-reaching. In particular, one tendency can be observed: with the retreat of the state from provider to regulator the state will no longer be the sole financer of knowledge. This development fundamentally alters the historical pact between knowledge and the state worked out in the late seventeenth century when the absolute state gained control over the production of knowledge, which was institutionalized in the new centres of knowledge such as the university and the royal academies. The first tendency, then, is the gradual break-up of that historical consensus (see Chapter 2 for an account of the historical trajectories of modernity and the university). This can be seen as a result of globalization, a process that challenges the logic of nationalization which has hitherto prevailed, leading to a gradual 'denationalizing' of science (Crawford *et al.*, 1993). The effects of globalization in many spheres of society – communications, welfare, migration, employment – have been much discussed but have not yet been discussed with respect to the production of knowledge in the university (see Chapter 8 for a fuller discussion).

Secondly, the established patterns in the production of knowledge are entering a crisis for reasons extending beyond the transformation in the role of the state. With the retreat of the state from its role as the primary provider and financer of knowledge we have entered a situation in which new knowledge producers are emerging. This is particularly evident in the case of the universities. Under the conditions of globalization and the application of reflexive methods of economic production, the site of knowledge production is shifting away from the university to a range of non-university locations, such as industrial laboratories, research centres, think-tanks and consultancies (Gibbons *et al.*, 1984: 6). Late modern society is a 'knowledge society' involving the increased production and dissemination of knowledge (Stehr, 1994). Knowledge, in other words, is no longer a meta-narrative but has entered the production process and is increasingly being generated in the context of application. This was Lyotard's (1984) main claim in his book, originally published in French in 1979, *The Postmodern Condition: A Report on Knowledge*: knowledge is productive, not emancipatory or autonomous (see Chapter 9 on the postmodern university). Thus a major challenge for the university in the future will be to find ways to respond to this situation of a proliferation of sites of knowledge production.

The third development relates to the emergence of new links between society and knowledge. It may be suggested that knowledge is rapidly becoming a new site of conflict in late modern society. This is evident on a number of fronts. Since the 1970s, at least in the western world, the recipients of knowledge have been not only elites but also mass publics. With the democratization of knowledge and the opening of higher education to all classes, knowledge has ceased to be the exclusive privilege of the elites. It may be argued that the public sphere has been very much shaped by knowledge. As a result of an increase in the volume of communication, the mass public is today much better informed about all sorts of issues – food, health, lifestyles, economy, politics, the environment, science – than ever before. Information has become an important resource, and in the affluent countries it may even challenge the primacy of material security. Knowledge has been democratized in the sense that it has not just become more available to more and more people but has also become a major site of contestation. This is apparent in the increasing demands on science to be made accountable to society. Social actors are increasingly becoming involved in the application of knowledge. In other words, there has been a shift from the politics of production to the politics of the application of knowledge. This development can be described as the reflexivity of knowledge, or the self-reflection of knowledge upon itself and its conditions of existence. Ulrich Beck (1992) has explored the implications of this with respect to the increased importance of risk, which has led to a situation of enhanced reflexivity as a result of the collapse of the self-legitimation of science. The risk society is a self-critical society. With the collapse in the unquestioned belief in the rationality of science, the idea of the neutrality of knowledge is no longer credible. More and more social actors are involved in the definition of problems and the application of the solutions (see Delanty, 1999; see also Chapter 10).

What conclusions can we draw from these developments? One implication of the new production of knowledge is that it ultimately points to the 'end of knowledge' (Fuller, 1993; Barnett and Green, 1997). But this must be qualified, for what has come to an end is one particular mode of knowledge. In the present context of the implications of the new production of knowledge for the university, what this means is the end of the concept of knowledge associated with the Enlightenment and which harks back to

Plato. In one way or another, the modern university has been the expression of the Enlightenment ideal or the 'republic of science': the autonomy of knowledge that has an emancipatory role to play. This model of knowledge – as coherent, autonomous, transcendent, self-referential – confers upon the university and its priestly caste of intellectuals the role of the guardian of knowledge that must be transmitted to society, the recipient of the knowledge systems of the elites. In Bauman's (1987) terms, the Enlightenment model of knowledge conferred upon the intellectual the role of 'legislator', a role Bauman believes has been overtaken today by the postmodern role of the 'interpreter'.

The university was the privileged site of knowledge conceived of as the legislation of modern society by intellectuals whose universalistic categories of truth, morality, humanity and reason defined the field of knowledge. The crisis of the university today exists because that conception of knowledge has finally been undermined by conditions established by the social production of knowledge. One of the principal findings of the Gulbenkian Commission's report on the social sciences (Wallerstein *et al.*, 1996) was that the end of knowledge has occurred as a result of the emergence of new relations between the knowledge producers and society on the one hand, and on the other, new relations between the sciences. Knowledge, in other words, has ceased to be something standing outside society, a goal to be pursued by a community of scholars dedicated to the truth, but is shaped by many social actors under the conditions of the essential contestability of truth.

Developing the three main themes in the production of knowledge mentioned above – the changing role of the state from provider to regulator, the emergence of new non-university knowledge producers, and the 'scientization' of the public – we can say that the role of the university is in crisis: the ivory tower is collapsing. The retreat of the state from Big Science means that the university will have to come to terms with the break-up of the historical pact that science and the state made in the late seventeenth century. The university can no longer depend on the state but will have to seek other providers. This will be one of the greatest challenges facing the new production of knowledge in the twenty-first century. Second, the university as the privileged site of knowledge is also in crisis as the university struggles to compete with new knowledge producers. Once knowledge enters the production process as opposed to having a meta-narrative function as in liberal modernity it ceases to be emancipatory and loses its autonomy. Under these circumstances knowledge becomes fragmented; it no longer exists in a unitary form under the control and definition of a privileged agency. Third, the university is becoming absorbed into the public sphere of mass society as new debates about accountability surface, challenging the Enlightenment idea of the autonomy and neutrality of knowledge. The culture of the experts was challenged by intellectuals in the 1960s and 1970s; today the critique of the intellectuals has been overtaken by the mobilization of mass publics who challenge the rationality of science and the scientistic self-legitimation of the older knowledge producers. Everywhere this is the case: the universities are forced to become more accountable to society. The Enlightenment framework is no longer capable of legitimating the production of knowledge. This is the condition widely called the 'end of knowledge' (Barnett and Green, 1997).

Underlying these developments is a dual process of globalization and fragmentation. On the one side, knowledge is increasingly being globalized and detached from its traditional reliance on the nation state and its custodians, the intellectuals and university professors; on the other side it is also being fragmented, that is, knowledge is losing its ability to provide a sense of direction for society and is breaking up into specialist discourses that arise in the context of application. These processes can be analysed in terms of a decoupling logic by which agency and knowledge are separated from each other and recombined in new ways.

I have already argued that the role of the university is undergoing a transition in late modernity as a result of structural shifts in the production and legitimation of knowledge. The older goal of the democratization of the university has been superseded by new challenges arising from the dual processes of the globalization and fragmentation of knowledge cultures. These challenges are related to the following developments: (1) the emergence of a new academic managerialism, (2) the emergence of the 'new production of knowledge', the main thesis of Gibbons *et al.* (1984), and (3) a separation of research from teaching (education). The remainder of this chapter looks at each of these developments in turn, and concludes with an assessment of the thesis that there is a new mode of knowledge production.

The new manageralism

While it is premature to make major prognoses, and it must be recognized that national governments are still the primary financers and providers of knowledge, we can detect a culture shift in the institution of the university and its relationship to the state. One way of capturing this shift is the arrival of what Michael Power (1997) calls the audit society. Universities are being forced to implement new regimes of management that more closely resemble businesses than the traditional sites of autonomous knowledge. Of diminished significance is the cherished belief of the Enlightenment that knowledge is a value in itself and can be pursued in the ivory tower of detached academe. Universities are increasingly forced to operate like businesses, competing with each other for students, the best professors and their share of the state's diminishing budget. The model science would appear to be no longer physics but accounting, with MBAs in the Anglo-American universities now constituting the greatest number of degrees. As universities are no longer dominated by the humanities, the intellectual has been overtaken by the administrator and the academic entrepreneur, Kant's 'businessman of science'.

These developments are reproduced in the internal organization of the university. Departments and faculties are increasingly becoming administrative units rather than being based on the traditional disciplines. The blurring of the traditional boundaries is not as a result of greater multi-disciplinarity but because of the imposition of audit cultures on the university. The department has been weakened as the location of research (Rothblatt, 1997a). Line managers exist in many British universities and strategic plans have become the norm as a new managerial ethos has invaded the scholar's space. Departments are under pressure to generate funding for research, and funded research is prized above individual research and often the highest mark of academic achievement is entrepreneurship. In the United States and Britain, where the crisis of the university is most apparent, tenure is under attack. In Britain, tenure was abolished in 1981 and the Research Assessment Exercise (RAE) has imposed a new regulatory regime on British academic life.

As a new managerial ethos is pervading the university, deans and heads of departments are coming more to resemble managers than academic figures. University presidents were once trained to be moral leaders, but in the transformation of higher education over the past few decades they are increasingly forced to become entrepreneurs. Manuals such as *Leadership and Ambiguity* by Cohen and March (1974) set a new orthodoxy for the American college president to act with purpose in an institution that does not have a clearly defined purpose. Keller's (1983) *Academic Strategy* has become a more up-to-date statement of art on corporate management of universities. There is some justification for the view that the managerial ethos has now penetrated to the level of the department and that as a result the university may be losing its sense of moral purpose as a managerial legitimacy takes root.

Dominelli and Hoogvelt (1996) have described the new managerialism as academic Taylorism. The key features of Taylorism are becoming increasingly apparent in university management practices: the compartmentalization of tasks, full managerial control and systematic costing of each step of the process. Although Taylorism relates to Fordist-style accumulation, it can be used to describe the new production of knowledge in that there has been a commodification of service delivery and the elimination of professional autonomy.

Reform through managerialism becomes a strategy of academic management (Currie and Vidovich, 1998). Power becomes centralized in the hands of a few senior managers who make decisions quickly. Academic self-governance is not time-efficient and consequently it is eroded in a world of corporate style decision-making. Although universities are embracing a managerialism borrowed from business, the new academic managerialism is one that has been discredited in business. With its tendency towards hierarchical structures, an organizational practice has been introduced in universities that has been abandoned in progressive business (Currie, 1998: 4).

The rise of the knowledge user

Much of the theory of the new production of knowledge is about the increasing importance of the user in the shaping of knowledge production. In this the distinction between the university and the firm is blurred. Gibbons *et al.* (1984: 36; also Gibbons and Wittrock, 1985) point out that as universities become more like firms, firms are becoming more like universities, for example firms give employees sabbaticals and other forms of training possibilities. Indeed, many corporations already possess some of the key features of universities (*The Economist*, 1997). The biggest boom in British universities throughout the 1990s has been business and management, with many universities having professorships sponsored by big business (Webster, 1995: 184). In what epitomizes the move to the corporate university, General Motors in the United States has established its own university in Chicago. Recognizing that knowledge is the key to competitive advantage, the corporate university aims to be an efficient provider of learning opportunities for the organization it serves as well as enabling the organization to formulate its goals.

The American corporate university may be an extreme case of the penetration of market values into academe and most universities practise what might be called market-like behaviour as opposed to really competitive market behaviour. However, universities are under increased pressure from the state to make their teaching programmes relevant to employment (Matkin, 1990). As a result of new relations between university and industry, 'knowledge for use' instead of 'knowledge for its own sake' has transformed the late modern university. For Gibbons *et al.* (1984) the rule of the user is one of the key features of the new production of knowledge. Knowledge is increasingly being tailored to a use rather than being an end in itself. This is because, in the advanced sectors of science and technology, knowledge is being generated in the context of application. Competition thus becomes the basis of the logic of discovery. This has major implications for the funding of research. As Gibbons *et al.* argue: 'Intensified international competition is forcing governments to reconsider the function of their S&T [science and technology] investments and firms to become more active participants in the production of knowledge' (1984: 55).

While the university is becoming more involved in instrumental goals, its centrality in the economy is in question as a whole range of knowledge producers have appeared on the scene, usurping the traditional role of the university as the exclusive producer of knowledge. In Britain the old universities and those established in the postwar period are seen by many to be challenged by the former polytechnics, which have acquired the status of universities and as a result the idea of the university as a place of excellence is becoming meaningless. However, this needs to be qualified by the fact that the broadening of university status allowed the UK to embark on mass higher education without seriously restructuring the older universities, which espouse simultaneously the virtues of liberal education and research leadership (Ryan, 1999). More significant might be the fact that industrial laboratories are becoming as important for the production of knowledge as the science departments in the universities. We are living in the information society, which means that capitalism needs more and more knowledge; this is a fundamental dimension of the current mode of production which depends to an ever-increasing extent on technical innovation (Castells, 1996). The kind of expertise that industry needs is problem-specific and is increasingly generated in the context of application (Gibbons *et al.*, 1984: 54). This is particularly the case with the small high-tech firm. Other competing knowledge producers are think-tanks, consultancy agencies, nongovernmental organizations, professional societies, governmental and corporate R&D laboratories. The 1980s saw an increase in the activities of these agents, which are characterized by flexibility and multifunctionality. A growing trend is the increased involvement of university personnel in consultancy and evaluation. Another trend is the tendency of the media to turn to think-tanks rather than to academics. This is also the case with government commissions, which are often disproportionately filled by university academics.

What these developments point to is that the university is having difficulty in adjusting to the conditions of post-Fordism. The 'massified' university is an example of Fordism applied to the production of knowledge. The massification of western higher education in the period following the Second World War and the explosion in research and development spending by governments benefiting from the unparalleled period of economic growth that most western economies experienced led to the creation of welfare states, which have entered a deep crisis today. The establishment of the university system was also a part of this gigantic experiment in social welfare democracy: the massification of welfare, communications and education. We have reached the end of this programme today in the sense that no further expansion in the welfare state can be expected comparable to what occurred in the past Second World War period. The post-Fordist economy has changed economic and social relations to the point at which economic growth can be sustained without a corresponding rise in full-time and secure employment. In the 1980s the state responded to the changed economic situation with an attack on the welfare state. Today the retreat of the state from its role as the primary provider is being felt, by higher education. In this context we can ask the question of what a post-Fordist university will look like. For Gibbons *et al.* the answer is the move to Mode 2 knowledge production.

How does Mode 2 differ from Mode 1? In Mode 1, problems are set and solved in a context governed by a small group of scientists, generally the academic community. The university is a place of research and it is within the university that the results of research are disseminated. In Mode 2, by contrast, knowledge is shaped in the context of its application, which is generally outside the university. In Mode 1, knowledge is primarily disciplinary and hierarchical while in Mode 2 it is transdisciplinary and fluid. Where

Mode 1 is homogeneous and relatively autonomous, Mode 2 is heterogeneous and, it is claimed, more socially accountable and reflexive. In sum, in the expanded process of knowledge production, universities are just one player.

The separation of teaching and research

The university is experiencing an internal transformation in its organization and production of knowledge. A central dimension to this pertains to the separation of teaching and research. In the Enlightenment model of the university the two were inseparable: professors gave lectures that formed the core of their writings. In their famous study, *The American University*, Parsons and Platt (1973) concluded that despite increased specialization in research the majority of the American university profession firmly believed in the unity of teaching and research. Today, in the age of the researcher and new links with industry, these domains of discourse have become separated. Research has become overly specialized and often irrelevant to the needs of students. Indeed, research has become so specialized that academics frequently have lost a sense of the overall significance of their research within their discipline – knowledge is no longer unitary and coherent and as a result has become diffuse, fragmentary and opaque.

This situation of de-differentiation has been accompanied by the increased blurring of the older disciplines. With the specialization of research, it is not the established disciplines that define the boundaries of knowledge but the context of the application of research, with target constituencies and user groups calling the shots. Knowledge, in other words, has become context-specific and is frequently problem-oriented. This situation has led to new commonalities in the sciences with the result that the internal divisions within the disciplines are becoming greater than the older divides across disciplines. According to Gibbons *et al.*, as a result of the diffusion of the new mode of knowledge, 'the boundaries between disciplines are dissolving and giving way to a more open structure where varieties of knowledge and competence are combined and recombined in novel configurations' (1984: 48–9). Increasingly, researchers are coming to see themselves as working in an area rather than in a discipline. This clearly has implications for the identity of disciplines (Crane and Small, 1987; Turner and Turner, 1990). Moreover, the traditional humanities and social sciences no longer dominate the university and are being overtaken by professional and vocational training. Emphasis has shifted towards problem-solving research, and in the social sciences policy-related research is growing in importance. In the UK, the binary system in which teaching and research was combined was abolished and two separate funding systems established.

Until now the primary struggle in the sciences was for institutionalization. This was particularly the case so far as the social sciences were concerned. Since the creation of permanent structures of knowledge that accompanied the rise of the modern state, the principal challenge for social science was its professional institutionalization in society (Delanty, 1997). However, it is a different story today, for the struggle for institutionalization has been achieved and indeed many of the problems facing social science today relate to the fragmentation of knowledge that has arisen precisely as a result of its professionalization and academization. These problems derive from the institutionalization of knowledge in specialized subdisciplines: it is, in short, a problem of specialization.

This situation raises many questions about the meaning of higher education. University lecturers whose real commitment is to research suffer a sense of hopelessness on two fronts. On the one side, their own research is frequently condemned to obscurity in an ever-expanding publishing industry and, on the other side, falling academic standards among students has the effect of a fundamental failure in academic communication. With respect to the first problem, the drive to publish in the massified research culture of the university has led to an explosion in publications that are rarely read. Steve Fuller (1997a: 148) comments on how organized research cultures supported by the university have become a massive industrial enterprise driven by a self-perpetuating system of self-referencing, of which the Science Citation Index (SCI) is the supreme example. Not too surprisingly, many academics become absorbed into teaching and administration. Particularly in the hard sciences, unless they continuously upgrade their skills, academics do their best work before they are 40 years old, before they become absorbed into teaching, for which they rarely have any formal training (Fuller, 1997b: 240). These problems are underlined by the declining popularity of a university career. Unlike careers in other spheres of professional life, a university career does not hold out the same prospects in terms of income and promotion, and the status of a university post is rapidly diminishing. In short, the neohumanist ideal of the university in which research and teaching are linked is no longer a reality taken for granted: research and teaching have gone their separate ways.

The problem of specialization is directly related to the double function of the university: its role as a producer of knowledge and its role as an educator. The massification of the university was primarily for the purpose of providing society with a means of reproducing technically exploitable knowledge in the creation of a trained labour force. Other forms of knowledge were secondary to this primary function of the university. The problem is that today this role can no longer be unproblematically fulfilled. There is no longer the same demand for a mass-educated population ready to be absorbed into the economy. The likely development will be towards a reduced mode of higher education, with students financing in part their own education to a greater extent than has been the case over the past thirty years. The World Bank's report on higher education in 1994 urged countries to shift from dependence on just one source of funding, that is, the state, towards multiple sources (Currie, 1998: 6). In Britain this is the outcome of the Dearing Report, which marks the end of the Robbins era of

expansion (Dearing, 1997). In the present context, what is particularly striking is that the disequilibrium between economy and university is occurring
at a time when the state is retreating from the university. The result is a
deep crisis in the functional logic of the university with respect to the state
and the economy.

According to Lyotard (1984), education is becoming less a fixed period
in one's life than an ongoing process shaped by the demands of rapidly
changing employment patterns. One of the themes in Bourdieu's great
study of the French university in the aftermath of May 1968 was that symbolic capital accruing from education did not always translate into occupational rewards (Bourdieu, 1988). As Gibbons *et al.* argue: 'Modern mass
higher education teaches people not to become too closely devoted to one
occupation or a single set of skills. It prepares them for the likelihood that
both will change often and they must travel fast' (1984: 75). The typical
student today is no longer under 25 and residential. In American higher
education, 43.5 per cent of the total student population is over 25, and 43
per cent are part-time (Manicas, 1998). Graduates are now aware that pos-
sessing a degree is no longer a passport to a job for life. Accordingly, many
are content to use their university education to develop transferable skills
(Webster, 1999). In order to be transferable, a skill must be flexible. Skills
such as time-management, problem-solving, self-reliance, adaptability rather
than actual formal credentials may be becoming more central to a university
education.

Beyond Mode 2 analysis

The theory of Mode 2 knowledge production accepts the inevitability of the
transformation in knowledge, and recognizes that at present Mode 1 and
Mode 2 continue to exist alongside each other. But the trend towards Mode
2 is evident, proponents believe, and offers positive and creative opportunities. The blurring of the sciences and the blurring of the divide between
science and society allows for novel and creative possibilities. I believe that
much of this characterization is correct although I think that some of
the conclusions are unwarranted. It is indeed true that the production of
knowledge is no longer confined to the university and that a whole range
of other knowledge producers have appeared challenging the university's
monopoly on knowledge. However, this does not justify the largely positive
picture that is painted of Mode 2 knowledge production as entailing a more
socially accountable kind of knowledge. In this chapter I have looked at
Mode 2 knowledge production as part of the progressive penetration of
market values into the shaping of knowledge. This is particularly evident in
the case of the university and the arrival of what Slaughter and Leslie call
'academic capitalism' (Slaughter and Leslie, 1997; see also Chapter 8). In
my view, Mode 2 is best seen as the penetration of the market into the
domain of knowledge production. It leaves unanswered the question of the

democratic and reflexive constitution of knowledge. Perhaps what is less accurate in this account is the characterization of Mode 1 as the basis of the university. Mode 1 may be specifically paradigm- and discipline-driven but the university as such has never been entirely defined by this kind of knowledge production. The theories of the university discussed in previous chapters, ranging from Parsons, to Habermas and Bourdieu, despite their different approaches and claims, offer a less stereotypical view of the university. This suggests that perhaps the university is in a better position to resist some of the more instrumentalizing aspects of Mode 2 knowledge.

It is important to see the new discourse of accountability as part of a move towards market values. Ostensibly, accountability strengthens democracy, but it is close to the values of the market in so far as it has provided legitimacy for privileging certain kinds of knowledge over others. In reality, accountability is another kind of accounting. The blurring of the boundaries between science and society is better described as a blurring of the border between science and the market. It is not evident that this has led to the enhancement of democracy. Gibbons *et al.* (1984) tend to embrace uncritically the managerial revolution as a step in a more democratic kind of knowledge society since those who appropriate knowledge will be those who produce it. It is seen as a more reflexive kind of knowledge than what prevailed under Mode 1. Despite some of the claims about the implications of Mode 2 knowledge for the university, the university has not only survived but also expanded. What is neglected in Mode 2 analysis is the fact that although the university may no longer be the only producer of knowledge it is still the most important dispenser of credentials and is also a significant arbiter of cultural capital, such as status. The crucial issue, however, is whether Mode 2 knowledge production within the university can be a basis of technological citizenship, whether the embracing of the user will allow technological innovation to be shaped by the demands of citizenship. For this to be possible, the university will have to be a forum for users drawn from not only industry but from other domains in society. The university is the institution in society most capable of linking the requirements of industry, technology and market forces with the demands of citizenship. Given the enormous dependence of these forces on university based experts, the university is in fact in a position of strength, not of weakness. While it is true that the new production of knowledge is dominated by an instrumentalization of knowledge and that as a result the traditional role of the university has been undermined, it is now in a position to serve social goals more fully than previously when other goals were more prominent. In the present context what must be emphasized is the question of connecting technology to citizenship in the articulation of technological citizenship. Technology, in particular information technology, is an inescapable fact of the modern world and its humanization is a condition of the advancement of citizenship. Universities are more equipped for this task than are other organizations. At the moment the problem is that goals are set for the university rather than by the university, which consequently does not utilize its full resources. To this end the older notion of academic freedom is still relevant so long as it is not an excuse to evade societal responsibility.

The next chapter deals with the downside of Mode 2 knowledge for the university which I shall be arguing can be seen as responding by adopting the values of the market. Instead of combating some of the instrumentalizing features of Mode 2 knowledge by cultivating a different kind of reflexivity based on some continuities with Mode 1, the university risks losing its identity in the corporate world of academic capitalism.

8

Globalization and Academic Capitalism: The New Knowledge Flows

The traditional university was located in a territorial space where the institution of the lecture was the primary form of communication and the solitary scholar the agent of knowledge. Today in our global age it is different. Verbal communication is being challenged by new kinds of non-verbal communication and new kinds of agency. The producer and recipient of knowledge are no longer the professor and student engaged in scholarly discourse in the tutorial. Knowledge is being depersonalized, deterritorialized and globalized. It is being taken out of its traditional context and disseminated by new media of communication (Becher, 1989). In the global age, the scholar's space is opening beyond the traditional spaces of the library, the seminar room and the study into a virtual level (Friese and Wagner, 1993). The new technologies of communication have made feasible the virtual university. Whether this is the negation of the idea of the university or a new level of reality with which we have to live will be debated for some time to come, for we are now only at the beginning of an epoch of far-reaching change.

This chapter begins by looking at some perspectives on globalization with respect to the transformation of the university. Much of the debate on globalization with respect to higher education polarizes into a perspective that emphasizes academic capitalism and one that sees in the new information technologies opportunities for a new kind of cultural and technological citizenship. In the past the ethos of the university was antithetical to entrepreneurialism (Robins and Webster, 1985). This was during a period when the social sciences were enjoying major expansion and Marxism and radical ideas were dominant. Today, with business schools and technoscience on the rise, entrepreneurial values are enjoying a new legitimacy. The critical voice of the university is more likely to be stifled than strengthened as a result of globalization. Yet, globalization has also opened a window on cosmopolitanism for universities, which have been too imprisoned in their national contexts. One of the logics of globalization – democratization – has also been an important dimension to the extension of higher education world-wide.

Although the university is in danger of becoming a site of global corporate capitalism, my contention is that it is still an important site of democratization, especially in technology, and the cultivation of cosmopolitan values.

Globalization, the state and the university

Proponents of globalization argue that the world is becoming an increasingly more integrated place as a result of the transnationalization of communication, markets and finance. But what is globalization? It is clearly a contested concept for it is used in a variety of ways. Most theories of globalization tend to deal either with processes of economic and political restructuring or with socio-cultural transformation. In general the globalization thesis has been dominated by a vision of the transnationalization of the world's economy in the areas of markets, finance and communications. Globalization becomes closely linked with the rise of international finance capitalism and technological change. In this sense, what is generally emphasized is the declining power of the state and the ascendancy of the market (Horsman and Marshall, 1994; Ohmae, 1995; Strange, 1996).

This situation can be seen as leading to a market driven uniformity, homogeneity, standardization or globalization can be seen as leading to fragmentation, plurality, even chaos. For with the declining ability of the state to control the environment in which it exists and the loss of national sovereignty, social and cultural forms of integration become weakened. Such developments lead many to a perspective on globalization as entailing heterogeneity and disorder. It is clear that the market cannot be a force of integration since it is not based on a principle of citizenship. In this view, processes of globalization from 'below' collide with globalization from 'above'. Thus Santos (1995: 262–96, 1999: 217–19) speaks of a 'globalized localism' (that is, the globalization of a local phenomenon, such as the internationalization of English) and 'localized globalism' (the impact of global process on local practices, such as deforestation) as two forms of globalization emanating 'from above'. In opposition to these kinds of globalization are counter-hegemonic projects, such as networks of international non-govermental organizations (INGOs) and movements related to citizenship and democracy. This second sense of globalization might be better termed cosmopolitanism, since it is something that runs counter to homogenizing processes. In any case, many theorists such as Robertson (1992) use the term 'globalization' to refer to the emergence of a world based on plurality and heterogeneity. In his use of the term it is the particularism of the universal, such the local adaptation of universal ideas, as in creolization that is important. Globalization allows as much the assertion of localism or particularism as does universalism. In this sense, then, Ritzer's argument concerning McDonaldization (referring to the hamburger chain) as a global popular culture is only one kind of cultural globalization (Ritzer, 1993). Globalization may bring about the progressive homogenization of all cultures and forms of communication but it can also be seen in terms of the recalcitrance of the particular and the fragmentation of experience and meaning. Appadurai (1996) thus sees globalization as the chaotic flow of cultural 'scapes', such as ethnoscapes, mediascapes, technoscapes, finance-scapes and ideoscapes, all of which provide particular cultural groups with models for their own organization and identity formation.

It is clear that theories of globalization share a view that the nation state is in decline and that transnational processes are becoming more important. While views differ as to whether this will lead to a more homogenized world or one that is fragmented as a result of the recalcitrance of the local, it is evident that some of the key determinants are linked to the diminishing role of the state. The thesis of the decline of the state has been subject to a good deal of critical scrutiny, for not all agree with the view that the state is in irreversible decline (Dunn, 1995; Berger and Dore, 1996; Hirst and Thompson, 1996; Holton, 1998). States are still the most powerful actors in the world context and capitalism is still largely organized on national lines. Yet, there is no doubting the massive decline in national sovereignty. Although states have retained considerable control over key policies, there are more competitors today, for instance the rise of the non-state actor, the INGO, the rise of regionalism and the city. Thus in one of the well known versions of this modified theory of globalization, Sassen (1992) writes of the rise of the 'global city'. The global cities are interconnected by means of international finance capitalism which is underpinned by the new technologies of information. These global cities become disconnected from their nation states accordingly as they become embedded in the global economy of informational finance capitalism. But this is clearly a very fragmented world in which cities lose their connection with their regional and national environments. In the global world there are big winners but many losers.

Perhaps, then, the most significant development is technological change. Manuel Castells's (1996) theory of the network society, while suffering from many of the deficits of globalization theory, offers an interesting way of conceiving of globalization. The global society is a network society. A network is a set of interconnected nodes, that is the point at which a curve intersects itself. These networks, Castells argues, are becoming more important and are based on the transmission of information:

> Networks are open structures, able to expand without limits, integrating new nodes as long as they are able to communicate within the network, namely as long as they share the same communication codes (for example, values or performance goals). A network-based social structure is a highly dynamic, open system, susceptible to innovating without threatening its balance.
>
> (Castells, 1996: 470)

As a system based on the flow of information, the network society is one that cannot be contained within national borders. In this sense, globalization is based primarily on information which feeds into different areas: culture, politics, economy. The postindustrial economy is not based on energy, as was the case with all earlier technological revolutions in the industrial age, but on information, application of science to a whole range of societal areas, including to itself.

In all these areas what is striking is the diminishing importance of space as territory or as place. Space becomes deterritorialized in the new space of flows that constitutes virtual reality. Lash and Urry (1994; Urry, 1998) thus refer to the flow of economies and images and signs in a dedifferentiated world in which the borders separating economy, politics and culture become diffuse. For them, globalization is the rapid movement of information as a result of the 'disorganization' of capitalism which is no longer able to constrain economy and culture within the national limits. In a more recent contribution, Urry writes of the replacement of society by mobilities (Urry, 2000).

The implications of these developments for the university have only begun to be discussed. For long the university has been seen as unaffected by the forces of social change, especially global forces. As argued in previous chapters, the university since the late nineteenth century had become a national institution. It helped to shape national culture and later became central to the production of national economies in terms of being the primary location for the training of the professions. Yet the university was more than a national institution; it also retained a cosmopolitanism of spirit, which was expressed for instance in the struggles over democracy with the rise of the counter-culture of the late 1960s. Cosmopolitan discourses and movements owed much to the university, as the example of feminism attests. These roles, the national and the cosmopolitan, were frequently at odds with each other in a century dominated by the nation state as the primary reference point for culture and economics. In the current situation, with many logics of globalization unfolding, there are the signs of a move beyond the nation state. However, what remains unclear is the extent to which we can speak of globalization enhancing the cosmopolitanism of the university.

The trend towards globalization with respect to the university would suggest that national models of higher education will become increasingly alike. Universities will become subject to the pressures of performativity and cultural homogenization. With the declining salience of the nation state as the sole provider, universities everywhere in the world will be forced to rely on other sources of funding to survive in a market-driven world. The university thus shifts from being an ideological apparatus of the nation state and the guardian of its heritage to being a relatively independent bureaucratic system. Developments such as increased student mobility, the internationalization of the curriculum and educational policy, and international research cooperation may be cited as examples of the globalization of knowledge as well as the rapid diffusion of knowledge leading to the formation of what Castells (1996) has called the 'network society' based on information.

The university in the past was an important institution in the building of national cultures, providing the dominant elites with a common culture and means of communication, such as the codification of a national language. As Turner (1998) has claimed, the university was also an important institution for defining western values, such as the value of universalism. He argues that while the 'nineteenth century university operating within the nation state produced individuals to function as national citizens, the new global universities, which may operate entirely through the World Wide Web, have not such a particularistic location in national cultures or even with a particular national corporation' (Turner, 1998: 75). Given the flow of information in the global age, the traditional university may be undermined by agencies more adept at the transmission of information from producer to user. One of the implications of this is that what is being transmitted is less knowledge than information.

Examples of the globalization of knowledge and the deterritorialization of higher education include the following points:

- Electronic mail and the internet have altered the nature of communication, locating much of knowledge in the non-places of cyberspace and eliminating time and distance as a barrier to knowledge and communication.
- Academics are travelling more often today. International conferences are becoming more frequent and academics have more opportunities to meet those with similar interests even when their research is highly specific.
- Academics are also networking more, forming multiple research networks that are spread across the globe.
- The number of co-authored or multi-authored publications is increasing, in particular in fields where the research depends on large-scale funding. Since this is rarely dominated by single academics, group publications are more frequent. This model suggests an end to the traditional model, described by Weber, of the solitary professor in personal possession of his tools.
- Higher education is becoming more standardized. Exchange programmes, such as the European Union's exchange programme Socrates, offer opportunities for students to travel more easily and there is also the increased occurrence of students taking a semester abroad as part of their studies. Students and staff are now more likely than before to be able to speak a foreign language.
- Transnational knowledge is also increasingly becoming a reality. This can be seen in the move towards a European science policy, as is evidenced by new funding opportunities for research supported by the European Union.
- There is a huge increase world-wide in the number of students participating in higher education. The number increased from 51 million in 1980 to about 82 million in 1995, representing an increase of about 61 per cent (Sadlak, 1998).
- Not only academics are travelling more but so too are students. Student flows are no longer determined by colonial or postcolonial links, Peter

Scott points out. Increasingly, student flows are within the developed world. These flows are more likely to be driven by the market rather than by the state (Scott, 1998b: 117–18).

While these can be seen as examples of globalization, they can also be seen as products of internationalization. What is the difference between internationalism and globalization? Higher education is a good illustration of the limits of globalization, much of which can be understood as the continuation of internationalism. Where globalization entails the undermining of the national state by markets, communication and deterritorialized processes, internationalism presupposes the existence of national centres which cooperate in certain areas. Thus the United Nations is based on internationalism rather than globalization, presupposing the existence of sovereign states. Universities have always been key players in international society, which set the limits of cosmopolitanism. There is not a great deal of evidence to suggest that the current situation has to any extent altered this.

Globalization, however, is certainly having an impact on universities. The argument that I advance below is that the encroaching discourse of globalization is taking shape in the form of a new kind of academic capitalism. Thus it is not the turn to the user as such that is undermining the possibility of universities enhancing citizenship but the subordination of knowledge to market values.

Academic capitalism and the triple helix

The nexus of globalization and capitalism lies in neoliberal ideology. It is this that fuels much of globalization. Released from the constraints of the nation state and the imperative of social citizenship, globalization has been shaped by neoliberalism. With respect to higher education this is apparent in the adoption by universities of the values from the corporate culture of industry (see Currie, 1998). Globalization has pushed universities in the direction of the market. According to Robert Reich, one of the central concerns of government is with making higher education service the needs of a technological civilization. He sees universities as the key to influence in the world economy, and governments will be keen to shape higher education accordingly (Reich, 1991). Etzkowitz and Leydesdorff (1997) have advanced the interesting thesis of the 'triple helix' of university, industry and government relations. What were once bilateral relations between government and university and between industry and university are now evolving in the direction of a triple set of links. By linking in with industry and at the same time responding to government pressures, universities are gradually moving into the global economy.

Rather than having the state as the exclusive provider of financial resources, universities are now depending on multiple sources, such as student fees, donations, consultancies and profitable research contracts with industry. One of the biggest university complexes in the world, the University of

California, receives less than 30 per cent of its funds from the state. In absolute terms, the state of California is putting more of its funds into prisons than into its colleges and universities (Manicas, 1998: 654). This is part of a world-wide tendency of the state to cease to be the exclusive provider of higher education. In the domain of research funding this is most striking. In 1930, only 10 per cent of research in the United States was funded by the government; by 1990 this had risen to 60 per cent (Robertson, 1999). This change can be explained by the need of the state for research in the area of defence, and that with the decline in this since the end of the cold war the university has been seeking to forge links directly with industry.

Most academics have experienced this in terms of the growth of corporate managerialism, that is the logic of financial accountability. An example of this is the practice of matched funding, whereby half of funded research is supplied by non-public money. In this way globalization and privatization are interwoven. University services are used by private-sector sponsors while the basic infrastructure remains publicly funded.

As Slaughter and Leslie (1997) argue, the changes that took place in higher education in the 1980s and 1990s were as great as the changes that took place in the last quarter of the nineteenth century. When the industrial revolution created the wealth that provided the base for higher education. But in the 1980s and 1990s, national systems of higher education were restructured in order to secure a greater share of global markets. The central argument of their book is that the structure of academic work is changing in response to the emergence of global markets. As national competition for global market shares increased, Australia, the United Kingdom, the United States and to a lesser extent Canada developed policies that reshaped higher education:

> Increased global competition interacted with national and state provincial spending priorities so that less money was available from government, when measured as a share of higher education revenue or in constant dollars per student. This precipitated campus reactions of a resource-dependent nature. In all four countries the block grant as a source of funding for higher education diminished as a share of higher education revenues, with the result that faculty and institutions began to compete or increased their competition for external funds.
>
> (Slaughter and Leslie, 1997: 209)

The shift to academic capitalism occurred because universities' search for extra funding coincided with the corporate quest for new products – products that required a high input of scientific knowledge. To achieve this, higher educational policies were devised to secure increased student enrolment at a lower national cost. There has been a general swing internationally from grants to loans. Universities in the United States, Canada, the UK and Australia began to embrace the market in order to secure increased funds and thus no longer to rely exclusively on the state. Slaughter and Leslie justify the term 'academic capitalism' on the grounds that it defines 'the reality of the nascent environment of public research universities, an environment full of contradictions, in which faculty and professional staff expend their human capital stocks increasingly in competitive situations' (Slaughter and Leslie, 1997: 9). Clearly, academic capitalism is not based on the private ownership of the means of production, but capitalism is also an economic system driven by market forces and it is in this sense that the term is used to describe the market behaviour of state-subsidized entrepreneurs.

This move towards academic capitalism is connected with the shift from industrial to postindustrial society, the latter being more dependent on higher education. The postindustrial society is also an information society needing a class of professional knowledge producers. Slaughter and Leslie write:

> The postindustrial technological revolution depends on universities. Universities provide the training necessary for the increasing numbers of professionals employed by corporations to invent, maintain, and innovate with regard to sophisticated technologies and products. In a growing number of cases universities are the sites where new technologies and products are developed, often in partnership with business, through funding provided in part by the state.
>
> (1997: 27)

Globalization has had a major impact on higher education, forcing it to engage with the market. As a result of globalization the state has fewer resources available for higher education, a development that has occurred at a time of expanded massification of higher education. Thus as the economy globalized, the business or corporate sector in industrialized countries pushed the state to concentrate recourses in the enhancement and management of technological innovation systems. At this time, the educational expansion begun in the 1970s declined as a result of expanding national debts due to increased borrowing. With less funding available to higher education and increased demands for funding from the universities, the state responded by forcing universities to be competitive, with league tables, quality assurance tests, research assessments and various performance indicators being used to determine the allocation of resources.

One of the most noticeable aspects of academic capitalism is the phenomenon of technoscience. This kind of postindustrial science is entirely market driven and in it the distinction between knowledge and commodity is broken down. Increasingly favoured by universities today, technoscience is becoming a major part of research, as the growth in biotechnology and telecommunications attests. It was in university laboratories that some of the major innovations were made in biotechnology (Kenney, 1986). As House argues, biotechnology was pioneered in universities and was the test case of the new commodification of knowledge because it crosses the divide between applied and basic research and the divide between theoretically and commercially driven research (House, 1998). She points out that the

Monsanto Chemical company was one of the first corporate enterprises to see the economic value of theoretical knowledge. In 1974, by providing Harvard University with grants and endowments worth US$23 million over twelve years, it in effect broke ground in establishing new norms in university–industry relations. Alliances with the pharmaceutical companies had been common in US universities in the first half of the twentieth century but industry–university links declined with the creation of independent national funding agencies for research. Relative to the federal government's share, it declined from 10 per cent of the total in 1955 to less than 5 per cent in 1960, and less than 3 per cent in 1970 (Dickson, 1984: 63). Biotechnology changed all this. From the late 1970s, leading academics began to sell their services to industry and others set up university-based business in technology-related areas. By 1980, affiliation with a company had become the norm in molecular biology departments (Dickson, 1984: 76; House, 1998). This is true too of information technology. In 1999, Melbourne University earned £34 million through floating on the Australian stock market a university spin-off company created to register internet users (*Times Higher Educational Supplement*, 24 December, 1999: 28).

It is also the case that this kind of research leads to the production of commodities that are highly competitive in global markets. Universities everywhere are heavily involved in building partnerships with business in the important areas of technoscience. What is emerging from this is unclear but it is certainly a move beyond the phenomenon of Mode 2 knowledge production discussed in the previous chapter. This analysis tended to see the university as increasingly isolated as research moves out of the university. But in fact what is happening is that the university is actively engaged in partnerships with industry, making possible a triad of industry–state–academe knowledge production. The universities provide the basic infrastructure for research, including the scientific expertise, which is state-funded to a large extent; industry supplies the wider context of distribution and links with the market. In this tripartite kind of knowledge production, universities use federal funds to generate inventions which are then licensed or contracted to the private sector. In a knowledge-based global economy the high level of training that is to be found in the university provides a crucial site for the global expansion of capitalism. In the United States since 1980 more than 1,500 start-up companies have been formed on technologies created at universities and research universities (Miyoshi, 1999: 8). This means that industrial utility is the principal objective of research. Developments such as these put an entirely different perspective on the argument that knowledge production is fundamentally altered in a way that opens knowledge to greater democracy. The university has in fact strengthened its position in the production of knowledge by attracting corporate interests. But, as Miyoshi highlights, a market-focused university may not be able to preserve its integrity. Academic freedom may be one of the casualities in the new principle of industrial utility. Instead of making knowledge more available, what is occurring is the utilization of public resources by corporate interests. This is reflected in developments in patenting – the conversion of knowledge into intellectual property. As universities become more immersed in partnerships with industry, knowledge will become more patented, which in effect means the exclusion of others sharing in it. Applications for international patents have increased in recent years with declining numbers of national patent applications.

At the moment, patented knowledge is widely believed to be the intellectual property of the scientists, akin to published work. But since these are university based, questions are now being asked concerning their right to intellectual ownership. Activities carried out for business purposes within the research context of the university may become the property of the university. Such issues are clearly complex and there is little consensus on the relationship between research and its commercial implications. While university administrators see the benefits in links with industry, others see major disadvantages. Universities take the risk out of much of industrial entrepreneurship by absorbing the costs of scientific experimentation. Were industry to undertake the same degree of time-intensive research, profit would be enormously reduced. Universities act as testing grounds for large-scale basic research which, when successful, can be applied in commercially viable areas. Aside from the element of risk there is also the fact that with access to universities, industry can indirectly allow the state to subsidize its concerns. The upshot of much of this is that it is becoming increasingly unclear what is profit and what is not.

Slaughter and Leslie (1997) make the important observation that the trend towards academic capitalism indicates a fundamental change in the professional identity of professors. Previously the professorate was a unique subset of professionals in that they had monopolies on advanced degrees and the training and credentials of other professionals. But with the incorporation of universities into the market this has changed:

> Participation in the market began to undercut the tacit contract between professors and society because the market put as much emphasis on the bottom line as on client welfare. The *raison d'être* for special treatment for universities, the training ground of professionals, as well as for professional privilege, was undermined, increasing the likelihood that universities, in the future, will be treated more like other organizations and professionals more like other workers.
>
> (Slaughter and Leslie, 1997: 5)

It is not only administrators who are engaging in academic capitalism but professors are themselves forging links with business. Slaughter and Leslie paint a depressing picture of widespread complicity of academics in a form of capitalism that will ultimately undermine the integrity of the university.

Academic capitalism is most advanced in the United States where universities have been sites of accumulation for some time but is by no means confined to the US (Branscombe *et al.*, 1999). Through the commercialization of teaching and research, universities have enhanced their wealth. I have discussed the commercialization of research until now. The other side of the coin of academic capitalism is teaching and the move towards seeing students as consumers. In the private colleges in the United States, student fees and endowments from graduates have always been major sources of funding. Today there are other mechanisms that make teaching profitable and to a point that the distinction between profit and no-profit is being blurred.

Enrolment management is a strategy of major universities as is off-campus teaching and accredited programmes. These are teaching programmes designed and prepared – or in many cases merely externally supervised – in a major western university (generally British or American) but administered by local universities or colleges. Another strategy in the larger North American universities is 'gentrification': the leasing out of university property. Advertising in universities is also becoming more common on North American campuses. Existing alongside these developments is increased casualization of teaching. In the United States the number of part-time university teachers has nearly doubled since 1970. Recruited from the nearly 38,000 PhDs produced annually in American colleges and universities, part-time teachers constitute the 'flexible' workforce of the post-Fordist economy. On the other side, the proportion of tenurable faculties is only about 50 per cent of the total number of full-timers.

Developments in information technology have put distance learning once again on the agenda. As David Noble has argued, the new interest in information technology for distance learning is entirely commercially driven. In his view it is not about technology or learning but about the commodification of higher education and resembles the mania for correspondence courses in the 1890s and which endured for the first half of the twentieth century (Noble, 1999). He argues that the trend towards automation of higher education as implemented in American universities today is a battle between teachers and students on the one side and administrators and businesses with educational products to sell on the other. In his view this is not progressive but is a regressive trend to the old era of mass production, standardization and commodification. The growth of vocational training, distance learning and the move to make course curricula the property of the university are also examples of how universities are reducing labour costs while expanding enrolment.

In this view industry–university links have undermined the autonomy of knowledge and academic freedom and reinforced the hierarchical structure of universities by giving control to central administration (Rhodes and Slaughter, 1991; House, 1998). This has become apparent in several cases of academics suffering reprisals for disclosing sensitive information for the public interest and thereby breaching contracts of secrecy. As Miyoshi argues: 'Global corporate operations now subordinate the state functions, and in the name of competition, productivity, and freedom, public space is being markedly reduced. And the university that was at times capable of independent criticism of corporate and state policies is increasingly less concerned with maintaining such a neutral position' (Miyoshi, 1998: 263).

In sum, then, there is some justification for the claim of Slaughter and Leslie that there is 'a loss of the university as a community, where individual members are oriented primarily toward the greater good of the organization' (1997: 22). Academic capitalists will gain power as middle-managers and professors will lose power. Teaching too will suffer, as instruction is commodified and the university becomes no different from any other commercial enterprise. In Slaughter and Leslie's view there is nothing natural about these developments, which are products of particular policies, and they can be reversed.

The reality of the virtual university?

One of the major innovations in higher education in recent years has been the emergence of the virtual university. Until now this has been associated with a futuristic design and far from reality. Current developments suggest a blurring of the real and the virtual university. The massive incorporation of information technology into the everyday life of the university provides evidence that the virtual university is now a part of reality.

Extreme examples of the virtual university can be found in a handful of deterritorialized universities, for example the University of Phoenix, the National Technology University, the California Virtual University College and the Western Governors University. However, the current reality in many universities world-wide is the embracing of virtual space as a place of learning. The recent announcement that 26 top North American universities (including the Massachusetts Institute of Technology, University of California at Berkeley, and the Universities of Columbia and Pennsylvania) have combined to produce a single online catalogue to market their distance learning products signals an acceleration of the spread of 'virtuality'. The virtual university is a university for profit and some of these are quite large, such as the University of Phoenix which has over forty thousand students (Manicas, 1998). It has been estimated that there are some three hundred colleges and universities offering virtual degrees with a total of over one million cyber-students (Sadlak, 1998: 103).

To date, most distance learning has been pitched towards the cheaper and less prestigious end of the higher education market (towards low-level qualifications, lifelong learning initiatives, and towards vocational training), but the increasing recognition that university 'brands' such as Harvard and Oxford are valuable commodities impels the adoption of 'virtual university' programmes (Robins and Webster, forthcoming).

The separation of place and space is becoming more common as a result of information technology. It is a regular occurrence today for staff to place material on websites and assignments to be delivered by email, and students are generally becoming more adept at using information technology to access staff and teaching materials. To an extent, then, there is an element of virtuality in present-day higher education systems but there is little to suggest that this will outstrip wider incorporation of technology into everyday life in the creation of a totally deterritorialized university. Against the spectre of a virtual university, Kristan Kumar insists that universities are, and must remain, places: 'Universities bring people together. They allow for a cross-fertilization of minds on a scale and in a manner not possible anywhere else in society' (1997: 29). This sense of place is what is being undermined by the virtual university. The idea of a 'home-based' university is a contradic-tion in terms, Kumar argues, because it is the nature of a university that it is the opposite of a home; it is a communal, residential place beyond the private sphere. The virtual university is a privatized institution in that it links the private world of the home with the equally privatized world of the market. In contrast it is public domain that the university embodies.

I believe Kumar is correct in defending the sense of place that is central to the university in modernity. There is no evidence that distance learning is more effective than traditional forms of learning. Indeed, there is much to suggest that lectures are effective tools in learning and the personal relationship with the lecturer is an important one in shaping the learning process. In depersonalized and deterritorialized forms of learning there is a particularly high drop-out rate. The danger now is that the big public uni-versities in the United States will give a second-class education while the private liberal arts colleges will provide an education for a small number who can afford it. In the UK this division is likely to be reflected in a similar divide between the ex-polytechnics and the old universities. In earlier chap-ters the mass university was shown to be one of the great innovations in the shaping of late modernity. In it the democratic values of citizenship were provided with an important basis. Those values are in danger if they are subordinated to the market.

However, a sense of proportion is necessary. For the moment it would appear that the virtual university is not an alternative to the traditional university but a modification of it. There is not a great deal to suggest that the virtual university will replace the traditional university, rather that the traditional university will increasingly embrace information technology. If the university is not to abandon its central mission to enhance human knowledge, ways will have to be found to ensure that technological innova-tion is wedded to citizenship. Thus one of the challenges of globalization for the university is the question of the feasibility of technological citizen-ship. The indications at the moment are that the university is making the move towards virtual technology via the market rather than through the public culture of citizenship. It is clear that information technology has much to contribute to the making of technological citizenship but at the moment there is little to see in the current drive towards virtuality other than market-driven forces.

The global age, with its foundations in communication technology, offers great opportunities for the enhancement of citizenship by making possible wider participation of citizens. Universities are in a particularly strong posi-tion to exploit the advantages of new technologies and to make technology serve the requirements of citizenship. Today technology – in particular biotechnology, military technology and information technology – is becoming not only more and more important in many spheres of life but is also becoming increasingly disengaged from any normative system. The challenge of universities is to occupy this new ground. Rather than retreating from technology and the market in the name of autonomy, universities should use their relative autonomy to humanize technology and to recreate new expressions of citizenship.

Cosmopolitanism versus globalization

Democratization world-wide is undoubtedly having an impact on the extension of higher education. Neoliberalism and the response by universities to it with academic capitalism and the trend towards the virtual university are only one aspect of the globalization. There is also the cosmopolitan dimension. Bryan Turner offers an important perspective on cosmopolitanism in the context of globalization of the university: the Islamization of knowledge. Universities function within the global context to define local cultures through the maintenance of minority languages and the creation of a national 'imaginary' community, he argues. Islamization, while on one level a defence of indigenous values from western ones, on another level expresses the desire of Muslim intellectuals for recognition and the aspiration to re-establish the authority of Islam:

> Although the Islamization of science is a real and significant challenge to the hegemony of Western university culture, it is interesting to note that most of the principal protagonists of Islamization are indeed either the products of Western university systems or are housed within them. In short, the Islamization of science debate has been produced by Muslims in Western university systems. The result is the Islamization of science may be as much a challenge to the traditional values of Islam as it is intended to a challenge to the values of Western culture'.
> (Turner, 1998: 76; see also Laruoi, 1976; Stenberg, 1996)

It is in this sense that globalization becomes a force of cosmopolitanism, that is, in promoting the self-transformation of cultures through a critical engagement with each other.

On a related level, universities are major vehicles of regionalization. Globalization is more than just the making of a global society but can also strengthen local powers against national centres. Many universities are evolving policies on their commitment to the regional as well as to the national and international context. Increasingly there has been a recognition that universities must have a role to play in the development of local and regional economies (Gray, 1999; Marks, 1999). In the UK there is a regional policy on higher education, with a growing difference between the English and Scottish university systems.

Globalization is then quite diverse. One view is that globalization is leading to the formation of a 'world scientific community' (Schott, 1991). But according to Stichweh, (1996) following Luhmann (1987), who sees the university as an organization, the university occupies a pivotal position in the evolution of a world society: globalization is as much about diffusion as it is about interconnectedness. Interconnectedness works through diffusion within localized contexts. In his view the dynamics of internal differentiation is the most important cause of the globalization of science:

> the globalization of science is not the result of one scientific community of scientists with a shared set normative and cognitive presuppositions emerging. Instead it is the incessant proliferation of ever-new communities of scientists with progressively restricted juridictions, which organizes the social and the cognitive space of science in a way which is incompatible with the boundaries of national scientific communities.
>
> (Stichweh, 1996: 332)

Thus while the economic exploitation of knowledge is becoming more and more globalized (as is witnessed by the fact that the growth rate for international patent applications has increased since 1980 at a much faster rate than that for national patents), science is still nationally organized and yet is globally interconnected. Nearly all the important organizations of science – *Centre Nationale de Recherche Scientifique* in France, the *Max-Planck-Gesellschaft* in Germany – are nationally funded. In the case of multinational corporations this is also the case in that while there is the global exploitation of technological knowledge, research and development are still concentrated in the country of origin. The persistence of national foundations for knowledge does not hinder the remarkable growth of global collaboration but makes it possible. Indeed, science has always been global by virtue of its universality.

These arguments are borne out by Andy Green who argues that rather than full-scale globalization of education, the evidence suggests that what is occurring is a partial internationalization of education systems. National education systems have become more porous in recent years as a result of globalization (Green, 1997: 171). However, that there is greater international penetration of national education systems does not mean that global forces will replace other determinants. The example of German higher education provides a remarkable example of resistance to global forces. After German unification in the early 1990s the West German model of higher education was extended to East Germany without requiring any reform. Transnational universities are few and far between, a notable exception being the Viadrina European University, located in the border city of Frankfurt/Oder and the Polish city of Slubice, with its special mandate to provide links between western and eastern Europe (Muller and Whitesell, 1996). Another example is the interlinking of the universities of Copenhagen, Malmo and Lund. Universities are becoming more important in the social construction of a shared Europe (Bertilsson, 2000).

9

The Postmodern University: Deconstructing Knowledge and Institutions

The foregoing chapters have traced the transformation of the role of the university: from its formative period following the Enlightenment the modern university took shape in the closing decades of the nineteenth century and in the course of the twentieth century the university came to occupy a key position within organized modernity. Originally based on a social contract with the Church, the university forged a new contract with the national state and, from the mid-twentieth century, became central to social citizenship and served the state and the modern professions in what was now a credential society. In the 1960s and 1970s, the university for the first time came to occupy the radical ground and offered an important space for the expression of democratic values and the transformative project of modernity. With the counter-culture of the 1960s, knowledge suddenly became politicized and the university ceased to be a bourgeois enclave, becoming a leading voice in mass society. In the 1980s, as organized modernity gave way to late modernity, a major change occurred when the university forged an alliance with industry and a new managerial ethos emerged. In what was now becoming a global age the university began to reach beyond the limits of the national state, but at the cost of greatly compromising its critical and democratic role. With decreased funding from the state and ever greater demands from rising student numbers, something like a new social contract emerged among the university, industry and the state. The basis of this is that knowledge production is to be shaped as much by the user as by the producer. Legitmated by a discourse of accountability, the university loses its sense of moral purpose. In the previous chapters I looked at the implications of the new production of knowledge that emerged in this time of globalization and noted that one dimension was the arrival of academic capitalism and the embracing of market and managerial values. But how extensive have these values become? Have we reached the end of knowledge? Are we now, as Readings (1996) argued, dwelling in the 'ruins of the university'? Can a constructivist, as opposed to a deconstructivist, philosophy offer a different approach?

The impact of globalization on the university has been immense, and while there is no underestimating the tremendous transformation of higher education in the 1980s and 1990s as a result of the double impact of neoliberalism and globalization which pushed the university closer to the market, my contention is that there is more to late modernity than the rule of the market. A useful way of assessing the current situation of the university is to take stock of the postmodern theory of knowledge. Four authors associated with different positions on postmodernism have written about the spectre of the postmodern university: Lyotard, Bauman, Derrida and Readings. Following a brief discussion of postmodernism, in the second part of this chapter I critically examine the interpretations of the postmodern university of Lyotard, Bauman and Derrida in order to assess the extent to which the thesis of the postmodern university offers an alternative model to current developments encroaching the end of knowledge. In the final section I look at Readings's particular interpretation of what he called the 'posthistorical university'.

Postmodernism and knowledge

Postmodernism in the most general sense concerns a revision of the cultural assumptions of modernity. For some it represents a move beyond modernity; for others it is the last stage of modernity in which modernity turns in upon itself. Three phases can be identified. The first is the emergence of the postmodern movement in the arts in the 1970s. The concern with aesthetic postmodernism was paralleled by a movement in French philosophy at about the same time and is best associated with the writings of Michel Foucault and poststructuralism. In these writings an explicitly epistemological thesis emerges about the nature of knowledge. Finally, in the 1980s, postmodernism becomes a theory of society and indicates a political endorsement of multiculturalism and a critique of capitalism. In this predominately American movement the concern is less with aesthetic and epistemological matters than with the question of the identity of the self in an age of fragmentation, multiplicity and difference (Hassan, 1987; Delanty, 2000a).

The postmodern movement in the arts began with postmodern architecture and signified a rejection of the formalism and abstract nature of the modern movement. Postmodern architecture sought to recover a sense of meaning lost in modernism and which it did by integrating style into everyday life. Thus the hallmark of postmodern architecture was context and montage. In it, as in the entire postmodern movement in the social, cultural and political thought of the late twentieth century, the situation defines the content of meaning. There can be no recourse to a higher principle, be it a principle of form, a universal law or a transcendent idea. Meaning is to be defined by its use. It was inevitable that this anti-foundationalist way of looking at things would embrace a certain relativism, and when developments in epistemology became linked with new theories of language, postmodernism became a theory of radical cultural relativism.

Poststructuralism emerged in the late 1960s and 1970s in the context of a disillusionment among French intellectuals with Marxism, phenomenology and existentialism, the prevailing modes of philosophical thought in France in the decades following the war. Declaring an end to modernity and its political movements, the new generation of French thinkers sought to deconstruct the modes of thought that prevailed in the modern age since the Enlightenment. These modes of thought are allegedly characterized by linearity and narrative, ways of thinking that are seen as oppressive and exclusionary. Deconstructionism came to mean an attack on meaning. By declaring that 'all was language', the poststructuralists – from Barthes and Lacan to Foucault and Derrida – aimed to show that every attempt to establish a meaningful statement was simply a strategy of language by which a discourse was established. The method of deconstructionism aimed to show that there was no privileged point outside the discourse from which the discourse could be criticized. In place of critique, poststructuralism offered only endless interrelations. One of the casualties in this was the very possibility of identity, and indeed also politics. The self was seen as the product of the illusion that the ego can unify the diversity of forces that surround it.

Poststructuralism, however, was largely a movement in psychoanalysis and literary studies. Even in philosophy it was marginal and was not very important in social science in its initial phase when it was dominated by French thought. However, by the 1980s, poststructuralism had been overtaken by postmodernism as a fully fledged philosophical movement and one that had a major impact on social science, in particular on sociology. As Marxism went into decline and entered its terminal phase in 1989, sociology began to look to alternative approaches to rethink the political and intellectual heritage of the modern age. In the post-Enlightenment ethos of the last decades of the century, poststructuralism offered a framework for this. The writings of Lacan, Barthes, Foucault and Derrida with their epistemological critiques of knowledge, power and the self were a way of overcoming not only tradition but also modernity. The writings of the philosophers Baudrillard and Lyotard, who preserved a stronger link with Marxism than literary figures like Derrida and Barthes, opened the door to sociology as did the work of Foucault. But it was in the United States that these thinkers had the greatest impact. Of particular appeal there was the question of the dissolution of the self and the implicit embracing of multiplicity and difference. Postmodernism thus became a philosophy of cultural fragmentation. Instead of seeing in the present the ruins of modernity, it saw new possibilities of meaning built around the acknowledgement of difference. It came to express American sensibilities about the impossibility of the modern project to sustain politics in an age of multiculturalism. In the writings of

Jameson (1991) and Harvey (1990), postmodernism took on a far more critical edge than in the poststructuralist ethos of French thought. The new kind of politics was very much a politics of the self and reflected a turning away from the social question, which was the basis of the political imagination of the modern era to the cultural question, that is the question of the relationship of the self to the other, the recovering of community and the re-creation of identity in an age that has seen the end of foundations and markers of certainty.

Postmodern theories of the university

It was not surprising that postmodern thought would address the question of the university (Paulston, 1999). No institution has more epitomized the modern project than the university. The university is both an institution of knowledge and a major player in the formation of the epistemic structure of the modern national state. The epistemic condition of modernity is encapsulated in the ethos of the modern university where knowledge was given a consecrating function in society and at the same time an autonomy from society. It was inevitable that the postmodern attack on modernity and its epistemic structures would be turned on the institution that underpinned the modern project.

In one of the seminal texts of postmodernism as a sociological theory, Jean-François Lyotard in *The Postmodern Condition: A Report on Knowledge* focused his attention on the university (Lyotard, 1984). In this well known book, originally published in 1979 and based on a report commissioned by the government of Quebec on the current state of knowledge, Lyotard provided what was to be a crucial bridge linking poststructuralism with sociological theories of the postindustrial society. Poststructuralism had broken with the modernist stance on knowledge as culturally universalistic, autonomous of society and politically emancipatory. Lyotard saw in the emerging postindustrial society the sociological reality of the poststructuralist thesis. In this kind of society there is no longer an integrating principle of unity – a grand narrative – that can serve either to legitimate or to overcome the social and political order. The postmodern condition which has prevailed in the postindustrial society is one of fragmentation.

The main dimension of this concerns the role of knowledge. In modernity, knowledge held out the possibility of political emancipation. The conditions of this possibility lay in the fact that in modernity knowledge was largely autonomous of the social order. The doctrine of the Enlightenment was that knowledge could emancipate people from the dogmatism of tradition. This vision of knowledge was the basis of many of the ideologies of the modern age: nationalism, socialism, liberalism, positivism. In these worldviews, knowledge contained a metaphysical principle that was in tension with the prevailing social order. This principle was an abstract one and could be realized only by radically transforming the reality. In one way or another all the great thinkers of the Enlightenment and its aftermath – Hegel, Comte, Marx – held to this idea of the liberating power of knowledge. For Hegel, human history was the progressive unfolding of narratives of self-consciousness; for Comte in his 'law of the three stages', the Enlightenment period, which succeeded the stage of theological thought, was dominated by a 'metaphysical' conception of knowledge which would in time give way to the stage of positivism once ways could be found to have its abstract principles realized; for Marx, human prehistory would come to a close once a new narrative of class consciousness could be formed. Part of this power of knowledge resided in its capacity to offer a unifying narrative which, if politically organized, could lay the foundations of a new kind of society. In Lyotard's terms, these architects of modernity held to a notion of narrative as metaphysical, in the sense that it transcended reality and held the promise of transforming reality if the appropriate political mechanism could be found.

According to Lyotard, the postmodern condition has rendered these visions of knowledge as a meta-narrative irrelevant. Knowledge today is no longer abstract, metaphysical and emancipatory. The postindustrial society is based on knowledge. We are living in an information society which has fragmented knowledge by commodifying and instrumentalizing it. Consequently, knowledge has lost the promise of emancipation. The integrating power of narrative has been lost in the mood of fragmentation that has come with the postindustrial society and the conversion of knowledge into information. The implications of this are far-reaching for the university. The university no longer occupies an autonomous space since such spaces have been eroded. Published around the same time as Bourdieu's studies on higher education, Lyotard's book reflected an even more far-reaching critique of the university. The university is an institution of modernity and is largely irrelevant to the political and cultural demands of the postmodern condition. Lyotard's attitude to the postmodern condition is ambivalent. On the one side, it is the latest stage of capitalism in its postindustrial form, that is a stage characterized by the predominance of the services, technology and information. On the other side, the postmodern condition expresses a new kind of politics of plurality whereby political struggles take place on many different levels and cannot be concentrated in any one particular struggle, such as the class struggle. Lyotard did not see the university as central to these struggles. The university is based on the principle of unity, that the diverse forms of knowledge and practices can be unified under a single institution.

Lyotard's stance on the university expressed his political position, which was a postmodern version of Marxism, or Marx read through the eyes of Nietzsche: the disintegration of the cognitive and institutional structures of modernity has been completed and radical politics must accept this. This was no less a declaration of the end of the university. The university was too much implicated in the control of society by the state. Thus Lyotard dismisses the entire neohumanist tradition, such as Humboldt's vision of the integration of teaching and research. He hoped that in the postmodern condition the university, along with the capitalist state, would wither away. Lyotard's hostility to the modernist project is perhaps best seen in the context of the restructuring of the French university system in the aftermath of the events of May 1968 when the government established new universities firmly under the control of the state and in which teaching would be integrated into the world of research. For Lyotard, teaching has a counter-revolutionary function, while research can offer subversive possibilities. It was clear that he was on the side of subversion, and indeed his book on the postmodern condition was written in this spirit, as a report on the state of knowledge. As Steve Fuller puts it: 'This sentiment neatly epitomises the postmodern normative posture – one that celebrates the endless proliferation of inquires and condemns the submission of this "information explosion" to the institutional containment of the university, which, after all, presupposes a clearly bounded "universe of discourse" that is traversed in a "curriculum"' (Fuller, 1999b: 583). Universities for Lyotard are based on bounded discourses – such as the department, the faculty, the curriculum – and modern forms of legitimation, such as the lecture and professorial authority.

Lyotard saw the reality of the postmodern condition to be the dominance of the performativity principle. This is not unlike the thesis of the new production of knowledge in the sense that it is the use of knowledge that legitimates its production. As I have already mentioned, Lyotard's stance on the postmodern condition was ambivalent, being simultaneously a form of capitalist restructuring and the ground of a new radical politics. This ambivalence feeds off the fact that whether the issue is economics or politics we are living at a time in which everything has been de-legitimated. This condition is the condition of the possibility of politics in a new key.

The de-legitimation of knowledge is one of the most pervasive aspects of the de-legitimation of authority. In the postmodern condition, the de-legitimation of knowledge came about as a result of the predominance of the performance criterion. One aspect of this is the depersonalization of knowledge. Thus, 'a professor is no more competent than memory bank networks in transmitting established knowledge, no more competent than interdisciplinary teams in imagining new moves or new games' (Lyotard, 1984: 53). In this view the university can be neither the site of communication, as in Habermas, nor the site of an alternative and more reflexive kind of symbolic capital as in Bourdieu. This is because the essence of the university is the modern attempt to construct totalizing narrative. As we have seen, both Bourdieu and Habermas in their different ways held on to the possibility of narrative as the ground of the university. This is what is rejected by Lyotard. The result in concrete terms is the impossibility of the neohumanist ideal of the university. Teaching is rejected as a meta-narrative and research must be released in the form of a plurality of little narratives.

This notion of the impossibility of the curriculum has become a major theme in postmodern critiques of education (Aronowitz and Giroux, 1991;

Donald, 1992; Usher and Edwards, 1994; Smith and Wexler, 1995). Not only is there a rejection of the idea of a common curriculum but there is also a growing suspicion of the possibility of a universal education. Postmodern critics of education typically argue for greater diversity and plurality in the teaching curriculum. The postmodern world is about choice and this ought to be available in education as it is in other aspects of life. Andy Green has criticized postmodern arguments concerning the possibility of a viable curriculum: 'Postmodernism has little value to offer educational theory but it has many dangers. The greatest of these is that the logic of the postmodern argument points towards an individualistic educational consumerism in many respects similar to that advocated by the free-marketeers of the new Right' (Green, 1997: 20). In his view, plurality and diversity have prevailed in the English educational system which is the most elitist and hierarchical in the world. Therefore there is no reason to believe that the diversity advocated by postmoderns would be any different.

In my view there is little difference between Lyotard's vision of the university and the spectre of academic capitalism discussed in the previous chapter. Both express the disintegration of the university. Lyotard's vision of the death of the university has become a reality in the modularization of courses, the privileging of research over teaching, the transition from disciplinary research within the context of distinct departments to postdisciplinary research. As Fuller argues: 'A vivid reminder of this development is the ease with which the research units of some academic departments can be transferred from the institutional setting of the university to another – say, a science park or a corporate facility – without seeming to lose any loss in the translation' (Fuller, 1999b: 586).

Lyotard's rejection of modernity for the political possibilities of the postmodern condition has suffered from a stark contrast between modernity and postmodernity. This is what Zygmunt Bauman has avoided in his characterization of the postmodern university. He argues that the university today is characterized by difference and diversity and therefore there is no point in either demanding a return of the older idea of the university or announcing the end of the university. There can be no *idea* of the university since there are too many different kinds of university. The older idea of the university, the Humboldt vision, was based on the assumption that there was one single institutional basis to the university and that therefore the idea of the university could be embodied in an institutional form. According to Bauman, the plurality and multivocality of universities is something liberating and could be the basis of new dialogues. 'It is the good luck of the universities are that there are so many of them, that there are no two exactly alike, and that inside every university there is a mind-boggling variety of departments, schools, styles of thoughts, styles of conversation, and even styles of stylistic concerns' (Bauman, 1997: 25). Bauman has recognized more fully than Lyotard that in the postmodern condition there is a greater diversity of universities and kinds of knowledge. This is an important point because it accepts the difference between knowledge and information on the one side and, on the other, the difference between teaching and research. Lyotard undoubtedly had one kind of university in mind, the pre-1968 Sorbonne. In the past three decades there has been a proliferation of different kinds of university such that there is no one dominant form. In some, teaching is privileged, in others research takes priority and in yet others vocational training is prioritized over liberal education. In the context of his wider theory of postmodernity, Bauman's position might be summarized by saying that the decline in the legislator's monopoly of the knowledge, which was tied to the framework of modernity and the nation state, releases the university from its older functions (Bauman, 1987, 1991, 1992, 1993, 1995).

Peter Scott (1995, 1997) has also defended a weak version of the postmodern thesis, the theme of a volume edited by Anthony Smith and Frank Webster (1997a), *The Postmodern University? Contested Visions of the Higher Education in Society*. In Scott's view the postmodern university is characterized above all by 'contested knowledge' and the emergence of local knowledges. Under the conditions of postmodernity, knowledge no longer enjoys the autonomy it previously had under the elite culture of modernity when it was tied to a privileged social stratum; there are many kinds of knowledge and there is growing scepticism about the claims of universalism made on behalf of the values of cognitive rationality. The postmodern university that is emerging will not simply reproduce the old hierarchies but will produce new structures of authority; at the same time this shift in power structures will be a source of self-assertion for many people who can turn to higher education to construct alternative identities. In short, the postmodern university will cease to be the domain of elites; the kind of knowledge it produces will have to compete with other kinds of knowledge.

At this point, it might be considered that postmodern thought in general has major problems with the very idea 'higher' education, which is the basis of the university. Postmodernism rejects the hierarchical ordering of knowledge into higher and lower forms, basic and applied forms of knowledge. One of the major proponents of postmodernism, Jacques Derrida, has offered an interesting interpretation of the identity of the university and the politics of teaching and research. In an essay based on a lecture given at Cornell University, 'The Principle of Reason: The University in the Eyes of its Pupils', Derrida criticized the 'frontier between basic and oriented research' (Derrida, 1983). The background to this lecture was Derrida's intellectual contribution to the creation of the International College of Philosophy in Paris. Historically, the university of modernity, he argued, has been legitimated by reference to the principle of reason: 'one cannot think the possibility of the modern university, without inquiring into that event, that institution of the principle of reason' (Derrida, 1983: 8). But this is to raise the issue of the foundation of the university and it is this that is problematical, for all acts of grounding must be severely criticized since this disguises an alternative reality, a different 'community of thought.'

Poststructuralism, with which Derrida's name has been associated, rejects both the instrumentalism of knowledge – which is represented by oriented or applied research – and the idea of a foundational kind of knowledge. Oriented research is programmed by utilitarian goals. Calling applied research 'oriented,' as is more common in France, or 'finalized', as in Germany, does not alter the fact that it is instrumentalized, Derrida argues. But basic research, too, must itself be questioned and not simply counterposed to applied research. His essay is a plea for a space for a new kind of self-questioning 'thought' that does not justify itself by reference to a principle of reason. In his view, the university has been too much dominated by the non-academic:

> Neither in its medieval nor in its modern form has the university disposed freely of its own absolute autonomy and of the rigorous conditions of its own unity. During more than eight centuries, 'university' has been the name given by a society to a sort of supplementary body that at one and the same time it wanted to project outside itself and to keep jealously to itself, to emancipate and to control. And in a certain way it has done so: it has produced society's scenography, its views, conflicts, contradictions, its play and its differences, and also its desire for organic union in a total body.
>
> (Derrida, 1983: 19)

Derrida argues that the opposition between basic and applied research is a fiction since the reality of research is quite different. It is not possible any more to distinguish between technology and science. Technoscience has become a reality, confirming what Heidegger said of technology, namely that the essence of technology is more than the technological:

> It is impossible, for example, to distinguish programs that one would like to consider 'worthy', or even technically profitable for humanity, from other programs that would be destructive. This is not new; but never before has so-called basic scientific research been so deeply committed to aims that are at the same time military aims. The very essence of the military, the limits of military technology and even the limits of its accountability are no longer definable.
>
> (Derrida, 1983: 12)

Derrida makes clear that he is not opposed to oriented research as such but is searching for a new community of thought:

> This thinking must also unmask – an infinite task – all the ruses of end-orienting reason, the paths by which apparently disinterested research can find itself indirectly reappropriated, reinvested by programs of all sorts. That does not mean that 'orientation' is bad in itself and that it must be combated, far from it. Rather, I am defining the necessity for a new way of educating students that will prepare them to undertake

new analyses in order to evaluate these ends and to choose, when possible, among them all.

(Derrida, 1983: 16)

Drawing on the works on higher education by the great German philosophers Kant, Nietzsche and Heidegger, Derrida argues that the essential feature of academic responsibility must not be professional education. Derrida is close to Kant in his conception of the responsibility of the university but does not accept Kant's appeal to the principle of reason that is embodied in the discipline of philosophy (Derrida, 1992). His essay has been influential in shaping deconstructionist theories of the university (Rand, 1992; Kanuf, 1997; Wortham, 1999). However Derrida's deconstructive approach has not been influential in debates about the postmodern university, which would appear to be more in tune with Lyotard's stance.

The university in ruins?

Within the context of poststructuralist thought, the most far-reaching interpretation of the postmodern university is Bill Readings's *The University in Ruins* (Readings, 1996). He describes the contemporary university as 'posthistorical' rather than postmodern in order to show that the university has outlived its historical justification and is today devoid of a mission in society. That historical justification, which derived from the Enlightenment, was to produce, protect and inculcate national culture. The modern university was designed to produce national subjects, and the decline of the nation state puts into question the university. The university and the state are both modern creations and the fate of the former is inextricably linked to that of the latter. Today the university is becoming a different kind of institution, shaped by corporate capitalism instead of the nation state. Consequently it is up for grabs, he argues. Globalization has put an end to the university of modernity as it has to the nation state. 'The University no longer has to safeguard and propagate national culture, because the nation state is no longer the major site at which capital reproduces itself' (Readings, 1996: 13). In place of national culture the university has found new ideology in the corporate ideology of 'excellence'. With this shift from culture to excellence the university as an institution shifts from being an ideological apparatus of the nation state to being a relatively independent bureaucratic system. The pursuit of excellence allows the university to use the commodity form to regulate the production of knowledge. Although claiming to make the university more accountable to society, the strategies that are adopted are not those of accountability but of accounting.

What is postmodern in the posthistorical university? The most striking feature is the emergence of 'dereferentialization'. Terms such as the 'culture', 'excellence', even the 'university' cease to have specific referents. Every university and every academic can become excellent just as today everything can be considered cultural, a term that no longer refers to a particular kind of content. '"Excellence" is rapidly becoming the watch-word of the University' (Readings, 1996: 21). This is an internally defined unit of value that has no external referent and can be reproduced in end-less discourses. In his view it has become a new integrating device, but one that erases the distinction between academe and capitalism: 'the appeal to excellence marks the fact that there is no longer any idea of the University, or rather that the idea has now lost all content. As a non-referential unit of value entirely internal to the system, excellence marks nothing more than the moment of technology's self-reflection' (Readings, 1996: 39). In the posthistorical university the student is a consumer.

Readings's account of the emergence of the posthistorical university is not couched in nostalgic terms. There can be no return to the modern university given the reality of globalization and the alleged demise of the nation state: 'We have to recognize that the University is a ruined institution' (Readings, 1996: 169). The current situation should lead us to recognize that a new space can be opened up for the university. The posthistorical university ceases to be a model of the ideal society, as it was in the Enlight-enment tradition. It is now possible to rethink the university without recourse to notions of unity, truth, consensus and communication. The alternative model that Readings seeks is a 'dissensual community'. Drawing on post-modern theories of community, such as those of Nancy (1990), Blanchot (1988) and Agamben (1993), Readings argues for a notion of community as absence, a yet to be achieved social bond (see Delanty, 2000a). The post-modern conception of community is not organic but based on difference in the sense that the self is perceived through the recognition of otherness and is therefore incomplete in itself. As far as teaching is concerned, this means that teaching must be more than the transmission of scientific know-ledge. Instead of the transmission of 'truth', teaching should be concerned with 'justice'. That is, teaching should be a matter of dialogue rather than the reproduction of a system of thought. Rather than looking for a new interdisciplinary space that will unify everything in place of the collapse of disciplinary knowledge, Readings proposes a shifting disciplinary structure that leaves open the question of how it all fits together. In sum, Readings argues: 'the University will have to become one place, among others, where the attempt is made to think the social bond without recourse to a unifying idea, whether culture or the state' (Readings, 1996: 191).

Like many postmodern arguments, Readings's thesis is largely a counter-thesis, a critique of the prevailing order and does not offer anything of substance for those seeking an alternative institutional embodiment. His critique of the neomanagerial discourse of excellence is what his book will be best remembered for, but like many theories of the death of the university it suffers from exaggerated claims. He exaggerates the end of the nation state as a result of globalization. There is some truth to his thesis that the university is no longer based on a historical project to create national sub-jects and that instead the university has reified its heritage by trying to imitate the technocorporate order by creating consumers. Knowledge may indeed be becoming commodified as information, but knowledge takes too many forms for the informational mode to be the dominant one. However, globalization does not necessarily run against the state. As I argued in the previous chapter, globalization can strengthen the state in certain key aspects while undermining it in others. The university as an institution is still largely framed in the image of the state though it is true that it no longer serves to reproduce national culture. An important consideration in this respect is that globalization can strengthen local resistances to global processes (Robertson, 1992). Thus cities can find themselves in positions of new power. This clearly has implications for universities, many of which try to steer a course between national and regional commitments.

This situation has not been determined entirely by the technocorporate culture of the posthistorical university as Readings claims. The university ceased to be a codifier of national culture much earlier. Readings's analysis neglects the fact that the university has been a crucial site of social and cultural citizenship for much of the twentieth century and that it was also one of the main locations in society where democratic values were developed. Although his analysis of the counter-culture of the 1960s does some justice to this, his approach too strongly stresses fundamental institutional and epistemic ruptures in the tradition of the university. My contention, in contrast, is that not only is there more continuity than Readings allows for but, more importantly, that there is more than one force shaping the contemporary university. Corporate culture's discourse of excellence is only one force. In these accounts the postmodern university is more than a zone of the accumulation of capital. As Smith and Webster conclude in their survey of the postmodern university: 'These trends cannot be denied as matters of empirical fact. However, against the interpretation that the university is being overturned, it can be insisted that the virtual monopoly the university retains in the awarding of legitimate credentials testifies to academe's vitality (Smith and Webster, 1997b: 107). Derek Bok, who served as president of Harvard from 1971 to 1991, believes that the university, although no longer an ivory tower, is still a powerful institution in society and is capable of adjusting to changed circumstances (Bok, 1982). While many accounts do remain nostalgic for the traditional model (Pelikan, 1992), the fact that the university has incurred social responsibilities does not mean that its end is in sight or that it ought be disestablished. In sum, I do not think the university is 'in ruins', to use Readings's metaphor. It is instead a site of conflicts. It is more a battleground than a ruin, as David Harvey (1998: 116) pointed out in a review of Readings's book. Given that there are more than 3,600 institutions of higher education in North America employing more than half a million faculty it is difficult to speak of the end of the university (Bender, 1997: 18). In my view, what a realistic assessment of the university suggests is more a constructivist perspective on new institutional possibilities than a deconstructivist one. In the following chapter I examine some aspects of the constructivist condition of the university today.

10

The New Politics of Knowledge: Culture Wars, Identity and Multiculturalism

In the previous three chapters I looked at the impact of changes in the economy on the university. It was noted that the new production of knowledge under the impact of globalization and neoliberalism has greatly altered the environment in which the university exists. The response of the university has been an embracing of market values in the formation of a triple alliance of university, industry and state. The postmodern critique of the university has mostly been directed against this development which is deemed to point towards the end of the modern university, for the university like the state is held to be a product of modernity. The decline of modernity – in its institutional and cognitive structures – is most visibly represented in the declining significance of the university as the site of knowledge. In this chapter I examine another facet of the postmodern scenario: culture wars over identity. The new production of knowledge is not only a matter of market values, the arrival of a new technocorporate culture of manageralism and academic capitalism; it is also about conflicts over identity.

One of the most striking developments in the university since the mid-1980s (more-or-less the same period when universities began to embrace market values) has been the penetration of what once was regarded as the private domain into the public domain of the university. In short, the western university became the site of major culture wars over race, ethnicity, religion and gender. These developments have had major repercussions for academic freedom which can no longer be seen as occupying a neutral space free of politics (Menand, 1997). To an extent this began with the counter-culture of the 1960s when universities became political hotbeds of radical democracy. But the debates of that period concerned to a far greater extent the relationship between university and society than those that were to surface in the 1980s. Class and academe made a short-lived alliance in the political movements that became prominent in western campuses in the

late 1960s. With the declining significance of Marxism and the fragmentation of the political ideology of the left, what moved into the vacant space
was culture. If 'all is politics' was the slogan for the generation of the 1960s,
the new catchphrase for the 1980s was to be 'all is culture,' a development
that was epitomized in the overtaking of sociology by cultural studies.

The political mood of the 1980s was shaped on the one side by the New
Right and, on the other side, by a multifarious cultural movement that was
partly a reaction to the market ideology of the New Right and in part a
reaction to the counter-culture of the preceding decades. This new cultural
movement is difficult to specify since it did not take a uniform nature,
combined as it was by a conservative backlash and at the same time embodying a diverse range of left-wing critiques. Postmodernism in a way encapsulated this cultural collage of positions which were never ideologically
coherent, and could not be since what was rejected was precisely any principle of unity. As a critique of the remnants of modernity and the New
Right, postmodernism gave expression to both cultural and political uncertainty and at the same time reflected new currents that began to gain
momentum by the 1990s. Thus, for instance, the increased presence of
globalization in cultural forms of communication and the political significance of the ending of the cold war opened up new perspectives on culture
and society.

It would be wrong to see globalization only in economic terms. As many
theorists have argued, globalization also entails a counter-hegemonic cultural project. While undermining 'from above' the power of states, globalization tends to release 'from below' nations which are consequently no
longer defined by states (see Chapter 8). Thus what is coming to an end in
the post cold war global age is the nation state, that is the fusion of nation
and state. Nations and states are going their separate ways and in this
parting of ways a range of national identities are being released from the
established order of nation states. But the new nationalism is only one
aspect of this unleashing of cultural identity from the older structures of
nation and class. The sociological phenomenon of the present age is that
cultural identity is no longer defined by social structures, be they those of
nation or class. It has lost its reference points as a result of globalization
and the undermining of the state. The modern age was dominated by the
state which was the political form in which all social conflicts developed.
With the institutionalization of class conflict in the welfare state by means
of social citizenship, the state became the final reference point for cultural
and political identity. It was then inevitable that once the state ceased to be
a universal sovereign entity cultural and political identities would be released from this framework.

The university offered the perfect receptacle for the articulation of new
kinds of cultural and political identity from the 1980s onwards. The older
cultural models of society began to collapse and in the resulting fragmentation of meaning, social groups began to experiment with new models. As an
older modernity began to give way to a new one, the university was the

incubator of new cultural identities. In the following sections I examine some of these: firstly, the culture wars around the curriculum, affirmative action and political correctness; secondly, the rise of cultural studies as a new discipline; and thirdly I look at some alternative scenarios in the context of reflexivity and cosmopolitanism.

Culture wars and the university

The debate about identity in western universities, but in particular in American universities, can be seen in the context of the crisis of modernity. It is a theme in much of recent social and political thought, and is especially pronounced in postmodernist writing, that the contemporary crisis is one of the identity of the self. In modernity the self was relatively secure in its identity and remained largely untouched by critical and reflexive developments. Modernity was based on the triumph of subjectivity over objectivity, be it nature, God, the state. In the name of nation, class, the individual the modern age asserted the fundamental priority of the self over everything else, even over 'the other'. The self was, to use Bauman's term, a 'legislator' (Bauman, 1987). It was this that lent to its project both an emancipatory edge and a violent thrust, since efforts to liberate the self from established forms of authority frequently became indistinguishable from campaigns to vanquish 'the other'. The distinctive feature of late modernity, or the postmodern period if one prefers that designation, is the extension of the modernist critique into the domain of the self which can no longer be taken to be self-legislating. Thus it is not one single self that emerges from modernity but a multiplicity of selves. The reconciliation of these selves is the basis of postmodern culture wars.

The university has been one of the main sites where these battles have been fought. Three developments have contributed to this: (1) the erosion of the distinction between the private and the public, (2) the growing challenge of cultural citizenship to social citizenship, and (3) the politicization of multiculturalism.

First, the older divide between the private world and the public domain has become blurred in recent times as a result of the rise of a range of new cultural politics, principally those associated with feminism and the politics of 'difference'. The private realm can no longer be said to be prepolitical given the immense politcization of gender roles and the assault on patriarchy. Although it has for much of its history been a prepolitical institution, the university has traditionally been part of public life. Bourgeois privatistic values found in academe a suitable resonance – individualistic achievement, status and prestige, professional renown, *Bildung* or the cultural shaping of personality – but the institution on the whole reflected the ideology of meritocratic reward for individual achievement and in it, too, national values were cultivated. The new cultural politics of identity have broken down the separation of the space of public life from private life. The university today must address a whole range of problems specific to what was once confined to the private domain. What has occurred is the emergence of institutional reflexivity in the sense of what Giddens calls 'self-monitoring' (Giddens, 1991). Examples of institutional reflexivity are the increased salience of identity politics over gender and race in the university. In the United States the debate over affirmative action and political correctness has transformed the institution of the university. The ideological battles of the late 1960s are over and have been replaced by these identity battles (Graff, 1992). On one side, these debates have made universities more responsive to changes in the wider society, and on the other the new political correctness has transformed the critical business of thought into a kind of anti-intellectualism, thinly disguised as anti-elitism. But there is no doubt that the new politics has been a positive development. Universities are increasingly operating self-monitoring practices with ever more student representation and responsiveness to the demands of the student body. Most universities have policies on anti-sexist and anti-racist language codes. Battles of 'intellectual copyright' and harassment are becoming a new zone of legal contention, thereby giving new roles to lawyers rather than committees in resolving conflicts and in regulating the conditions under which research is conducted (Gibbons *et al.*, 1984: 37). Like other institutions in the private and public sectors, universities are also becoming more flexible: the new production of knowledge is forcing universities to leave behind the era of hierarchical power relations in favour of more reflexive ones.

Second, social citizenship is today being challenged by cultural citizenship (Isin and Wood, 1999; Delanty, 2000b). The political impetus of modernity was the search for equality which eventually became the basis of social citizenship in the welfare state. Today the centrality of equality has been challenged by demands for difference. To be equal and to be different are the two main problems facing citizenship today (Touraine, 1997, 1998). Education has become a major site of this double conflict. Demands for affirmative action have undermined the older principle of equality of opportunity (Cahn, 1995; Bacchi, 1996). For many groups a commitment to equality is not adequate in that universities reflect their social environment. In the United States, such debates have been particularly pronounced since there, more than in Europe, factors other than class have greater political visibility. In Britain the debate about making universities more representative of their social environment has mostly been about class; the representation of ethnic groups, cultural minorities of various types, has been less pronounced. Although a debate has revolved around people with disabilities, British universities have not embarked on affirmative action policies with regard to either student or staff recruitment. Most institutions of higher education are, however, committed to policies of equality of opportunity. In short, cultural citizenship in the sense of positive discrimination for particular groups has not been a feature of British or continental European universities. In fact, in most European countries affirmative action is illegal, since it entails the official recording of ethnic markers and in many ways contradicts the established policies of equality of opportunity. In the United States, where such issues are more prominent, the debate on affirmative action has continued, with several notable changes in policy, such as the decision of the University of California, Los Angeles, to abandon affirmative action in student recruitment (Sacks and Thiel, 1995).

The debate on affirmative action will continue but it is likely that some of the issues will change. Until now it has mostly been seen as a means of increasing the visible representation of non-whites. But the problem with this is that the increase in non-whites does not necessarily bring about the representation of marginalized *views*. This is because, as Fuller has observed, members of marginalized groups who might benefit from affirmative action policies are more likely to want to conform to the dominant paradigms and will not want to admit that their success is due to their ethnic, gender or class identity (Fuller, 1999b: 593–4). The affirmative action debate has not fully addressed the question of the ends of such policies; for instance, is the end to promote a diversity of 'views', to overcome discrimination or to overcome social disadvantage, or to increase social representations? Problems of increasing the social representation of marginalized groups run into the problems of doing what multiculturalists object to: essentializing groups. This is an inevitable reifying consequence of the need to define groups.

Third, multiculturalism has taken on a new meaning. The conventional understanding of multiculturalism is that cultural diversity is largely to be institutionalized in the private domain, with the public sphere as the realm of a shared political culture. In this model, group differences are tolerated in so far as there is a trade-off between cultural identity and political identity. In a multicultural society, what has been pluralized is cultural identity. To varying degrees, most western societies adopt some version of this, with France taking a more extreme commitment to the absolute universality of the public domain as the location of republican values. In the United States, the shared political culture of the public domain is more open to particularistic values, but there too the basic commitment to a common culture is apparent. Only in Canada has there been any official attempt to dissolve this trade-off in the form of an official recognition of ethnic groups in favour of whom the public authorities may positively discriminate. With the growing salience of cultural citizenship the dominant liberal and republican model of multiculturalism has been transformed. For some time the liberal foundations of multiculturalism as an integrating force has been the subject of growing debate (Schlesinger, 1992; Smelser and Alexander, 1999). This has had a huge impact on the university, which previously existed outside the multicultural society, for the university was allegedly based on only one culture, the common heritage of humankind. The politicization of multiculturalism has destroyed this illusion of universality. Nowhere has the onslaught on liberal multiculturalism been more apparent than in the curriculum. The debate in the humanities on the western canon and the debate on hidden histories in history and the social sciences has transformed the teaching programmes of the leading American universities (Fish, 1995). One thing that emerges from these debates, which have been characteristically American, is that political energies have been dominated more by ethnicity than by class. However, it is unlikely that ethnicity will overshadow gender, and in the view of some, America is already a 'postethnic' society, with other divisions but also common ground emerging (Hollinger, 1995; Smelser and Alexander, 1999).

Views differ greatly on the cognitive implications of such debates for the university. For some, such as Bloom in his controversial book *The Closing of the American Mind*, the new culture wars are a betrayal of traditional forms of knowledge, such as the western canon in literature (Bloom, 1987). This too is the position of D'Souza in his tellingly titled *Illiberal Education: the Politics of Race and Sex on Campus* and Kimball in *Tenured Radicals* (D'Souza, 1991; Kimball, 1990; see also Alter, 1989). Others, for instance the *Report of the Gulbenkian Commission on the Restructuring of the Social Sciences*, see it in more open terms as a sign of the relevance of the university to society (Wallerstein *et al.*, 1996). In his book *Beyond the Culture Wars*, Graff argues that the university today is vastly superior to the restricted university of a few decades ago because of these debates. That the crisis of culture is occurring in education is positive: 'It is a sign of the university's vitality that the crisis is happening so openly there. The academic curriculum has become a prominent arena of cultural conflict because it is a microcosm, as it should be, of the clash of cultures in America as a whole' (Graff, 1992). It might be suggested that the politicization of the curriculum is a reflection of the transformation of the dominant cultural models of western society. For Graff the challenge is to teach the conflicts themselves: 'the best solution to today's conflicts over culture is to teach the conflicts themselves, making them part of our object of study and using them as a new kind of organizing principle to give the curriculum the clarity and focus that almost all sides now agree it lacks' (Graff, 1992: 12).

The turn to culture and theory

Throughout the humanities and social sciences in the 1980s and 1990s there has been a revival of theory. Why is this? In literary studies, in history and in sociology, theory has surfaced in what had been empirical domains of enquiry? Graff offers a profound view on this turn to theory:

> We do not normally reflect on our assumptions and practices unless something forces us to, however, and what usually provides that stimulus is conflict, some challenge to promises that previously seemed so obvious that we did not have to be aware of them as such. 'Theory' is a name for the kind of self-consciousness that results when a community ceases to agree on these heretofore seemingly obvious, 'normal' assumptions.
>
> (Graff, 1992: 55)

I agree with his diagnosis that the revival of theory is related to the erosion of any consensus on what constitutes such concepts as politics, tradition, universality, culture, literature. Theory is not confined to academic intellectuals but goes on in society as a whole in the encounter between different orders of justification, as Boltanski and Thevenot argue (1999). The revival of theory can be seen as a reflexive response to the wider transformation of cultural models in society. Attacks on theory are often, then, disguised attacks on cultural change (Alter, 1989).

In the context of the eruption of cultural wars there is one development that justifies some discussion, namely cultural studies. The significance of this new discipline is that it has taken some of the ground from history, literary studies and sociology. This ground is culture, which is in the traditional humanities and social sciences and has always been relatively delineated. In sociology, culture generally refers to values, norms and beliefs, distinct from society and politics. In anthropology, culture referred to primitive 'cultures' as distinct from modern 'society' and was characterized by an immediate identification of culture and society. In intellectual history, culture as a domain of ideas was generally held to be distinct from the material level of 'civilization'. In literary studies, culture was embodied in the western canon and its national subtypes. Cultural studies emerged out of the democratization of culture, in the recognition that all forms of value creation can be called culture. It was also a response to postmodernism, the notion that discourses do not have to contain an external meaning such as that intended by a particular subjectivity. According to Readings, culture as discourse devoid of meaning fitted the ethos of the university in the age of corporate capitalism. His thesis is that cultural studies utilizes the same understanding of culture as in the technocorporate ethos of excellence: it is a discourse devoid of a reference. 'Cultural Studies, in its current incarnation as an institutional project for the 1990s, proceeds from a certain sense that no more knowledge can be produced, since there is nothing to be said about culture that is not itself cultural, and vice versa. Everything is culturally determined, as it were, and culture ceases to mean anything as such' (Readings, 1996: 17). Like the rhetoric of excellence, culture now has no meaning because everything can become culture. Readings's point is that culture once defined the historical mission of the university. In this historical project culture was held to be the culture of the national state and with the decline of the state, culture loses its ability to define the rationale and identity of the university: 'Cultural Studies must be understood to arise when culture ceases to be the animating principle of the University and . . . becomes instead an object of study among others, a discipline rather than a metadisciplinary idea' (Readings, 1996: 92).

This may be a harsh judgement on cultural studies. In my view, despite his highly perceptive account of changes in the legitimating function of culture, Readings misses the point concerning the significance of the cultural turn in the human and social sciences. Although it lacks the disciplinary strength of, for instance, sociology with its established methodological and theoretical approaches and rooted in a historical tradition of thought, cultural studies must be seen in the wider context of the revival of interest in culture in the human and cultural sciences, for the impact of the cultural turn has also been strongly felt in sociology. Across a whole range of theories much of contemporary theorizing concerns the question of major cultural transformation in the symbolic and cognitive structures of late modern societies (Delanty, 1999; Strydom, 1999b). Indeed, the revival of theory in the social sciences and humanities is connected to the transformation of cultural models. The point, then, should be that the recent interest in culture and the revival of theory are not done justice by cultural studies. Cultural studies, under the impact of the confluence of postmodernism, postcolonialism and multiculturalism, has tended to focus instead on the question of the self and other. Much of multiculturalism has been inspired by Edward Said's book *Orientalism* (Said, 1979). His approach might be described as selective essentialism: western thinking about the Orient and the non-western world attributes to it an essentialism, which is merely a western construction and a reflection of imperialist ambitions. Thus all western writing about the Orient is dismissed as expressing a desire for intellectual mastery. Yet, this theory of culture as a constructed discourse, in which the other is always a fabrication of the self, is separated from politics, as is witnessed by Said's support for the Palestinian political cause. As Fuller (1999a: 68) remarks, it would seem that Said has reinvented Max Weber's notoriously sharp separation of science and politics. However, postcolonial studies has now largely overcome this separation: if all is culture in post-modern theory; all is politics once again in postcolonialism. Thus, margin-ality studies, women's studies, African American studies, gay and lesbian studies have on the whole dominated recent cultural studies. In general, cultural studies has been animated by the desire to include the previously excluded into the category of culture. But this is hardly subversive for, as Readings (1996) argued, culture no longer matters given that it is now capitalism and not the state that rules and capitalism is not perturbed by cultural critique. Indeed, as Schumpeter argued: 'unlike any other type of society, capitalism inevitably and by virtue of the very logic of its civiliza-tion creates, educates and subsidizes a vested interest in social unrest' (Schumpeter, 1954: 146).

In my view, current developments in sociology and, more broadly, in social theory address the question of culture from a more adequate theor-etical standpoint than notions of inclusion and exclusion, self and other. Although there is little consensus on the meaning of culture, social theory offers some innovating ways of rethinking the relationship between the cultural and the social. The ideas of discursivity, reflexivity, creativity in contemporary social thought offer challenging ways of understanding the present time. Crucial to all these accounts is the centrality of communication. The cultural turn must be seen in the context of the much more historic-ally long-run linguistic turn in modern thought. With its origins in the hermeneutical tradition coming from the later philosophy of Wittengenstein and Heidegger, the tradition of symbolic interaction from George Herbert Mead, poststructuralism and, more recently, the theories of Searle, the critical communication theories of Habermas and Apel, culture and language have been closely connected. The philosophy of language opened modern thought to language as a level of social reality. The significance of this for social science is only beginning to become apparent. A view is emerging which sees contemporary societies as increasingly integrated through communication, rather than by ideology, dominant value systems, elites, or institutions. This means that choices have to be made. In order for the self – be it the individual or the collective actor – to make sense of their situation and make cultural choices they need to have access to information and participation in communication. Contra rational choice theory, it is important to recognize that these choices are culturally mediated. Contemporary societies are culturally highly mediated in a particular sense. While all societies are culturally mediated in that symbolic and cognitive structures offer various interpretations of reality, contemporary society places a stronger role on individual or a group's capacity to make interpretations from the available cultural structures. Contemporary society is characterized by a high degree of complexity and abstractness, and because of this, reality is rarely directly experienced. Therefore it is not always a matter of making straightforward choices. The cultural mechanisms by which social reality is mediated is communication. Thus late modern societies need to devise communicative structures capable of matching the needs of people for cultural interpretation in order to make choices on the many options that exist for social action in our highly differentiated and complex societies. It might be suggested, then, that the contemporary challenge of cultural reflexivity consists of the extension of communication into the realms most central to the working of society. It is in this context that the question of cultural citizenship arises for the university.

Beyond instrumentalism and relativism

Two forces are transforming the university today: instrumentalism and relativism. In previous chapters we have seen how market forces have forced the university into a new instrumentalism of purpose. In this chapter I have discussed some of the key features of another path of change: the descent into relativism. Culture wars and the growing relativism in the humanities and social sciences have eroded the Enlightenment conception of the university at precisely the time that market forces are entering the university. Against the conservative critique of cultural politics, my interpretation is that we have to accept much of it and explore ways in which these battles can be seen as renewing the moral purpose of the university as opposed to simply eroding the very possibility of the university having a moral purpose. However, the solution, as I argue below, is only partly cultural. The other aspect of the contemporary challenge to the university is the question of overcoming the growing instrumentalism that has crept into it due to market forces.

The question more fundamentally is what constitutes a principle of unity. Neither cultural politics nor the market offer a principle of unity. The politics of cultural identity is fundamentally divisive and does not offer a means of restoring any sense of moral purpose. My point is that although the culture wars may have broken down, the older cultural moulds of the university, the political and ethical imagination that they offer, cannot be a basis for the identity of the university. Since we also cannot retreat into the lost world of the nineteenth century, other possibilities need to be explored. It is evident, too, that the market cannot offer a principle of unity. My contention is that the university must find ways to go beyond both relativism and instrumentalism. Since these are the two most powerful movements in contemporary society, the university is assured of an important role in defining the direction of change in the realms of culture and in economy. Having lost its once privileged role in defining the national culture, the university can take up this more cosmopolitan function. This it can do because the instrumentalism of the market and relativism in culture are today global forces, no longer specific to any national society. The university has the chance to become a major player in the shaping of cosmopolitan culture out of the diverse elements that characterize globalization. However, it is crucial to recognize that this cosmopolitanism is not purely cultural, it is also technological and economic. The role of the university with respect to technological and cultural citizenship is discussed in the following conclusion.

Conclusion: Knowledge, Citizenship and Reflexivity

In this book I have been arguing that universities are losing their role as the sole site of knowledge production, for knowledge is now being produced, or at least shaped, by many other social actors. But this does not mean the demise of the university which instead becomes more and more drawn into the communicative structure of society. Although it is still one of the most important *producers* of knowledge, it is not the main *user* of knowledge. In the knowledge society the users of knowledge extend over a wide range of institutions and social groups. Knowledge is central to the information economy, to telecommunication systems, to technological systems, to politics, to everyday life. However, it is crucial to see that our knowledge societies are also characterized by the extension of knowledge into the cultural domain. This is because it is produced and used within publicly structured communication. In my view this is what makes the knowledge society more than an information society in Castells's (1996) sense of the term or a knowledge society in the specific sense used by Stehr (1994). The knowledge society refers to a situation in which knowledge is being used to produce knowledge and the conditions of knowledge production are no longer controlled by the mode of knowledge itself. In this reflexive application of knowledge to itself, something else is also being generated: the production of new cognitive fields. These extend beyond knowledge as such, that is knowledge in the sense of what is or what might be known, bodies or branches of knowledge or what might be more generally characterized as information, to include new schemes of classification in the sense of cultural models making possible the interpretation of the natural, social and subjective worlds. In the knowledge society, cognitive processes not only produce knowledge as content but also give rise to new cognitive structures and identities, a deeper and more far-reaching epistemic shift in horizons. This thesis implies, then, that the role of the university is enhanced, not undermined, in the knowledge society, for the university occupies a space in which different discourses interconnect.

In theory, the role of the university could be conceived in terms of the interconnectivity of different modes of knowledge but more importantly among the cognitive processes embodied by a whole range of social actors (for example social movements, the public, scientific actors) who produce cultural models and knowledge. In my view, this is the theoretical basis of a communicative understanding of the university. In order to make the connection between communication and knowledge clearer I would like to explore the idea of reflexivity, for according to the argument put forward here, knowledge is becoming more reflexive in so far as it is becoming more linked with communication.

The concept of reflexivity has been a major theme in sociology and social theory since the 1970s (Gouldner, 1971; O'Neill, 1972; Habermas, [1968] 1978; Luhmann, 1990; Bourdieu and Wacquant, 1992) and has also been implicit in postmodern thought (Lawson, 1985) and in more recent work on late modernity. Giddens uses reflexivity to refer to the tendency in late modernity for institutions and individuals to increasingly monitor their action by means of knowledge (Giddens, 1990, 1991). This is represented in the importance of expert systems which offer interpretations of social reality for individuals. This view sees knowledge as a cognitive means by which individuals can invent their own biographies. His broader social theory paints a picture of how knowledge is a means of making agency and structure a more fluid arrangement. Structures are rule systems which require interpretative rule-learning by social actors (Giddens, 1984). Although the relation between this theory of 'structuration' and the theory of reflexive modernity has not been clarified, the suggestion appears to be that knowledge offers the possibility of the reflexive constitution of institutions. Ulrich Beck (1992) has offered a similar view on reflexivity, though one that stresses more its critical thrust. Distinguishing between primary scientization and reflexive scientization, he argues that while, in the past, knowledge was used to act upon an object – for instance nature – today it is being used to act upon itself. This kind of reflexivity in science is mirrored in growing reflexivity in society which grows distrustful of organized science. Science, in short, becomes a system of public knowledge. Like the fall of high culture, science has entered public discourse in the universal crisis of the risk society. Thus whereas Giddens stresses reflexivity embodied in institutions and in particular in expert systems, Beck emphasizes reflexivity as a critical force in society as a result of the collapse of the rationality of science (see Beck *et al.*, 1994).

Building upon these conceptions of reflexivity, I want to use the term in a way that stresses its transformative force with respect to cognitive structures as opposed to a perspective focused on either agency or structure. Reflexivity is enhanced by the experience of crisis in cognitive structures. In a useful contribution to the debate on reflexivity, May distinguishes between what he calls endogenous reflexivity and referential reflexivity, the former pertaining to an agent's understanding of the knowledge that is used in the immediate context of the life-world and the latter to a process of re-cognition in which knowledge generated allows the social actor to gain a better understanding of their situation (May, 1999, 2000). In contrast, my conception of reflexivity extends beyond the level of the individual social actor to the expression of crisis in public communication and discourse in which intersubjectively shared assumptions are problematized in open-ended discourses. In this use of the term, which is more constructivist and less self-referential, the reflexive moment refers to the articulation of crisis and social construction by processes that are far from being under the control of any social actor.

The upshot of this is that reflexivity entails a relation to the communication of problems and the experience of contingency. It can be seen in the relation between knowledge and society. Thus expert systems of various kinds and publicly structured systems of communication are reflexively linked in the formulation of problems, the production and utilization of knowledge. Crucial to an understanding of this thesis is the openness of knowledge, an openness that is linked to the incompleteness of communication. In other words, there is something between the level of knowledge production and the level of knowledge utilization by social actors. The space between these two levels is the space of cognitive transformation. It is this level that is not adequately theorized in the various accounts of the new production of knowledge where the assumption in general is that knowledge production and wider cognitive structures have reached the level of 'finalization' and, as a result, knowledge can be reduced to its 'uses'.

The relationship between users and producers is more complex than often suggested. The two scenarios of 'knowledge as an end' or 'the end of knowledge' do not capture the current situation. Neither the Enlightenment model of knowledge produced for its own end in the splendid isolation of the academy – the ideal of liberal education – nor the postmodern scenario of the end of knowledge in the age of academic capitalism captures the current reality of epistemic change in the sense of cognitive change in cultural models and changes in the mode of knowledge. These accounts are too dominated by the institutional context or by a reductive understanding of knowledge as information. Changes in the role of the state do not fundamentally alter the incompleteness of communication and the openness of knowledge. The importance of the university resides in the fact that it occupies precisely this space in the production and communication of knowledge. I see this space as growing and not declining as a result of changes in technology, in the market, and in the role of the state. As the university may lose some of its functions, for instance its exclusive role in the production of knowledge and more so in the application of knowledge, its role will increase in the communication of knowledge. Reflexive communication is not merely the transmission of an established body of knowledge – for instance, a canon, or basic research – to users in the wider society. It involves the inclusion of as many voices as possible in the construction of knowledge. This is far more than applied knowledge, the so-called Mode 2 type of knowledge. It is a more creative and experimental kind of knowledge and one that is more responsive to the transformation of cultural models. Responsiveness to the market is only one possible reaction to the withdrawal of the state as the exclusive provider of higher education. There is also another kind of reflexivity which comes into play and which may be more representative of the university than Mode 1 knowledge, namely the reflexive encounter of knowledge with cognitive change in cultural models.

Friese and Wagner make an important point is this respect:

> the current critique of knowledge may coincide with the withdrawal of the state as the main sponsor of knowledge of universities. However, that is not what it is about. It proposes a return to emphasize the use of reflexive capacity over the acquisition of information and the erection of solid conceptual structures. As such, it points to a tradition of thinking about the university which is probably as old and as persistent as the institution itself but which has never become dominant.
>
> (Friese and Wagner, 1998: 30)

This reflexive capacity of knowledge, which is not unique to the late modernity, is a different kind of knowledge from either Mode 1 or Mode 2, that is modernist knowledge as an end or the fragmentation of knowledge into its applied uses. Knowledge-seeking in this sense, as Friese and Wagner argue, has always been in danger, but it is constitutively so: 'If there is a specific danger in the current situation, it lies in the fact that much of organized science has forgotten about this, its own constitutive feature and keeps looking for institutional solutions for doing away with the remainder of it' (1998: 30–1). Citing Granel and Lyotard they argue that the university should renew itself as 'a kind of poetic–political–philosophical whirlwind through which historical experience is at work at the knowledge itself' (Granel, 1982: 78, cited in Friese and Wagner, 1998). Or, as Lyotard writes, 'thoughts are clouds ... Thoughts never stop changing their location one with the other' (Lyotard, 1988: 5, cited in Friese and Wagner, 1998). The future of the university lies in preserving this relatively non-institutional space. Seeing the university as the site of reflexively constituted knowledge allows us to appreciate its role in contemporary society. One feature of this is what Barnett has correctly identified as the challenge of living with uncertainty in an age of chaos and supercomplexity (Barnett, 1999; see also Barnett, 1990). The university can allow society to live at greater ease with uncertainty. In his book on the university in an age of supercomplexity, Barnett shows how our frames of thinking are being constantly challenged by cultural, social, political and economic change. The role of the university must be to make sense of this situation of endless change and, secondly, it must enable people to live more effectively in this chaotic world.

Building upon this theory, the argument I have been putting forward in this book is that the challenge of the university today is to have a critical and hermeneutic role in the orientation of cultural models. The university must be capable of giving society a cultural direction. The national state once fulfilled this function, as the Church had earlier. With the diminishing power of national culture at least to provide a sense of cultural direction the university can take on this role. This, it is to be stressed, is a cultural as opposed to a political task, since the university must restrict itself to the hermeneutic encounter of the mode of knowledge with the cultural model of society. Wallerstein argues that the university can be seen as the meeting place of cultures, the universal as the embodiment of the particular, in the sense of particular communities (Wallerstein, 1991: 197). 'World culture', then, is merely the expression of this engagement. The university is the place of cultural resistance, the thesis of Fuller who argues likewise that the university needs to institutionalize opposition. His point is that the university 'should become the clearing house for all the voices that would otherwise be silent or muted beyond recognition' (Fuller, 1999a: 78). I agree that this is one of the roles of the university today, but I do not think that the university is primarily a place of cultural resistance. There is also the question of whether addressing instrumentalism and cultural resistance alone runs the risk of degenerating into subjectivism. Yet there is no denying that the transformation of cultural models is one of the most important tasks of the university and this can succeed only if as many voices as possible can be included. In short, it is a question of cultural citizenship. By this I mean that the role of the university extends beyond knowledge to participation in and the creation of cultural production more broadly. Cultural citizenship refers to the relationship between self and other, that is the rules governing membership of cultural community. While the state – and more generally political community – is the domain of social, political and civic rights, the growing salience of cultural citizenship is more relevant to the university. Today the whole area of cultural rights is becoming more and more important and is manifest in debates about the recognition of group difference and thus of group differentiated rights, the protection of cultural resources such as heritage and language, atonement for historical grievances. In sum, the question of political community is being more and more challenged by the need to rethink the question of cultural community now that it can no longer be assumed that political community rests on a relatively uniform cultural identity. This is an area of cultural contestation that is particularly relevant to the university as an institution concerned with the encounter between knowledge and cognitive structures.

The second function of the university is to make a contribution to what is increasingly being called technological citizenship (Isin and Wood, 1999). Along with cultural citizenship, technological citizenship has become a new form of citizenship, going beyond social citizenship and, indeed also, of cultural citizenship. At the present time technology is shaping the world according to the dictates of capitalism and global markets. As a global force it is not linked to citizenship, which has predominantly been confined to national contexts and has been historically linked to the welfare state. Universities have an important role to play in linking technology to citizenship. Technological citizenship concerns a new terrain of rights relating to the forces unleashed by technological rationality in the media, environment, the internet and information technology, biotechnology, food and water, health. It is more than social citizenship in so far as this has traditionally been understood as access to public goods and guaranteed by the state. Technological citizenship relates more to the global world of what Urry calls mobilities (Urry, 2000). In an age characterized by the mobility of capital, labour, communication, food and images, new kinds of rights will emerge which cannot be organized around the centrality of the state and national societies. It is evident that many of these kinds of rights will increasingly depend on new technologies which will in turn shape the discourse of rights.

The challenge facing the university today is to link cultural reproduction and technological production. In the university as in the wider society these two forces are disengaged. On the one side are battles of cultural identity and on the other a market-driven capitalism is pervading the university, shaping the university in the image of technoscience. In a way this conflict encapsulates the broader conflict of modernity between life-world and system, between culture and power. Against the postmodern interpretation, there is enough evidence to justify the view that the university is able to retain a post-metaphysical principle of unity. I am arguing that this relates to its ability to establish zones of interconnectivity between the opposing domains of technology and culture. In this regard the cosmopolitan faces of citizenship, that is, cultural and technological citizenship, are central to its mission.

If this interpretation is correct then the chances that the university will evolve a new institutional role in society in the twenty-first century are good. As argued above, this will not be a total departure from the modern project any more than the modern project was a departure from the medieval and ancient academy. In fact, the history of the university can be written as the extension of knowledge beyond the realm of ivory tower to the social world. In short, the university now inhabits a postscientific culture. Scientific knowledge is no longer the privileged repository of culture or the sole voice of cultural direction. This means not the end of the university but the beginning of its new role.

This diffusion of knowledge in society has been for much of the modern age a delicate balance between the national and the cosmopolitan faces of the university. The university, as we have seen, served the nation state by codifying national culture, security systems and the accreditation of its professional classes. It was one of the bulwarks of organized modernity. At the end of this period which brought prosperity, security and peace to much of the western world the university became the site for the cultivation of counter-cultural values, and the ethos of pluralization found in it a foothold that was to prove crucial to the world-wide enhancement of democracy. In the last great period of its history, in the three decades after the end of the Second World War, when the university expanded to become an institution of social citizenship, its cosmopolitan identity was preserved by the inclusion of new cultural voices. Today, while the struggle for inclusion will continue, making the university more truly representative of its social environment, the cosmopolitan challenge remains to be fulfilled in an age no longer dominated by the national project. It is not that this project has come to an end in the sense of the 'end of the nation state' thesis, but that this project has largely been accomplished. The implication of this for the university is that it will have to look beyond the nation for its cultural mission. Neither the capitalist-driven market nor postdisciplinary managerialism will provide the solution on the other side to the challenges that technology pose. The solution resides in linking the challenge of technology with cultural discourses. Universities are among the few locations in society where these discourses intersect. As sites of social interconnectivity, they can contribute to the making of cosmopolitan forms of citizenship.

The university is the institution in society most capable of linking the requirements of industry, technology and market forces with the demands of citizenship. Given the enormous dependence of these forces on university based experts, the university is in fact in a position of strength, not of weakness. While it is true that the new production of knowledge is dominated by an instrumentalization of knowledge and that as a result the traditional role of the university has been undermined, it is now in a position to serve *social* goals more fully than previously when other goals were more prominent. The university was once defined by its cultural mission, becoming later defined by the conflicting imperatives of 'system integration' and 'social integration', to use Habermas's terms (Habermas, 1987). At the moment the university stands at the cross-roads between these scenarios. Because it is now fully permeated by its environment, the university can become more influential in the knowledge society that has now emerged. The university no longer merely reflects the social transformations of modernity, but is itself now a major site in which different social projects are articulated.

I have emphasized the task of connecting technology to citizenship in the creation of technological citizenship. Technology, in particular information technology, is an inescapable fact of the modern world and its humanization is a condition of the advancement of citizenship. Universities are more equipped for this task than are other organizations. At the moment the problem is that goals are set for the university rather than by the university which consequently does not utilize its full resources. To this end the older notion of academic freedom is still relevant so long as it is not an excuse to evade societal responsibility. The university must recover the cosmopolitan project that was central to its identity from the beginning. Once a cosmopolitan institution in a world of regions, it became with modernity a national institution in an increasingly global world and, today, it is on the threshold of a new beginning, which can be characterized as the renewal of the cosmopolitan project.

References

Abbott, A. (1988) *The System of Professions: An Essay on the Division of Expert Labour.* Chicago: University of Chicago Press.

Adorno, T. (1983) 'The sociology of knowledge and its consciousness', in *Prisms.* Cambridge, MA: MIT Press.

Agamben, G. (1993) *The Coming Community.* Minneapolis: University of Minnesota Press.

Allen, V. and Axiotis, A. (1998) 'Nietzsche on the future of education', *Telos*, 111: 107–21.

Alter, R. (1989) *The Pleasure of Reading in an Ideological Age.* New York: Simon & Schuster.

Althusser, L. (1971) 'Ideology and the ideological state apparatus', in *Lenin and Philosophy and Other Essays.* London: NLB.

Anrich, E. (ed.) (1956) *Die Idee der deutschen Universität: Die fünf Grundschriften, Fichte, Schleiermacher, Steffens, Schelling, Humboldt.* Darmstadt: Hermann Gentner Verlag.

Apel, K-O. (1980) *The Transformation of Philosophy.* London: Routledge & Kegan Paul.

Appadurai, A. (1996) *Modernity at Large: Cultural Dimensions of Globalization.* Minneapolis: University of Minnesota Press.

Arendt, H. (1967) 'Truth and politics', in P. Laslett and W. C. Runciman (eds) *Philosophy, Politics and Society.* Oxford: Basil Blackwell.

Armytage, W. H. G. (1955) *Civic Universities: Aspects of a British Tradition.* London: Benn.

Arnold, M. (1960) *Culture and Anarchy.* Cambridge: Cambridge University Press.

Aronowitz, S. and Giroux, H. (1991) *Postmodern Education: Politics, Culture and Social Criticism.* Minneapolis: University of Minnesota Press.

Bacchi, C. (1996) *The Politics of Affirmative Action: 'Women', Equality and Category Politics.* London: Sage.

Bacon, F. (1973) *The Advancement of Learning.* London: Dent.

Baker, K. (1975) *Condorcet: From Natural Philosophy to Social Mathematics.* Chicago: University of Chicago Press.

Barnett, R. (1990) *The Idea of Higher Education.* Buckingham: Open University Press.

Barnett, R. (1994) *The Limits of Competence: Knowledge, Higher Education and Society* Buckingham: Open University Press.

Barnett, R. (1999) Realizing the University in an age of supercomplexity. Buckingham: Open University Press.

Barnett, R. and Green, A. (eds) (1997) The End of Knowledge in Higher Education. London: Cassell.

Bauman, Z. (1987) Legislators and Interpreters: On Modernity, Postmodernity and Intellectuals. Cambridge: Polity Press.

Bauman, Z. (1991) Modernity and Ambivalence. Cambridge: Polity Press.

Bauman, Z. (1992) Intimations of Postmodernity. Cambridge: Polity Press.

Bauman, Z. (1993) Postmodern Ethics. Oxford: Blackwell.

Bauman, Z. (1995) Life in Fragments: Essays in Postmodern Morality. Oxford: Blackwell.

Bauman, Z. (1997) 'Universities: old, new and different', in A. Smith and F. Webster (eds) The Postmodern University? Contested Visions of Higher Education in Society. Buckingham: Open University Press.

Becher, T. (1989) Academic Tribes and Territories. Milton Keynes: Open University Press.

Beck, U. (1992) The Risk Society. London: Sage.

Beck, U., Lash, S. and Giddens, A. (1994) Reflexive Modernization. Cambridge: Polity Press.

Bell, D. (1966) Reforming of General Education: The Columbia College Experience and its National Setting. New York: Columbia University Press.

Bell, D. (1974) The Coming of the Postindustrial Society. London: Heinemann.

Benda, J. (1969) The Treason of the Intellectuals. New York: Norton.

Bender, T. (ed.) (1988) 'Retrospect', in The University and the City: From Medieval Origins to the Present. Oxford: Oxford University Press.

Bender, T. (1993) Intellect and Public Life. Baltimore: Johns Hopkins University Press.

Bender, T. (1997) 'Politics, Intellect, and the American University', in T. Bender and C. Schorske (eds) American Academic Culture in Transformation. Princeton: Princeton University Press.

Bender, T. and Schorske, C. (eds) (1997) American Academic Culture in Transformation. Princeton: Princeton University Press.

Berger, S. and Dore, R. (eds) (1996) National Diversity and Global Capitalism. Ithaca, NY: Cornell University Press.

Berger, T. and Luckmann, T. (1967) The Social Construction of Reality. Harmondsworth: Penguin.

Bertilsson, M. (1992) 'From university to comprehensive higher education: on the widening gap between Lehre and Leben', Studies in Higher Education, 24: 333–49.

Bertilsson, B. (2000) 'From elite to mass – what is next?', in C. Lindquist and L.-L. Wallenuis (eds) Globalization and its Impact. Stockholm: FRV.

Berube, M. and Nelson, C. (eds) (1995) Higher Education Under Fire. London: Routledge.

Birnbaum, N. (1969) The Crisis of Industrial Society. New York: Oxford University Press.

Blanchot, M. (1988) The Unavowable Community. Barrytown, NY: Station Hill Press.

Bloom, A. (1987) The Closing of the American Mind. New York: Simon & Schuster.

Bloor, D. (1976) Knowledge and Social Imagery. London: Routledge & Kegan Paul.

Boggs, C. (1993) Intellectuals and the Crisis of Modernity. New York: SUNY Press.

Böhme, G. (1997) 'The structure and prospects of the knowledge society', Social Science Information, 36(3): 447–68.

Bok, D. (1982) Beyond the Ivory Tower: Social Responsibilities of the Modern University. Cambridge, MA: Harvard University Press.

Boltanski, L. and Thevenot, L. (1999) 'Critical and pragmatic sociology', European Journal of Social Theory, 2(3): 359–77.

Bottomore, T. (1964) *Elites and Society*. London: Watts.
Boudon, R. (1981) 'The French university since 1981', in C. Lemert (ed.) *French Sociology: Rapture and Renewal Since 1968*. New York: Colombia University Press.
Bourdieu, P. (1977) *Outline of a Theory of Practice*. Cambridge: Cambridge University Press.
Bourdieu, P. (1984) *Distinction: A Social Critique of the Judgement of Taste*. London: Routledge and Kegan Paul.
Bourdieu, P. (1988) *Homo Academicus*. Cambridge: Polity Press.
Bourdieu, P. (1990a) *The Logic of Practice*. Cambridge: Polity Press.
Bourdieu, P. (1990b) 'The intellectual field: a world apart', in *In Other Words: Essays Towards a Reflexive Sociology*. Stanford: Stanford University Press.
Bourdieu, P. (1991a) *Language and Symbolic Power*. Cambridge: Polity Press.
Bourdieu, P. (1991b) *The Political Ontology of Martin Heidegger*. Cambridge: Polity Press.
Bourdieu, P. (1991c) 'On symbolic power', in *Language and Symbolic Power*. Cambridge: Polity Press.
Bourdieu, P. (1993) *The Field of Cultural Production*. Cambridge: Polity Press.
Bourdieu, P. (1996a) *The State Nobility*. Cambridge: Polity Press.
Bourdieu, P. (1996b) *The Rules of Art: Genesis and Structure of the Literary Field*. Cambridge: Polity Press.
Bourdieu, P. (1997) *Practical Reason*. Cambridge: Polity Press.
Bourdieu, P. (1998a) 'The scholastic point of view', in *Practical Reason*. Cambridge: Polity Press.
Bourdieu, P. (1998b) *On Television*. Cambridge: Polity Press.
Bourdieu, P. (1998c) *Acts of Resistance*. Cambridge: Polity Press.
Bourdieu, P. (1999) *Pascalian Meditations*. Cambridge: Polity Press.
Bourdieu, P. and Haacke, H. (1995) *Free Exchange*. Cambridge: Polity Press.
Bourdieu, P. and Darbel, A. (1991) *The Love of Art: European Art Museums and their Public*. Cambridge: Polity Press.
Bourdieu, P. and Passeron, J-C. (1977) *Reproduction in Education, Society and Culture*. London: Sage.
Bourdieu, P. and Passeron, J-C. (1979) *The Inheritors: French Students and their Relation to Culture*. Chicago: University of Chicago Press.
Bourdieu, P., Passeron, J-C. and Saint Martin, M. de (1992) *Academic Discourse: Linguistic Misunderstanding and Professorial Power*. Cambridge: Polity Press.
Bourdieu, P. and Wacquant, L. (1992) *Introduction to Reflexive Sociology*. Cambridge: Polity Press.
Bove, P. (1986) *Intellectuals in Power: A Genealogy of Critical Humanism*. New York: Columbia University Press.
Bowen, W. and Shapiro, H. (eds) (1998) *Universities and their Leadership*. Princeton: Princeton University Press.
Branscombe, L., Kodema, F. and Florida, R. (eds) (1999) *Industrializing Knowledge: University–Industry Cleavages in Japan and the US*. Harvard, MA: MIT Press.
Brick, H. (1986) *Daniel Bell and the Decline of Intellectual Radicalism*. Madison: University of Wisconsin Press.
Brint, S. (1994) *In an Age of Experts: The Changing Role of Professionals in Politics and Public Life*. Princeton: Princeton University Press.
Cahn, S. (ed.) (1995) *The Affirmative Action Debate*. London: Routledge.
Calhoun, C. (1994) *Neither Gods nor Emperors: Students and the Struggle for Democracy in China*. Berkeley: University of California Press.

Cambell, R. H. and Skinner, A. S. (eds) (1982) *The Origins and Nature of the Scottish Enlightenment.* Edinburgh: Donald Publishers.

Carey, J. (1992) *The Intellectuals and the Masses.* London: Faber & Faber.

Castells, M. (1996) *The Rise of the Network Society.* Oxford: Blackwell.

Castoriadis, C. (1987) *The Imaginary Institution of Society.* Cambridge: Polity Press.

Cicourel, A. (1973) *Cognitive Sociology.* Harmondsworth: Penguin.

Cobban, A. (1975) *The Medieval Universities, Their Organization and Development.* London: Methuen.

Cohen, M. and March, J. (1974) *Leadership and Ambiguity: The American College President.* New York: McGraw-Hill.

Collins, R. (1979) *The Credential Society.* New York: Academic Press.

Collins, R. (1998) *The Sociology of Philosophies: A Global Theory of Intellectual Change.* Cambridge, MA: Harvard University Press.

Crane, D. and H. Small (1987) 'American sociology since the seventies: the emerging identity crisis in the discipline', in T. C. Halliday and M. Janowitz (eds) *Sociology and its Publics: The Forms and Fates of Disciplinary Organization.* Chicago: University of Chicago Press.

Crawford, E., Shinn, T. and Sorlin, S. (eds) (1993) *Denationalizing Science: The Contexts of International Scientific Practice.* Dordrecht: Kluwer.

Crook, S., Patulski, J. and Waters, M. (1992) *Postmodernization: Change in Advanced Society.* London: Sage.

Currie, J. (1998) 'Introduction', in J. Currie and J. Newson (eds) *Universities and Globalization: Critical Perspectives.* London: Sage.

Currie, J. and Newson, J. (eds) (1998) *Universities and Globalization: Critical Perspectives.* London: Sage.

Currie, J. and Vidovich, L. (1998) 'Micro-economic reform through managerialism', in J. Currie and J. Newson (eds) *Universities and Globalization: Critical Perspectives.* London: Sage.

Dant, T. (1991) *Knowledge, Ideology and Discourse: A Sociological Perspective.* London: Routledge.

Davis Graham, H. and Diamond, N. (1996) *The Rise of the American Research University.* Baltimore: Johns Hopkins University Press.

Dearing (1997) *Higher Education in the Learning Society. Report of the National Committee of Inquiry into Higher Education.* London: HMSO.

de Certeau, M. (1997) *Culture in the Plural.* Minneapolis: Minnesota University Press.

Delanty, G. (1997) *Social Science: Beyond Realism and Constructivism.* Buckingham: Open University Press.

Delanty, G. (1998a) 'The idea of the university in the global era: from knowledge as an end to the end of knowledge?', *Social Epistemology: A Journal of Knowledge, Culture and Policy,* 12(1): 3–25.

Delanty, G. (1998b) 'Rethinking the university: the autonomy, reflexivity and contestation of knowledge', *Social Epistemology: A Journal of Knowledge, Culture and Policy,* 12(1): 103–13.

Delanty, G. (1999) *Social Theory in a Changing World: Conceptions of Modernity.* Cambridge: Polity Press.

Delanty, G. (2000a) *Modernity and Postmodernity: Knowledge, Power, Self.* London: Sage.

Delanty, G. (2000b) *Citizenship in a Global Age: Culture, Politics, Society.* Buckingham: Open University Press.

Derrida, J. (1983) 'The principle of reason: the university in the eyes of its pupils', *Diacritics,* 13 (Fall): 3–20.

Derrida, J. (1992) 'Mocholos, or, the conflict of the faculties', in R. Rand (ed.), *Logomachia: The Conflict of the Faculties*. Lincoln, NB: University of Nebraska Press.

Dewey, J. (1930) *The Public and its Problems*. New York: Holt.

Dickson, D. (1984) *The New Politics of Science*. New York: Pantheon.

Diderot, D. (1971) 'Plan d'une université', *Oeuvres completes*. Paris: Club Française du Livre.

Dominelli, L. and Hoogvelt, A. (1996) 'Globalization, contract government and the Taylorization of intellectual labour in academia', *Studies in Political Economy*, 49: 71–100.

Donald, J. (1992) *Sentimental Education*. London: Verso.

D'Souza, D. (1991) *Illiberal Education: The Politics of Race and Sex on Campus*. New York: Free Press.

Dunn, J. (ed.) (1995) *Contemporary Crisis of the Nation State?* Oxford: Blackwell.

Durkheim, E. (1960) *The Division of Labour in Society*. Glencoe, IL: Free Press.

Durkheim, E. (1977) *The Evolution of Educational Thought*. London: Routledge & Kegan Paul.

Eder, K. (1996) *The Social Construction of Nature*. London: Sage.

Eder, K. (1999) 'Societies learn and yet the world is hard to change', *European Journal of Social Theory*, 2(2): 195–215.

Eisenstadt, S. N. (1966) *Modernization: Protest and Change*. Englewood Cliffs, NJ: Prentice-Hall.

Eliot, T. S. (1940) *The Idea of a Christian Society*. New York: Harcourt, Brace & Co.

Etzioni-Halevy, E. (1985) *The Knowledge Elite and the Failure of Prophecy*. London: Allen & Unwin.

Etzkowitz, H. and Leydesdorff, L. (eds) (1997) *Universities in the Global Economy: A Triple Helix of University, Industry, Government Relations*. London: Cassell Academic.

Eyerman, R. (1994) *Between Culture and Politics: Intellectuals in Modern Society*. Cambridge: Polity Press.

Eyerman, R. and Jamison, A. (1991) *Social Movements: A Cognitive Approach*. Cambridge: Polity Press.

Ferruolo, S. C. (1985) *The Origins of the University: The Schools of Paris and their Critics, 1100–1215*. Stanford: Stanford University Press.

Feyerabend, P. (1975) *Against Method: Outline of an Anarchistic Theory of Knowledge*. London: Verso.

Feyerabend, P. (1978) *Science in a Free Society*. London: New Left Books.

Fink, L., Leonard, S. and Reid, D. (eds) (1996) *Intellectuals and Public Life: Between Radicalism and Reform*. Ithaca: Cornell University Press.

Fish, S. (1995) *Professional Correctness: Literary Studies and Political Change*. Oxford: Clarendon Press.

Foucault, M. (1977) 'The political function of the intellectual', *Radical Philosophy*, 17: 12–14.

Foucault, M. (1980) *Power/Knowledge: Selected Interviews and Other Writings, 1972–1977*, edited by D. Bouchard. Oxford: Blackwell.

Freitag, M. (1998) *Le Naufrage de L'Université*. Montreal: Éditions Nota Bene.

Friese, H. and Wagner, P. (1993) *Der Raum des Gelehrten*. Berlin: Edition Sigma.

Friese, H. and Wagner, P. (1998) 'The other space of the university', *Social Epistemology: A Journal of Knowledge, Culture and Policy*, 12(1): 27–32.

Frisby, D. and Featherstone, M. (eds) (1997) *Simmel on Culture*. London: Sage.

Fuller, S. (1993) *Philosophy, Rhetoric and the End of Knowledge*. Madison: University of Wisconsin Press.

Fuller, S. (1994) 'Rethinking the university from a social constructivist standpoint', *Science Studies*, 7(1): 4–16.
Fuller, S. (1997a) 'Life in the knowledge society', *Theory, Culture and Society*, 14(1): 143–55.
Fuller, S. (1997b) 'Putting people back into the business of science', in J. Colliers (ed.), *Scientific and Technical Communication*. London: Sage.
Fuller, S. (1999a) *The Governance of Science*. Buckingham: Open University Press.
Fuller, S. (1999b) 'Making the university fit for critical intellectuals: recovering from the ravages of the postmodern condition', *British Educational Research Journal*, 25(5): 583–95.
Fuller, S. (2000) *Thomas Kuhn: A Philosophical History for Our Time*. Chicago: University of Chicago Press.
Gadamer, H-G. (1979) *Truth and Method*. London: Sheed & Ward.
Gadamer, H-G. (1992) *Hans-Georg Gadamer on Education, Poetry and History: Applied Hermeneutics*, edited by D. Misgeld and G. Nicholson. New York: SUNY Press.
Galbraith, J. K. (1967) *The New Industrial State*. Boston: Houghton Mifflin.
Geertz, C. (1983) *Local Knowledge*. New York: Basic Books.
Geiger, R. (1986) *To Advance Knowledge: The Growth of the American Research University, 1900–1940*. Oxford: Oxford University Press.
Geiger, R. (1993) *Research and Relevant Knowledge: American Research Universities since World War II*. Oxford: Oxford University Press.
Gibbons, M. and Wittrock, B. (eds) (1985) *Science as a Commodity: Threats to the Open Community of Scholars*. London: Longman.
Gibbons, M., Limoges, C., Nowotny, H. *et al.* (1984) *The New Production of Knowledge*. London: Sage.
Giddens, A. (1984) *The Constitution of Society: Outline of a Theory of Structuration*. Cambridge: Polity Press.
Giddens, A. (1990) *The Consequences of Modernity*. Cambridge: Polity Press.
Giddens, A. (1991) *Modernity and Self-identity*. Cambridge: Polity Press.
Giddens, A. (1994) *Beyond Left and Right*. Cambridge: Polity Press.
Goldfarb, J. (1998) *Civility and Subversion: The Intellectual in Democratic Society*. Cambridge: Cambridge University Press.
Goldman, A. (1999) *Knowledge in a Social World*. Oxford: Claredon University Press.
Goodman, R. and Fisher, W. (eds) (1995) *Rethinking Knowledge: Reflections Across the Disciplines*. New York: SUNY Press.
Gouldner, A. (1965) *Enter Plato*. London: Routledge & Kegan Paul.
Gouldner, A. (1971) *The Coming Crisis of Sociology*. London: Heinemann.
Gouldner, A. (1973) 'Romanticism and classicism: deep structures in social science' *For Sociology: Renewal and Critique in Sociology Today*. London: Allen Lane.
Gouldner, A. (1979) *The Future of Intellectuals and the Rise of the New Class*. London: Macmillan.
Graff, G. (1992) *Beyond the Culture Wars: How Teaching the Conflicts can Revitalize American Education*. New York: Norton.
Grafton, A. and Jardie, C. (eds) (1986) *From Humanism to Humanities: Education and the Liberal Arts in Fifteenth and Sixteenth Century Europe*. London: Duckworth.
Gramsci, A. (1971) *Selections from Prison Notebooks*. London: Lawrence & Wishart.
Granel, G. (1982) *De l'université*. Mauzevin: Trans-Europ-Repress.
Gray, H. (1999) 'Re-scoping the university', in H. Gray (ed.) *Universities and the Creation of Wealth*. Buckingham: Open University Press.
Green, A. (1997) *Education, Globalization and the Nation State*. London: Macmillan.

Gurvitch, G. (1971) *The Social Frameworks of Knowledge.* Oxford: Blackwell.

Habermas, J. (1969) *Protestbewegnung und Hochschulenreform.* Frankfurt: Suhrkamp.

Habermas, J. (1971a) 'The university in a democracy: democratization of the university', in *Toward a Rational Society.* London: Heinemann.

Habermas, J. (1971b) 'Student protest in the Federal Republic of Germany', in *Toward a Rational Society.* London: Heinemann.

Habermas, J. (1972) *Theory and Practice.* London: Heinemann.

Habermas, J. ([1968] 1978) *Knowledge and Human Interests,* 2nd edition. London: Heinemann.

Habermas, J. (1979) *Communication and the Evolution of Society.* London: Heinemann.

Habermas, J. (1984) *The Theory of Communicative Action,* vol. 1: *Reason and the Rationalization of Society.* London: Heinemann.

Habermas, J. (1987) *The Theory of Communicative Action,* vol. 2: *Lifeworld and System: A Critique of Functionalist Reason.* Cambridge: Polity Press.

Habermas, J. (1989) *The Structural Transformation of the Public Sphere.* Cambridge: Polity Press.

Habermas, J. (1992) 'The idea of the university – learning processes', in *The New Conservatism: Cultural Criticism and the Historians' Debate.* Cambridge: Polity Press.

Habermas, J. (1996) *Between Facts and Norms: Contribution to a Discourse Theory of Democracy and Law.* Cambridge: Polity Press.

Halsey, A. H. (1992) *The Decline of Donnish Dominion.* Oxford: Oxford University Press.

Harvey, D. (1990) *The Condition of Postmodernity: An Inquiry into the Origins of Cultural Change.* Oxford: Blackwell.

Harvey, D. (1998) 'University, Inc', *Atlantic Monthly,* October: 112–16.

Hassan, I. (1987) *The Postmodern Turn: Essays in Postmodern Theory and Culture.* Columbus: Ohio State University Press.

Heidegger, M. (1985) 'The self-assertion of a German university', *Review of Metaphysics,* 38: 467–502.

Heilbron, J. (1995) *The Rise of Social Theory.* Cambridge: Polity Press.

Hirst, P. and Thompson, G. (eds) (1996) *Globalization in Question.* Cambridge: Polity Press.

Hofstadter, R. (1963) *Anti-intellectualism in American Life.* New York: Knopf.

Hollinger, D. (1995) *Postethnic America: Beyond Multiculturalism.* New York: Basic Books.

Holland, D. and Quinn, N. (eds) (1991) *Cultural Models in Language and Thought.* Cambridge: Cambridge University Press.

Holton, R. (1998) *Globalization and the Nation-state.* London: Macmillan.

Horsman, M. and Marshall, A. (eds) (1994) *After the Nation-State.* London: HarperCollins.

House, D. (1998) 'Agent of change with change: the development of biotechnology in universities'. Unpublished paper.

Humboldt, W. von (1970) 'University reform in Germany: reports and documents' *Minerva,* 8: 242–50.

Huxley, T. H. (1902) '1876 address on university education', in *Science and Education,* vol. 3: *Collected Papers.* London: Macmillan.

Isin, E. and Wood, P. (1999) *Citizenship and Identity.* London: Sage.

Jacoby, R. (1987) *The Last Intellectuals: American Culture in the Age of Academe.* New York: Basic Books.

Jameson, F. (1991) *Postmodernism, or, the Cultural Logic of LateCapitalism.* Durham, NJ: Duke University Press.

Jaspers, K. (1960) *The Idea of the University.* London: Peter Owen.

Jones, D. (1988) *The Origin of Civic Universities: Manchester, Leeds, and Liverpool.* London: Routledge.

Judt, T. (1992) *Past Imperfect: French Intellectuals, 1944–1956.* Cambridge: Cambridge University Press.

Kant, I. (1979) *The Conflict of the Faculties.* New York: Abaris Books.

Kant. I. (1996) 'An answer to the question: what is Enlightenment?', in J. Schmidt (ed.), *What is Enlightenment? Eighteenth-century Answers and Twentieth-century Questions.* Berkeley: University of California Press.

Kanuf, P. (1997) *The Division of Literature: Or the University in Deconstruction.* Chicago: University of Chicago Press.

Kassow, S. (1989) *Students, Professors and the State in Tsarist Russia.* Berkeley: University of California Press.

Keller, G. (1983) *Academic Strategy: The Management Revolution in American Higher Education.* Baltimore: Johns Hopkins University Press.

Kenney, M. (1986) *Biotechnology: The University–Industry Complex.* New Haven, CT: Yale University Press.

Kerr, C. (1963) *The Uses of the University.* Cambridge, MA: Harvard University Press.

Kerr, C. (1991) *The Great Transformation in Higher Education 1960–1980.* Albany, NY: SUNY Press.

Kimball, R. (1990) *Tenured Radicals: How Politics has Corrupted Higher Education.* New York: Harper & Row.

Kittelson, J. and Transue, P. (eds) (1984) *Rebirth, Reform and Resilience: Universities in Transition, 1350–1770.* Columbus: Ohio State University Press.

Knorr-Cetina, K. (1981) *The Manufacture of Knowledge.* Oxford: Pergamon.

Konrad, G. and Szelenyi, I. (1979) *The Intellectuals on the Road to Class Power.* Brighton: Harvester.

Kuhn, T. (1970) *The Structure of Scientific Revolutions,* 2nd edition. Chicago: Chicago University Press.

Kumar, K. (1997) 'The need for place', in A. Smith and F. Webster (eds) *The Postmodern University? Contested Visions of Higher Education in Society.* Buckingham: Open University Press.

Laroui, A. (1976) *The Crisis of the Arab Intellectual.* Berkeley: University of California Press.

Lasch, C. (1979) *The Culture of Narcissism.* New York: Norton.

Lasch, C. (1985) *The Minimal Self: Psychic Survival in Troubled Times.* London: Pan.

Lash, S. and Urry, J. (1994) *Economies of Signs and Space.* London: Routledge.

Latour, B. (1987) *Science in Action.* Milton Keynes: Open University Press.

Lazerfeld, P. and Thielens, T. (1958) *The Academic Mind: Social Scientists in a Time of Crisis.* Glencoe, IL: Free Press.

Law, J. (1994) *Organized Modernity.* Oxford: Blackwell.

Lawson, H. (1985) *Reflexivity: The Post-modern Predicament.* London: Hutchinson.

Leavis, F. R. (1948) *Education and the University: A Sketch for an 'English School'.* London: Chatto & Windus.

Leavis, F. R. (1969) *English Literature in our Time and the University.* London: Chatto & Windus.

Lefort, C. (1986) *The Political Forms of Modern Society.* Cambridge: Polity Press.

Lepenies, W. (1988) *Between Literature and Science: The Rise of Sociology.* Cambridge: Cambridge University Press.

Lipset, S. M. (ed.) (1967) *Student Politics.* New York: Basic Books.

Locke, J. (1968) *The Educational Writings of John Locke*, edited by J. Axtell. Cambridge: Cambridge University Press.

Lowenthal, R. (1975) 'The university's autonomy versus social priorities', in P. Seabury (ed.) *Universities in the Western World*. New York: Free Press.

Luhmann, N. (1987) 'Zwischen Gesellschaft und Organisation: Zur Situation der Universitäten', in N. Luhmann (ed.) *Soziologische Aufklärung 4: Beiträge zur funktionalen Differenzierung der Gesellschaft*. Opladen: Westdeutscher Verlag.

Luhmann, N. (1990) *Essays in Self-Reference*. New York: Columbia University Press.

Luhmann, N. (1995) *Social Systems*. Stanford: Stanford University Press.

Lynd, R. (1939) *Knowledge for What? The Place of Social Science in American Culture*. Princeton: Princeton University Press.

Lyotard, J-F. (1984) *The Postmodern Condition: A Report on Knowledge*. Manchester: Manchester University Press.

Lyotard, J-F. (1988) *Peregrinations. Law, Form, Event*. New York: Columbia University Press.

McCarthy, D. E. (1996) *Knowledge as Culture: The New Sociology of Knowledge*. London: Routledge.

McClelland, C. (1980) *State, Society and University in Germany*. Cambridge: Cambridge University Press.

McDonald, C. (1992) 'Institutions of change: notes on education in the late eighteenth century, in R. Rand (ed.) *Logmachia: The Conflict of the Faculties*. Lincoln, NB: University of Nebraska Press.

Manicas, P. (1998) 'Higher education at risk', *Futures*, 30(7): 651–6.

Mannheim, K. (1936) *Ideology and Utopia: An Introduction to the Sociology of Knowledge*. London: Routledge & Kegan Paul.

Mannheim, K. (1952) *Essays in the Sociology of Knowledge*. London: Routledge & Kegan Paul.

Marcuse, H. (1941) *Reason and Revolution: Hegel and the Rise of Social Theory*. London: Routledge & Kegan Paul.

Marcuse, H. (1955) *Eros and Civilization*. Boston: Beacon Press.

Marcuse, H. (1964) *One-dimensional Man*. London: Routledge & Kegan Paul.

Marcuse, H. (1969) *An Essay on Liberation*. Boston: Beacon Press.

Marcuse, H. (1979) *The Aesthetic Dimension*. London: Macmillan.

Marks, A. (1999) 'A united European higher education system: the problems for trans-national institutional convergence', *New Era in Education*, 80(3): 78–83.

Marshall, T. H. (1992) *Citizenship and Social Class*. London: Pluto.

Matkin, G. (1990) *Technology Transfer and the University*. New York: Macmillan.

May, T. (1999) 'Reflexivity in the age of reconstructive social science', *International Journal of Social Research and Methodology*, 1(1): 7–24.

May, T. (2000) 'A future for critique: positioning, belonging and reflexivity', *European Journal of Social Theory*, 3(2): 157–73.

Melluci, A. (1996) *Challenging Codes: Collective Action in the Information Age*. Cambridge: Cambridge University Press.

Menand, L. (ed.) (1997) *The Future of Academic Freedom*. Chicago: University of Chicago Press.

Mendelsohn, E., Weingart, P. and Whitley, R. (eds) (1977) *The Social Production of Scientific Knowledge*. London: Routledge & Kegan Paul.

Merton, R. (1970) *Science, Technology and Society in Seventeenth Century England*. New York: Fertig.

Merton, R. (1973) *The Sociology of Science: Theoretical and Empirical Investigations.* Chicago: University of Chicago Press.

Miyoshi, M. (1998) ' "Globalization", culture, and the university', in F. Jameson and M. Miyoshi (eds) *The Cultures of Globalization,* Durham NJ: Duke University Press.

Miyoshi, M. (1999) 'The dash of cash', *Times Higher Educational Supplement,* 17 December, p. 8.

Müller, E. (ed.) (1990) *Gelengenliche Gedanken Über Universitäten.* Leipzig: Reclam Verlag.

Muller, S. and Whitesell, H. (eds) (1996) *Universities in the Twenty-first Century.* Oxford: Berghahn Books.

Nancy, J-L. (1990) *The Inoperative Community.* Minneapolis: Minnesota University Press.

Newman, J. H. (1996) *The Idea of the University,* edited by F. Turner. New Haven, CT: Yale University Press.

Nichols Clark, T. (1973) *Prophets and Patrons: The French University and the Emergence of the Social Sciences.* Cambridge, MA: Harvard University Press.

Nisbet, R. (1971) *The Degradation of the Academic Dogma: The University in America, 1945–70.* London: Heinemann.

Noble, D. (1999) 'Digital diploma mills: the automation of higher education', *First Monday.*

Nowotny, H. (2000) 'Transgressive competence: the narrative of expertise', *European Journal of Social Theory,* 3(1): 5–21.

Ohmae, K. (1995) *The End of the Nation State.* New York: Free Press.

O'Mahony, P. and Delanty, G. (1998) *Rethinking Irish History: Nationalism, Identity and Ideology.* London: Macmillan.

O'Neill, J. (1972) *Sociology as a Skin Trade: Essays Towards a Reflexive Sociology.* London: Heinemann.

Ortega y Gasset, J. (1932) *The Revolt of the Masses.* New York: Harper.

Ortega y Gasset, J. (1944) *Mission of the University.* Princeton: Princeton University Press.

Parsons, T. (1974) 'The university "bundle": a study of the balance between differentiation and integration', in N. Smelser and G. Almond (eds) *Public Higher Education in California: Growth, Structural Change, and Conflict.* Berkeley: University of California Press.

Parsons, T. (1979) *Action Theory and the Human Condition.* New York: Free Press.

Parsons, T. and Platt, G. (1973) *The American University.* Cambridge, MA: Harvard University Press.

Paulston, R. (1999) 'Mapping comparative education after postmodernity', *Comparative and International Education Society,* 43(4): 438–63.

Pelikan, J. (1992) *The Idea of the University.* New Haven, CT: Yale University Press.

Perkin, H. (1989) *The Rise of Professional Society: England since 1880.* London: Routledge.

Popper, K. (1945) *The Open Societies and its Enemies.* New York: Harper & Row.

Power, M. (1997) *Audit Society.* Cambridge: Cambridge University Press.

Price, D. (1963) *Little Science, Big Science.* New York: Columbia University Press.

Rand, R. (ed.) (1992) *Logomachia: The Conflict of the Faculties.* Lincoln, NB: University of Nebraska Press.

Rashdall, H. (1987) *The University in Europe in the Middle Ages,* (3 vols). Oxford: Oxford University Press.

Readings, B. (1996) *The University in Ruins.* Cambridge, MA: Harvard University Press.

Reich, R. (1991) *The Work of Nations: Preparing Ourselves for 21st Century Capitalism.* New York: Random House.

Reuben, J. (1996) *The Making of the Modern University: Intellectual Transformation and the Marginalization of Morality*. Cambridge, MA: Harvard University Press.

Rhodes, R. (1996) 'The new governance: governing without government', *Political Studies*, 44: 652–67.

Rhodes, G. and Slaughter, S. (1991) 'The public interest and professional labor: research universities', in W. G. Tierney (ed.) *Culture and Ideology in Higher Education*. New York: Praeger.

Riesman, D. (1950) *The Lonely Crowd: A Study of the Changing American Character*. New Haven, CT: Yale University Press.

Riesman, D. (1998) *On Higher Education: The Academic Enterprise in an Era of Rising Student Consumerism*. New Brunswick: Transaction Publishers.

Riesman, D. and Jencks, C. (1968) *The Academic Revolution*. New York: Doubleday.

Ringer, F. (1969) *The Decline of the German Mandarins*. Cambridge, MA: Harvard University Press.

Ritzer, G. (1993) *The McDonaldization of Society*. London: Sage.

Robbins, B. (ed.) (1993a) *The Phantom Public Sphere*. Minneapolis: Minnesota University Press.

Robbins, B. (1993b) *Secular Vocations: Intellectuals, Professionalism, Culture*. London: Verso.

Robertson, D. (1999) 'Knowledge societies, intellectual capital and economic growth', in H. Gray (ed.) *Universities and the Creation of Wealth*. Buckingham: Open University Press.

Robertson, R. (1992) *Globalization: Social Theory and Global Culture*. London: Sage.

Robins, K. and Webster, F. (1985) 'Higher education, high tech, high rhetoric', *Radical Science Journal*, 18: 36–7.

Robins, K. and Webster, F. (eds) (Forthcoming) *The Virtual University?* Oxford: Oxford University Press.

Ross, A. (1989) *No Respect: Intellectuals and Popular Culture*. London: Routledge.

Rothblatt, S. (1997a) 'The "place" of knowledge in the American academic profession', *Daedalus*, 126(4): 245–64.

Rothblatt, S. (1997b) *The Modern University and its Discontents: The Fate of Newman's Legacies in Britain and America*. Cambridge: Cambridge University Press.

Rothblatt, S. and Wittrock, B. (eds) (1993) *The European and American University since 1800*. Cambridge: Cambridge University Press.

Ryan, A. (1999) *Liberal Anxieties and Liberal Education*. London: Profile Books.

Sacks, D. and Thiel, P. (1995) *The Diversity Myth: 'Culturalism' and the Politics of Intolerance at Stanford*. Oakland, CA: Independent Institution.

Sadlak, J. (1998) 'Globalization and concurrent challenges for higher education', in P. Scott (ed.) *The Globalization of Higher Education*. Buckingham: Open University Press.

Said, E. (1979) *Orientalism*. New York: Vintage Books.

Said, E. (1994) *Representations of the Intellectual: The 1993 Reith Lectures*. London: Vintage.

Sanderson, M. (ed.) (1975) *The Universities of the Nineteenth Century*. London: Routledge and Kegan Paul.

Santos, de Sousa B. (1995) *Toward a New Common Sense: Law, Science and Politics in the Paradigmatic Transition*. London: Routledge.

Santos, de Sousa B. (1999) 'A multicultural conception of human rights', in M. Featherstone and S. Lash (eds) *Spaces of Culture*. London: Sage.

Sartre, J-P. (1967) *What is Literature?* London: Methuen.

Sassen, S. (1992) *The Global City: New York, London, Tokyo.* Princeton: Princeton University Press.
Schelsky, H. (1963) *Einsamkeit und Freiheit: Idee und Gestalt der deutschen Universität und ihrer Reformen.* Hamburg: Rowohlt.
Schlesinger, A. (1992) *The Disuniting of America: Reflections on a Multicultural Society.* New York: Norton.
Schmaus, W. (1994) *Durhkeim's Philosophy of Science and the Sociology of Knowledge.* Chicago: Chicago University Press.
Schott, T. (1991) 'The world scientific community: globality and globalization', *Minerva*, 29(4): 440–62.
Schumpeter, J. (1954) *Capitalism, Socialism and Democracy.* London: Allen & Unwin.
Schutz, A. (1967) *The Phenomenology of the Social World.* London: Heinemann.
Scott, P. (1995) *The Meanings of Higher Education.* Buckingham: Open University Press.
Scott, P. (1997) 'The postmodern university?', in A. Smith and F. Webster (eds) *The Postmodern University? Contested Visions of Higher Education in Society.* Buckingham: Open University Press.
Scott, P. (ed.) (1998a) *The Globalization of Higher Education.* Buckingham: Open University Press.
Scott, P. (1998b) 'Massification, internationalization and globalization', in P. Scott (ed.) *The Globalization of Higher Education.* Buckingham: Open University Press.
Sennett, R. (1978) *The Fall of Public Man.* New York: Vintage.
Shils, E. (1973) *Max Weber on Universities: The Power of the State and the Dignity of the Academic Calling in Imperial Germany.* Chicago: University of Chicago Press.
Shils, E. (1997) *The Calling of Higher Education: The Academic Ethic and Other Essays on Higher Education.* Chicago: Chicago University Press.
Slaughter, S. and L. Leslie (1997) *Academic Capitalism: Politics, Policies, and the Entrepreneurial University.* Baltimore: Johns Hopkins University Press.
Smelser, N. and Alexander, J. (eds) (1999) *Diversity and its Discontents: Cultural Conflict and Common Ground in Contemporary American Society.* Princeton: Princeton University Press.
Smith, A. and Webster, F. (eds) (1997a) *The Postmodern University? Contested Visions of Higher Education in Society.* Buckingham: Open University Press.
Smith, A. and Webster, F. (1997b) 'Conclusion: an affirming flame', in A. Smith and F. Webster (eds) *The Postmodern University? Contested Visions of Higher Education in Society.* Buckingham: Open University Press.
Smith, R. and Wexler, P. (eds) (1995) *After Postmodernism: Education, Politics and Identity.* London: Falmer Press.
Somers, M. (1996) 'Where is sociology after the historic turn? Knowledge cultures, narrativity, and historical epistemologies', in Terrence, J. McDonald (ed.) *The Historic Turn in the Human Sciences.* Ann Arbor: University of Michigan Press.
Somers, M. (1999) 'Privatising citizenship', in V. Bonnell and L. Hunt (eds) *Beyond the Culture Turn.* Berkeley: University of California Press.
Sommer, J. (ed.) (1995) *The Academy in Crisis: The Political Economy of Higher Education.* New Brunswick: Transaction Publishers.
Sorkin, D. (1983) 'Wilhelm von Humboldt: the theory and practice of self-formation (*Bildung*), 1791–1810', *Journal of the History of Ideas*, 44: 55–73.
Stehr, N. (1994) *Knowledge Society.* London: Sage.
Stehr, N. and Meja, V. (eds) (1984) *Society and Knowledge: Contemporary Perspectives in the Sociology of Knowledge.* London: Transaction Books.
Stenberg, L. (1996) *The Islamization of Science*, vol. 6. Lund: Novapress.

Stichweh, R. (1996) 'Science in the system of the world society', *Social Science Information*, 35(2): 327–40.

Strange, S. (1996) *The Retreat of the State: The Diffusion of Power in the World Economy*. Cambridge: Cambridge University Press.

Strydom, P. (1987) 'Collective learning: Habermas's concessions and theory implications', *Philosophy and Social Criticism*, 13(3): 265–81.

Strydom, P. (1992) 'The ontogenetic fallacy: the immanent critique of Habermas's developmental logical theory of evolution', *Theory, Culture and Society*, 9: 65–93.

Strydom, P. (1993) 'Sociocultural evolution or the social evolution of practical reason? Eder's critique of Habermas', *Praxis International*, 13(3): 304–22.

Strydom, P. (1999) 'Triple contingency: the theoretical problem of the public in communication societies', *Philosophy and Social Criticism*, 25(2): 1–25.

Strydom, P. (2000) *Discourse and Knowledge: The Making of Enlightenment Sociology*. Liverpool: Liverpool University Press.

Sutherland, G. (ed.) (1973) *Matthew Arnold on Education*, edited with an introduction by G. Sutherland. Harmondsworth: Penguin.

Swartz, P. (1997) *Culture and Power: The Sociology of Pierre Bourdieu*. Chicago: Chicago University Press.

The Economist (1997) 'Survey: universities', 4 October.

Thompson, E. P. (1970) *Warwick University Ltd*. Harmondsworth: Penguin.

Times Higher Education Supplement (1998) 'A world wide web of elite universities', 13 March.

Toulmin, S. (1992) *Cosmopolis: The Hidden Agenda of Modernity*. Chicago: Chicago University Press.

Touraine, A. (1965) *Sociologie de l'action*. Paris: Seuil.

Touraine, A. (1971a) *Post-industrial Society*. New York: Random House.

Touraine, A. (1971b) *The May Movement: Revolt and Reform*. New York: Random House.

Touraine, A. (1977) *The Self-production of Society*. Chicago: Chicago University Press.

Touraine, A. (1981) *The Voice and the Eye: An Analysis of Social Movements*. Cambridge: Cambridge University Press.

Touraine, A. (1988) *The Return of the Actor: Social Theory in the Post-industrial Society*. Minneapolis: University of Minnesota Press.

Touraine, A. (1995) *Critique of Modernity*. Oxford: Blackwell.

Touraine, A. (1997) *What is Democracy?* Oxford: Westview.

Touraine, A. (1998) 'Can we live together, equal and different?', *European Journal of Social Theory*, 1(2): 165–78.

Turner, B. (ed.) (1993) *Citizenship and Social Theory*. London: Sage.

Turner, B. S. (1998) 'Universities, elites and the nation-state: a reply to Delanty', *Social Epistemology*, 12(1): 73–7.

Turner, B. S. (1999) 'Postdisciplinarity'. Unpublished manuscript.

Turner, J. H. and S. P. Turner (1990) *The Impossible Science: An Institutional Analysis of American Sociology*. London: Sage.

Unger, R. (1975) *Knowledge and Politics*. New York: Free Press.

Urry, J. (1998) 'Contemporary transformations of time and space', in P. Scott (ed.) *The Globalization of Higher Education*. Buckingham: Open University Press.

Urry, J. (2000) *Sociology Beyond Society*. London: Routledge.

Usher, R. and Edwards, R. (1994) *Postmodernism and Education: Different Voices, Different Worlds*. London: Routledge.

Van den Dale, W. (1977) 'The social construction of science: institutionalization and definition of positive science in the latter half of the seventeenth century', in E. Mendelsohn, B. Weingart and R. Whitley (eds) *The Social Construction of Scientific Knowledge.* Dordrecht: Reidel.

Veblen, T. (1962) *The Higher Learning in America.* New Haven, CT: Yale University Press.

Wacquant, L. (1996) Foreword to P. Bourdieu *The State Nobility.* Cambridge: Polity Press.

Wagner, P. (1994) *A Sociology of Modernity: Liberty and Discipline.* London: Routledge.

Wagner, P., Wittrock, B. and Whitley, R. (eds) (1991a) *Discourses on Society: The Shaping of the Social Science Disciplines.* Dordrecht: Kluwer.

Wagner, P., Weiss, C., Wittrock, B. and Wollman, H. (eds) (1991b) *Social Sciences and Modern State: Natural Experiences and Theoretical Crossroads.* Cambridge: Cambridge University Press.

Wallerstein, I. (1969) *University in Turmoil: The Politics of Change.* New York: Atheneum.

Wallerstein, I. (1991) 'Can there be such a thing as word culture', *Geopolitics and Geoculture.* Cambridge: Cambridge University Press.

Wallerstein, I. *et al.* (1996) *Open the Social Sciences: Report of the Gulbenkian Commission on the Restructuring of the Social Sciences.* Stanford: Stanford University Press.

Walzer, M. (1987) *Interpretation and Social Criticism.* Cambridge, MA: Harvard University Press.

Walzer, M. (1988) *The Company of Critics: Social Criticism and Political Commitment in the Twentieth Century.* New York: Basic Books.

Weber, M. (1948) 'Science as a vocation', in H. H. Gerth and C. Wright Mills (eds) *From Max Weber.* London: Routledge & Kegan Paul.

Weber, M. (1958) *The City.* New York: The Free Press.

Weber, M. (1973) 'The alleged "academic freedom" of the German universities' (1908), trans. Edward Shils, *Minerva* 11.

Webster, F. (1995) *Theories of the Information Society.* London: Routledge.

Webster, F. (1999) 'Higher education', in G. Browning, A. Halcli and F. Webster (eds) *Understanding Contemporary Society: Theories of the Present.* London: Sage.

Whitehead, A. (1929) 'Universities and their functions', in *The Aims of Education and Other Essays.* London: Williams and Norgate.

Wieruszowski, H. (1966) *The Medieval University: Masters, Students, Learning.* Princeton, N.J.: Van Nostrand.

Wittrock, B. (1993) 'The modern university: the three transformations', in S. Rothblatt, and B. Wittrock (eds) *The European and American University Since 1800.* Cambridge: Cambridge University Press.

Wolff, K. H. (ed.) (1993) *From Karl Mannheim.* London: Transaction.

Woolgar, S. (1988) *Knowledge and Reflexivity: New Frontiers in the Sociology of Knowledge.* London: Sage.

World Bank (1994) *Higher Education: The Lessons of Experience.* Washington, DC: World Bank.

Wortham, S. (1999) *Rethinking the University: Leverage and Deconstruction.* Manchester: Manchester University Press.

Wuthnow, R. (1989) *Communities of Discourse: The Reformation, the Enlightenment and Nineteenth-century Socialism.* Cambridge, MA: Harvard University Press.

Young, M. (ed.) (1971) *Knowledge and Control: New Directions for the Sociology of Education.* London: Collier Macmillan.

Young, R. (1992) 'The idea of a chrestomathic university', in R. Rand (ed.) *Logomachia: The Conflict of the Faculties.* Lincoln, NB: University of Nebraska Press.

Znaniecki, F. (1968) *The Social Role of the Man of Knowledge.* New York: Harper & Row.

Index

The Society for Research into Higher Education

The Society for Research into Higher Education (SRHE) exists to stimulate and coordinate research into all aspects of higher education. It aims to improve the quality of higher education through the encouragement of debate and publication on issues of policy, on the organization and management of higher education institutions, and on the curriculum, teaching and learning methods.

The Society is entirely independent and receives no subsidies, although individual events often receive sponsorship from business or industry. The Society is financed through corporate and individual subscriptions and has members from many parts of the world.

Under the imprint *SRHE & Open University Press*, the Society is a specialist publisher of research, having over 80 titles in print. In addition to *SRHE News*, the Society's newsletter, the Society publishes three journals: *Studies in Higher Education* (three issues a year), *Higher Education Quarterly* and *Research into Higher Education Abstracts* (three issues a year).

The Society runs frequent conferences, consultations, seminars and other events. The annual conference in December is organized at and with a higher education institution. There are a growing number of networks which focus on particular areas of interest, including:

Access	Learning Environment
Assessment	Legal Education
Consultants	Managing Innovation
Curriculum Development	New Technology for Learning
Eastern European	Postgraduate Issues
Educational Development Research	Quantitative Studies
FE/HE	Student Development
Funding	Vocational Qualifications
Graduate Employment	

Benefits to members

Individual

• The opportunity to participate in the Society's networks

- Reduced rates for the annual conferences
- Free copies of *Research into Higher Education Abstracts*
- Reduced rates for *Studies in Higher Education*
- Reduced rates for *Higher Education Quarterly*
- Free copy of *Register of Members' Research Interests* – includes valuable reference material on research being pursued by the Society's members
- Free copy of occasional in-house publications, e.g. *The Thirtieth Anniversary Seminars Presented by the Vice-Presidents*
- Free copies of *SRHE News* which informs members of the Society's activities and provides a calendar of events, with additional material provided in regular mailings
- A 35 per cent discount on all SRHE/Open University Press books
- Access to HESA statistics for student members
- The opportunity for you to apply for the annual research grants
- Inclusion of your research in the *Register of Members' Research Interests*

Corporate

- Reduced rates for the annual conferences
- The opportunity for members of the Institution to attend SRHE's network events at reduced rates
- Free copies of *Research into Higher Education Abstracts*
- Free copies of *Studies in Higher Education*
- Free copies of *Register of Members' Research Interests* – includes valuable reference material on research being pursued by the Society's members
- Free copy of occasional in-house publications
- Free copies of *SRHE News*
- A 35 per cent discount on all SRHE/Open University Press books
- Access to HESA statistics for research for students of the Institution
- The opportunity for members of the Institution to submit applications for the Society's research grants
- The opportunity to work with the Society and co-host conferences
- The opportunity to include in the *Register of Members' Research Interests* your Institution's research into aspects of higher education

Membership details: SRHE, 3 Devonshire Street, London
W1N 2BA, UK. Tel: 020 7637 2766. Fax: 020 7637 2781.
email: srhe@mailbox.ulcc.ac.uk
world wide web: http://www.srhe.ac.uk./srhe/
Catalogue: SRHE & Open University Press, Celtic Court,
22 Ballmoor, Buckingham MR18 1XW. Tel: 01280 823388.
Fax: 01280 823233. email: enquiries@openup.co.uk

CITIZENSHIP IN A GLOBAL AGE
SOCIETY, CULTURE, POLITICS

Gerard Delanty

- What is citizenship?
- Is global citizenship possible?
- Can cosmopolitanism provide an alternative to globalization?

Citizenship in a Global Age provides a comprehensive and concise overview of the main debates on citizenship and the implications of globalization. It argues that citizenship is no longer defined by nationality and the nation state, but has become de-territorialized and fragmented into the separate discourses of rights, participation, responsibility and identity. Gerard Delanty claims that cosmopolitanism is increasingly becoming a significant force in the global world due to new expressions of cultural identity, civic ties, human rights, technological innovations, ecological sustainability and political mobilization. Citizenship is no longer exclusively about the struggle for social equality but has become a major site of battles over cultural identity and demands for the recognition of group difference. Delanty argues that globalization both threatens and supports cosmopolitan citizenship. Critical of the prospects for a global civil society, he defends the alternative idea of a more limited cosmopolitan public sphere as a basis for new kinds of citizenship that have emerged in a global age.

Contents

c.184pp   0 335 20489 9 (Paperback)   0 335 20490 2 (Hardback)

SOCIAL SCIENCE
BEYOND CONSTRUCTIVISM AND REALISM

Gerard Delanty

This concise and comprehensive volume provides an accessible overview of the main debates on the sociology and philosophy of the social sciences from the contemporary perspective of radical reflexivity and democratization. From its origins in the sixteenth and seventeenth centuries when a new system of knowledge was created around the idea of modernity, the author traces the transformation of modern conceptions of social science as a cognitive system and as an institution. Focusing on the rise of positivism in the age of the Enlightenment to its final collapse in the twentieth century, Delanty argues how social science is today recovering its role as the critical voice of modernity and examines the positivist dispute from post-empiricist perspectives. It is argued that the conception of social science emerging today is one that involves a synthesis of radical constructivism and critical realism. The crucial challenge facing social science is a question of its public role: growing reflexivity in society has implications for the social production of knowledge and is bringing into question the separation of expert systems from other forms of knowledge.

This is one of the most ambitious and wide-ranging texts in recent years on debates about the contemporary situation of social science. It will be of strong interest to undergraduates and postgraduates in the social sciences as well as to professional researchers working in the areas of the philosophy of social science, the sociology of science and knowledge, and social and political theory.

Contents
Introduction: crisis or transition – Positivism, science and the politics of knowledge – Hermeneutics and interpretation: the search for meaning – The dialectical imagination: Marxism, critique and emancipation – Communication and reconstruction: Habermas, Apel and the search for a synthesis – Deconstructionism and postmodernism: the problem of interdeterminacy – New debates: constructivism and realism – Conclusion: social science as discourse practice – Bibliography – Index.

176pp   0 335 19861 9 (Paperback)   0 335 19862 7 (Hardback)

THE FUTURE OF KNOWLEDGE PRODUCTION IN THE ACADEMY

Merle Jacob and Tomas Hellström

- What are the most significant challenges posed by new modes of organizing knowledge production in the academy?
- How are academic-industry partnerships managed?
- What is the future role of the university in the knowledge society?

The new knowledge society is characterized by a growing partnership between the university and industry. What are the implications for academics of such partnerships? What happens when the production of academic research is reorganized to reflect corporate structures and ambitions? What will future academic institutions be like? Does the nation state still have a role in determining how national science systems should be organized?

This volume explores knowledge management in the university and beyond from the perspective of researchers working in academic-industry partnerships. Its re-examination of the role of the academy in knowledge production (and in society) is important reading for all academic researchers, for academic managers, and for students and scholars in science studies and the sociology of knowledge.

Contents

192pp   0 335 20616 6 (Paperback)   0 335 20617 4 (Hardback)

REALIZING THE UNIVERSITY
IN AN AGE OF SUPERCOMPLEXITY

Ronald Barnett

The University has lost its way. The world needs the university more than ever but for new reasons. If we are to clarify its new role in the world, we need to find a new vocabulary and a new sense of purpose.

The university is faced with *supercomplexity*, in which our very frames of understanding, action and self-identity are all continually challenged. In such a world, the university has explicitly to take on a dual role: firstly, of compounding super-complexity, so making the world ever more challenging; and secondly, of enabling us to live effectively in this chaotic world. Internally, too, the university has to become a new kind of organization, adept at fulfilling this dual role. The university has to live by the uncertainty principle: it has to generate uncertainty, to help us live with uncertainty, and even to revel in our uncertainty.

Ronald Barnett offers nothing less than a fundamental reworking of the way in which we understand the modern university. *Realizing the University* is essential reading for all those concerned about the future of higher education.

Contents
Introduction – Part 1: The end is nigh – Death and resurrection – The end of enlightenment? – The ends of knowledge – The fading constellations – Part 2: Supercomplexity and the university – The constellation of fragility – Supercomplexity: the new universal – The conflict of the faculties – Part 3: Reframing the university – Conditions of the university – A suitable ethos – Part 4: Realizing the university – Constructing the university – Research in a super-complex world – Teaching for a supercomplex world – Conclusions – Notes – Bibliography – Index – The Society for Research into Higher Education.

224pp   0 335 20248 9 (Paperback)   0 335 20249 7 (Hardback)